# THE STORY OF TRANSATLANTIC FLIGHT

# THE STORY OF TRANSATLANTIC FLIGHT

## DAVID BEATY

**Airlife**
CLASSIC

For B – as always

First published in the UK in 1976
by Martin Secker & Warburg Ltd as *The Water Jump*

This edition published 2003
by Airlife Publishing Ltd

**British Library Cataloguing-in-Publication Data**
A catalogue record for this book
is available from the British Library

ISBN 1 84037 428 4

Printed in England by St Edmundsbury Press Ltd, Bury St Edmunds, Suffolk

Distibuted in North America by
STACKPOLE BOOKS
5067 Ritter Road, Mechanicsburg, PA 17055
www.stackpolebooks.com

For a complete list of all Airlife titles please contact:
**Airlife Publishing Ltd**
101 Longden Road, Shrewsbury, SY3 9EB, England
E-mail: sales@airlifebooks.com
Website: www.airlifebooks.com

# Contents

# List of Illustrations

# Foreword

In writing this book, my intention was twofold: first, to try and capture the colour and flavour of the North Atlantic sky while many of those who took part in its conquest could be consulted and while documents and papers (much was destroyed in the war or shredded afterwards) remain available: second, to try and show from hindsight as clearly as I could the pattern behind the story, how things came to happen, what stood in the way of development, what pushed it forward.

Such an intention imposed its own limitations within the compass of a manageable volume. I am conscious most of all of the omissions. Many individual accomplishments in the narrative have had books written about them, others which I omit or barely mention deserve such treatment. A further pressure on space was the fact that the story of the North Atlantic sky could not be told in isolation. It had to be fitted into the context, however briefly described, of the development of aviation —its problems, politics, people and technicalities.

As a result, many achievements on the South and Mid-Atlantic only come into this account if in my view they contributed greatly to the present North Atlantic civil aviation service. The same line had to be taken over just as many fine military flights, particularly by the USAAF and the RAF. The main concentration is on the formative early years—technical, administrative, political—not so much on the later proliferations and offshoots. As far as possible, I have kept to the main trunk growth in order to show how tiny beginnings developed into such a highly sophisticated achievement.

Due acknowledgement must be made to many people, more than I can individually name: to authors, libraries, ministries, airlines and manufacturers as well as to those who were actively involved in the pattern of the operation and generously gave me their information. There are a number of discrepancies between published accounts, so that wherever possible I have consulted primary authorities or the people and organisations concerned. However, the emphasis and the views expressed, and the errors, remain my own.

My grateful thanks are particularly due to Captain Michael Carroll, former Flight Superintendent of BOAC's 707 Fleet, who researched with me throughout and without whose unfailing help, enthusiasm and resourcefulness this book would not have been completed.

I am also grateful to Mr John C. Leslie, former Manager of Pan American's Atlantic Division, who kindly read the draft and made many useful suggestions. Both Mr Charles Smith, Manager, Statistical Services Section, British Airways, and Mr T. E. Scott-Chard of British Airways Information Services, also read the draft and kindly gave me advice and information. Captain Jack Nicholl, former General Manager Flight Training and now Principal of C.S.E. Oxford, and Captain Philip Brentnall, present General Manager Flight Training, advised on Training, as did Captain John Willett, Flight Engineer Officer Branson and Mr Tony Banks on the operational side and Mr John Ritchie, Navigation Superintendent 707 Fleet—all of British Airways—on navigation aspects, while Mrs Lakritz and her staff gave us much help with files and papers in British Airways archives.

I would also like to express my thanks to Mr Charles Abell, former Manager Atlantic Division, Captain Barrow, Captain Calvert, Captain Cole and members of the 747 and Concorde fleets, Air Vice-Marshal D. C. T. Bennett, Mr Gerry Bull, Mr Len Davies, Office Services Manager, Mr Clifford Dodds and Mr L. Smee and members of Cabin Services Training, Mr Frederick Gillman, Captain O. P. Jones, Captain J. C. Kelly-Rogers, former Manager Atlantic Division, Mr W. D. Koster, Captain D. Limbrey, Miss Minnie Mann, Major McCrindle, former Deputy Director-General, Mr John Moore, Mr Douglas Newham, Mr Geoffrey Ratcliffe, Mr Robbie Robinson, Lord Thomas of Remenham, Captain Frank Walton, Director Flight Operations—all former BOAC and/or British Airways: to Sir William Hildred, former Director-General, Captain Lincoln Lee and Mr A. Vandyk and Mr L. C. White of IATA: to Mr James Oughton and Mr Walter Gibb of the British Aircraft Corporation: to Mr Philip Barnett, Statistics, Mr J. C. Connor, Head of Information and Mr M. H. Vivian, Controller, Safety, of the Civil Aviation Authority; to Mr J. A. Giel and Mr Zandvlist of KLM: to Mr A. W. L. Nayler, Librarian, RAeS: to Captain C. C. Jackson, Dr P. D. McTaggart-Cowan, Executive Director, Science Council of Canada, Mr A. J. Watson, Ministry of Transport, and Mr Robert Dodds, Head of Transport Weather Services: to Lady Olive Wood, Mr Timothy Bird, Mr J. H. Fraser, National Air Traffic Services, Prestwick, Mr Douglas Scoffham, Mr Henning Rikard-Petersen, and FlugKapitan Gerhard Wasserkampf.

For photographs and information, I am also indebted to Air Canada, Albert F. Simpson Historical Research Centre, American Embassy, London, Associazione Nazionale Transvolatori Atlantici, Atmospheric Environment Service, Boeing Aeroplane Company, British Aircraft

Corporation, British Airports Authority, British Airways Overseas Division and Photographic Unit, Bundesarchiv-Freiburg, Civil Aviation Authority, Daily Mail Picture Library, Department of the Navy, Navy Historical Centre, Department of Trade and Industry, Deutsche Lufthansa, Deutsche Museum, Munchen, Dornier GmbH, Douglas Aircraft Corporation, *Flight International*, Flight Refuelling, Hawker Siddeley Aviation, Imperial War Museum, International Air Transport Association, International Civil Aviation Organisation, KLM Royal Dutch Airlines, Lockheed Aircraft Corporation, McDonnell Douglas Corporation, Ministry of Defence, Ministry of Transport, National Air & Space Museum, Smithsonian Institution, Pan American World Airways, Redifon Flight Simulation Ltd, Royal Aero Club, Royal Aeronautical Society, Smith Industries Ltd, Sperry Gyroscope Division, Zentralstelle fur Luftfahrt-Raumfahrtdokumentation und Information, Munchen, Federal German Republic.

I have been fortunate in having David Farrer as friend and editor for twenty-two years, and I am also grateful to Frances Lindley and John Blackwell for valuable editorial advice on this book.

Grateful acknowledgements for the use of photographs are made to Associated Newspapers, Popperfoto, US Navy, Vickers, CAA, John Underwood, Topical Press, *Flight*, Fox, Dornier, Gurra, Lockheed, Keystone, John Taylor, Pan American World Airways, British Airways, 25 Club, Air Canada, Flight Refuelling Ltd, BAC, McDonnell Douglas, Science Museum, and Redifon Ltd.

## One: The Race to be First

As you come out of the tunnel in the coach, just before you turn towards the Overseas Terminal and at the base of the Airport Control Tower, ahead you catch a glimpse of what appears to be a white pillar. Closer to, you can see it is a stone statue of two figures wearing flying clothes, standing close together side by side.

Just for a moment, you may wonder what those two young men are doing there amongst all the bustle of cars and aircraft, facing westwards, the way you are going. And then you are caught up in the departure procedure. You leave the coach. You check in at the ticket counter, where your reservation has been made in a world-wide computer called Babs. Your baggage is weighed, and then disappears. You are given a boarding pass. Your passport is checked. In you go to the departure lounge where already they are calling you.

'Passengers for the New York service should now proceed to Gate Thirteen.'

This is London Airport and the girl speaks first in English. But it might be Paris or Frankfurt or Stockholm or Amsterdam. Or it might be an eastbound service from Montreal or New York. The huge plate glass windows looking out on a prairie of winter grass and rain-soaked concrete, the turnstile to the shop selling duty-free liquor, cigarettes and perfume, the clicking of the indicator that looks like a vast tote board on which are flight numbers and destinations and the instructions *boarding*, *wait here*, or *last call* complete with red flashing light, could indicate the departure lounge of most capital city airports in the world. What is certain is that you are about to do the water jump over the 3456 miles across the Atlantic to New York—perhaps as a veteran of many crossings, more probably for the very first time.

As you walk out of the lounge towards the aircraft, your hand luggage is examined, you pass through an empty gate, through which an invisible beam seeks out any metallic objects—then on down the glass-lined corridor to Gate Thirteen

[1]

Over on the left, corralled in the grey ramp, you can see a herd of multi-coloured aircraft—the blue and white of a Pan American Clipper, the red-tipped tail of a British Airways VC10, the slim silver of an Air Canada DC8. There is a scent, rather pleasant and old-fashioned like an oil lamp burning, as huge tankers fill a Jumbo with 52,470 gallons of kerosene. Men in overalls move in and out of a forest of undercarriage legs—but there is no sign yet of your crew.

They will already have arrived one hour before departure—fifteen years ago it was two and a half. Then if there was fog or a strong westerly wind, the Operations Officer would have telephoned the Captain with details of the load and the route and terminal weather and awaited his decision on whether or not to go. But today, unless the visibility is near zero, there is no question of your flight not leaving.

Now there are only three operating crew—Captain, First Officer, Flight Engineer Officer. In an aircraft one-eighth the size thirty years ago there were in addition a Navigating and a Radio Officer and an additional Engineer. They will have signed on, collected their mail from their pigeon-holes, read the latest orders and proceeded to Flight Operations, where the Captain will have been presented with the Flight Plan completed by Babs, now only awaiting his signature, a weather briefing sheet, and Notams (notices to airmen on the state of radio and other facilities). Twenty-five years ago, the Captain or First Officer would have gone along to the meteorological office and discussed the weather situation, while the navigator wrestled with the Flight Plan, trying to circumvent the strong westerlies by going on a Rhumb Line track (straight), or Great Circle (shortest distance), or Composite (a cocked hat to get round the top of a low pressure area to pick up an easterly). With a full load it was inevitable then that a landing would have to be made at Goose or Gander—but often the big problem, in winter particularly, was whether a landing would also have to be made in Iceland. Eastbound aircraft flew at odd thousands of feet, westbound at even thousands in order to avoid collision. Otherwise, the choice was open on heights to fly, though these had to be agreed with Control. While all this was going on, the Engineer would have been carrying out a long external and internal check—dipping the fuel tanks with a stick, being careful to see there were a few extra gallons over the specified amount 'for Mum'.

Now there is far less to do. Everything is streamlined and mechanised. Even the dipstick works magnetically from under the wing. There is no juggling around with routes and distances and landings at Goose and Gander. The computer dictates that you will fly non-stop on one of six tracks agreed by the UK and Canada Air Traffic Control, separated by 60 miles, and your altitude (now called Flight Level) will be around 33,000 feet, where a jet aircraft operates most economically. Electronic eyes far more efficient than human ones will have checked the aircraft throughout, including the security aspects of the cargo holds. Even as you walk through Gate Thirteen, the Flight Engineer will have checked the fuel and gone through the Technical Log, noting any previous faults. He will have set the exact latitude and longitude of London Airport in the Inertial Navigation System. This will again be checked by both Captain and First Officer. The crew will almost have completed the starting engines check. The cabin crew will have checked the food containers loaded through the galley outside doors, and the Chief Purser in a blue coat is already at the top of the steps to say to all the passengers 'Good afternoon . . . nice to see you!'

You are piped on board the Boeing 747 to the sound of soft music. A stewardess in a red overall with blue cuffs shows you your seat, one with a porthole. All the doors are shut. The cabin crew demonstrate the wearing of life jackets, and the oxygen masks that descend automatically in the unlikely event of pressurisation trouble, indicate the fourteen inflatable life-rafts each holding 32 persons and point out the ten emergency exits.

Already you can feel the gentlest vibration as number four engine is started. On the flight deck, all instruments will have been checked. The other three engines roar into life, and the aircraft is hauled backwards out of the dock by a tractor.

Before leaving the ramp, the Captain briefs the First Officer and Flight Engineer on lift-off and climb-out procedures, and what actions are to be taken in the event of a failure or an emergency, so that they are in the forefront of the crew's mind.

Suddenly over the radio, your Air Traffic Clearance: 'Cleared to Kennedy by Brecon 22 departure. Squawk A6261'.

The First Officer reports it back. He switches on the Squawk Ident— the radio transmission that will increase the size of the aircraft blip on the Controller's radar screen.

As the aircraft taxies out to the take-off point, take-off flap is lowered, the Engineer calls the Before Take-off Check List, and all three crew check that the vital actions are carried out.

At the holding point, the Tower gives clearance for take-off.

The Captain releases the brakes. He puts his left hand on the nose-wheel steering, his right on the four thrust levers and moves them forward. In his position, the Engineer also has his right hand on the thrust levers. The First Officer holds the control column.

Very slowly, the heavy aircraft begins to accelerate.

The First Officer calls, '80 knots!'

The Captain transfers his left hand from the nosewheel steering to the control column. The Flight Engineer Officer has already set all four engines to their predetermined take-off settings, but the Captain still keeps his right hand on the thrust levers.

There is no vibration. Outside the jet engine noise sounds muted, and there is little exhaust smoke. Only a push against the back of your seat gives indication of the immense power forward.

At 140 knots, the First Officer calls, 'V 1!'

Both the Captain's hands grip the control column. Now, no matter what happens, it is too late to stop. For just these few moments, everyone holds their breath. The idea of 350 tons of metal flying—it is impossible. Over on the right now, you see the Control Tower and just catch a glimpse below it of that statue of those two airmen standing together. They were the very first to do the water jump in one hop in a Vimy bomber that weighed six tons. They were told it was impossible, but on the night of 14/15 June 1919, they did it. Their names were John Alcock and Arthur Whitten Brown.

At 152 knots, the First Officer calls, 'Rotate!'

The Captain eases back on the control column. Softly, your sixteen main wheels leave the ground. Gently, England falls away. You are achieving the impossible. You have begun the water jump.

*       *       *

'It is impossible.'

Such was the official and technical view on flying the North Atlantic by aeroplane after the First World War.

All the available evidence supported it.

The most powerful engines were then only around 400 horse-power. Aircraft were still fragile-looking biplanes with speeds around 100 mph, open cockpits and ranges of around 600 miles. Air navigation was in the railway-line-following stage, and large pointers were constructed on beaches and place names painted on roofs. Instruments were quite inadequate, consisting only of an airspeed indicator, revolution counter, altimeter, magnetic compass and a spirit-level type attitude gauge.

How could any pilot hope to get across even the two thousand miles of ocean between the two nearest points of land?

The map of the Atlantic illustrates the dilemma. Round the houses on the northern route via the Faroes, Iceland, Greenland, Labrador to Montreal was the nearest possibility—but the 900-mile last leg was beyond the range of ordinary aircraft not fitted with extra tanks and, therefore, carrying simply a load of petrol. In any case, there were no aerodromes en route, and seaplanes or flying boats would have to be used. The weather along that route was reported unflyable, and the harbours were frozen up for seven months of the year.

The range of the direct route from Ireland to Newfoundland (1950 miles) put it quite out of the question—and Botwood was also frozen over for half the year.

The route via the Azores offered the best weather but again the

Azores–Bermuda leg (2100 miles) was quite hopeless, and the Azores–Newfoundland alternative (1460 miles) was little better, and there again there was the ice problem.

British civil aviation had started in 1911 on the occasion of the coronation of George V when an aircraft flew from Hendon to Windsor with franked mails. Nevertheless, aeroplanes were still regarded as 'a new species of steed for sport and spectacle'. The Under Secretary of State for War had told British aircraft manufacturers, 'Gentlemen, much as we would like to help you by placing orders, we regret that we cannot do this, as we are guardians of the public purse, and we do not consider that aeroplanes will be of any possible use for war purposes.' It had needed the beneficence of four rich patriotic citizens who donated four aircraft to the Navy—who allowed officers to learn to fly on them with the proviso 'no flying on Sundays'.

Nevertheless, Great Britain came out of the First World War with the means to match her maritime achievements by making herself the greatest civil aviation power in the world. There were 347,102 employed in her aircraft industry—the French had half that and the Germans less than a third. The RAF was the largest air force in the world with 22,647 aeroplanes, 103 airships and nearly 700 aerodromes. A Civil Aerial Transport Committee, chaired by Lord Northcliffe and with H. G. Wells as a member, had produced a report pointing out that the government must subsidise the industry to develop. Frank Pick of the London Underground had vigorously dissented with the Committee's view that Britain should stand, together with every other country except Germany, for the sovereignty of the air above their territories. He also dissented from the decision to place control of civil aviation in the Air Ministry.

H. G. Wells wrote: '. . . a people who will not stand up to the necessity of Air Service planned on a world scale and taking over thousands of aeroplanes and thousands of men from the very onset of peace, has no business to pretend to anything more than second-rate position in the world. We cannot be both Imperial and mean . . .'

But Winston Churchill told the Commons in 1920 that 'Civil aviation must fly by itself, the Government cannot possibly hold it up in the air,' and the influence of godfathers from the Foreign Office, the Colonial Office, the Dominions Office, the Post Office, the Treasury and the Air Ministry on the new-born babe (British civil aviation *officially* began in 1919) increased with the years.

Germany was hampered in civil aviation development by the Versailles Treaty. France, Holland and Belgium began policies of sensible subsidisation. Russia had been well advanced in aviation but the revolution caused the experts to emigrate. Amongst others, Sikorsky eventually went to America—to that country's inestimable advantage.

*Overleaf:* A map prepared in 1930 showing projected alternative routes across the Water Jump.

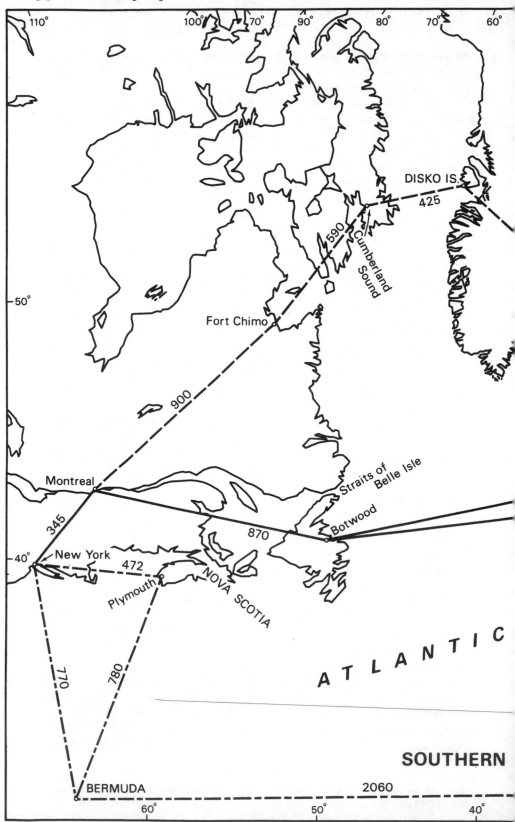

110°   100°   70°   90°   80°   70°   60°

DISKO IS.
425

590
Cumberland
Sound

50°

Fort Chimo

900

Montreal

345

Straits of
Belle Isle

Botwood

870

40°   New York

472

Plymouth

NOVA SCOTIA

A T L A N T I C

770   780

SOUTHERN

BERMUDA   2060

60°   50°   40°

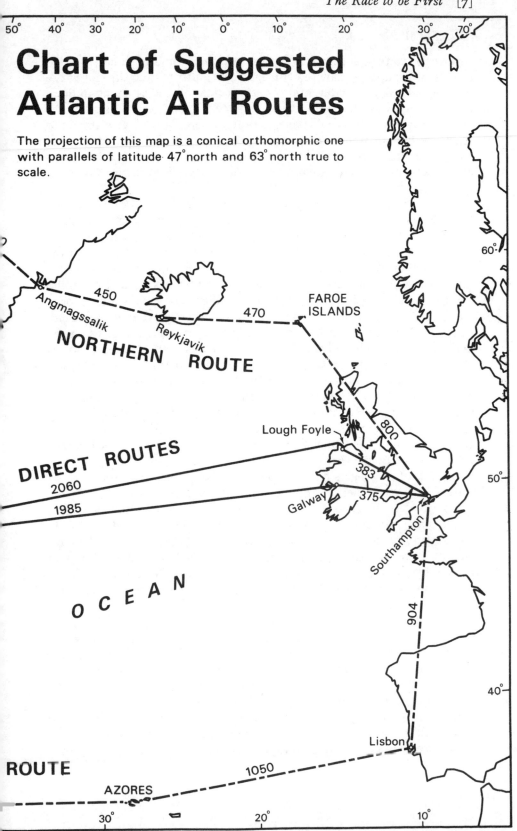

# Chart of Suggested Atlantic Air Routes

The projection of this map is a conical orthomorphic one with parallels of latitude 47°north and 63°north true to scale.

From 1908 to 1913 Congressional appropriations for aircraft had totalled less than $100,000 a year. In contrast, from April 1917 to the end of the war eighteen months later, appropriation was totalled at $1200 million, half of which was returned to the Treasury. No American-designed aircraft had reached the Western Front, where at the armistice the American aerial strength was reportedly 196 British-designed aircraft with American Liberty engines. The huge stock of unused warplanes was embarrassing, and the government was busy disposing of them at giveaway prices.

As regards flying the North Atlantic, few contradicted the official view that the whole thing reeked of horse-racing with more than a whiff of gambling. This effect was further borne out by the fact that many pilots wore riding breeches, and the London Air Terminal in 1920 at Heathrow was shared on the south side by the Remount Regiment and the Light Cavalry. Apart from the problem that there were no steeds to last the course, there was the North Atlantic weather. The very words 'North Atlantic' have an expressive ring—so cold and remote that the wind can be heard whistling through them and the breakers crashing down on the beaches. Their colour has always been black and white, darkness relieved by the white caps of waves. Those considering the possibilities of Atlantic flight would have seen the huge anvils of solid cloud filled with rain, hail, snow, lightning, ice and upcurrents. They would have felt the power of west winds so strong that they were capable of blowing slow aircraft backwards and giving them a negative ground speed. Huge ships had been blown over and capsized. Larger ones like the *Titanic* had struck icebergs and sunk. Waves had split open steel hulls, thousands of passengers had perished. More ships lie buried under these waters than any other ocean, and most of them are British.

No wonder people considered the North Atlantic, sated on ships, would make mincemeat of any airmen foolhardy enough to take it on. It had already made mincemeat of the American Wellman who had set off on 15th October 1910 from Atlantic City with a British navigator and three other crew in an airship called *America*. After three days, with the airship quite out of control and drifting helplessly, they were rescued by the Royal Mail Steamer *Trent*.

Even Nature was against man in the Atlantic sky. The world's atmosphere becomes less dense with height, so that if an airman managed to climb above the weather he would get the bends from bubbles in his blood stream, be subject to immense fatigue and lack of oxygen. Since temperature drops by 1°F every 300 feet, he would be half frozen in his open cockpit. Added to such unalterable elements was the fact that the noise of the early engines was deafening, and the vibration such that no man could be expected to stand it for more than a few hours.

And what was the point anyway? It only took six days in a ship that

was the height of luxury, with dance halls and casinos, every entertainment and eight-course menus. Cunard liners like the *Mauretania* made
good profits for the British, and the idea of competing in such butterfly
craft against such safe and solid comfort appeared lunatic.

In fact, a chorus of 'lunatic' had greeted Lord Northcliffe when in
1913 he offered a prize of £10,000 for the first man to fly non-stop across
the Atlantic. This was only one of many aviation prizes put up by the
*Daily Mail*, invariably in the teeth of public opinion and against official
government views. The effect of these competitions for generous money
prizes—put up by rich industrialists, sportsmen and private firms—on
the advancement of aviation, and the phenomenal progress of Atlantic
flying, can hardly be exaggerated. Governments and Civil Services not
unnaturally tend to bury the talents collected from the taxpayer and do
not risk them on gambles like the water jump.

However, there were individuals who had other views. A young naval
pilot was predicting that trans-Atlantic flying was 'a perfectly safe and
sane commercial proposition, not a gigantic gamble'. His name was
Juan Trippe, later to become founder and President of Pan American
World Airways.

There were other individuals who also saw the possibilities. Opti-
mistically entering into World War I on the slogan that it 'would be over
by Christmas', the British had gone in for big bombers in an attempt to
pulverise Berlin. But the real threat were the U-boats, which were
sending thousands of tons of shipping to the bottom of the ocean, and
there was a danger that Britain would be starved into submission. When
America entered the war, Rear Admiral Taylor, Chief Constructor to the
US Navy, wrote in a memorandum, 'It seems to me the submarine
menace can be abated, even if not destroyed, from the air. The ideal
solution would be big flying boats . . . able to fly across the Atlantic to
avoid difficulties of delivery.'

Now unlimited American money released by war necessity—always the
big governmental boost for the scientific advancement of the ideas of
individuals—became available. The Americans called in Glenn Curtiss,
the first man who had flown an aeroplane successfully from water and
consumed with a passion to be first to fly across the Atlantic. He had
already built a flying boat, again an individual effort, four years before
(again called *America*) and had trained a young man called Towers to fly
it. Now money was no object, Curtiss set about building a large anti-
submarine flying boat. An aircraft with a broad-based hull that made it
look like a Dutch clog was flying within a year. Powered by four new 400
horsepower Liberty engines, the Navy-Curtiss 4's all-up weight was a
fantastic 28,000 lb. Two pilots sat side by side in an open cockpit, with a
gunner in front of them and a radio officer and two engineers deep in the
hull. The design was regarded as heretical, and an investigating British

An R.A.F. Chaplain gives a benediction to Major Wood (*left*) and Captain Wyllie before they took off from Eastchurch in a Short *Shirl*, for an attempt at the east-west crossing, 8 April 1919.                                                                                  (Kessell)

The Short *Shirl*—upside down, wings awash, roundels just showing—is towed into Holyhead Harbour after coming down in the Irish sea. Both crew were saved.                                                                                  (copyright unknown)

Aviation Commission had commented, 'The machine is impossible and is not likely to be of any use whatever.'

By this time, World War I was over. But the American Navy pressed forward with their plan. There was a need to show the taxpayers the calibre of their unused warplanes. It was emphasised that 'as it seems probable that Great Britain will make every effort to attain the same relative standing in aerial strength as she has in naval strength, the prestige that she would attain by successfully carrying out the first trans-Atlantic flight would be of great assistance to her . . . it would seem most fitting that the first trans-Atlantic flight should be carried out upon the initiative of the US Navy.'

Such an assessment of Britain with her immense aerial strength at that time was totally justified—and totally wrong. The British Government hardly lifted a finger in the race across the Atlantic. Pressure was brought on the Admiralty to beat the Americans with the 33,000 lb five-engined Felixstowe Fury triplane which was then the biggest flying boat in the world, but the Treasury refused. Meteorological assistance was rather grudgingly provided in Newfoundland, but otherwise the effort was left to British individuals and aircraft manufacturers, and in the spring of 1919 there had disembarked from ships and booked into the snowbound and fogbound Cochrane Hotel, St John's, Newfoundland, a motley bunch of British airmen, with weird crates of aircraft pieces— Hawker and Grieve with a Sopwith Atlantic, Raynham and Morgan with their red Martinsyde and Vice-Admiral Kerr with a huge Handley Page V1500 bomber designed to bomb Berlin. A Short Shirl had already made a plucky attempt on the westbound crossing from Britain, but after only a few miles had come down with engine trouble in the Irish Sea. All were

The Handley Page V1500, the huge four-engined contender for the Daily Mail prize. (Associated Newspapers)

The crew of the V1500: Major Brackley (left), Major Gran (centre) and Admiral Kerr.                                                            (Popperfoto)

intent on being the first across the Atlantic and winning the *Daily Mail* £10,000 prize.

While the British were having a hilarious time watching each other like hawks so that no one pulled a fast one, dashing all over Newfoundland trying to find a few hundred yards of level ground that had not got too many rocks and fir trees on it and playing pranks on each other in the hotel, the American Navy was proceeding with a massive campaign to conquer the Atlantic sky.

Three NC4 flying boats—now known as Nancies—were going to use the two stepping stones of Newfoundland and the Azores to reach Lisbon, and then fly on to Britain. The captains of the aircraft were the navigators, a practice surviving in the British Navy till World War II and beyond. Towers, the same man whom Curtiss had taught to fly, was appropriately in command of the endeavour and captained NC3, Lieutenant-Commander Bellinger NC1 and Lieutenant-Commander Read NC4. Sixty-eight destroyers were stationed at intervals of fifty miles along the entire route. Five battleships were assigned every four hundred miles and, together with every fourth destroyer, acted as meteorological stations. As soon as any Nancy approached, each ship was to start making smoke and continue till all three were accounted for. The smoke would indicate wind speed and direction. At night, the ships were to 'torch' their funnels by improperly firing their boilers, and searchlights were to be trained into the wind to give the wind direction. Every five minutes, star shells were to be fired from three-inch guns until all aircraft were safely over. Just in case these flying boats failed, a four-man airship, C5, was stationed in Newfoundland to make the attempt.

Almost unnoticed, on 8th May 1919, with a four-leaf clover, the gift of the Aviation Director, in the pocket of each crew man, the large yellow wings and grey hulls of the three Nancies lifted off the water at Rockaway, NY, in formation for the first leg to Newfoundland. All crewmen were strapped in by the Curtiss belt, invented after Towers had survived a fall from 1500 feet in an out-of-control aircraft, and standard aviation equipment ever since.

NC4 had already had trouble before even starting, being damaged by a fire in the hangar. Now almost immediately it began falling behind the others. Before it reached the first station destroyer, it had lost the centre pusher engine due to low oil pressure. Shortly afterwards, a connecting rod exploded out of the remaining centre engine in a cloud of steam. Unable to maintain height, Read landed on a misty sea, and taxied eighty miles east, reaching Chatham harbour by dawn.

The engines were changed, but now gales delayed them. For five days, NC1 and NC3 waited in Trepassey Bay, Newfoundland for NC4 to join them, while in banner headlines in the newspapers, public indignation erupted at the vast expense being wasted on this futile attempt.

Already christened the *Lame Duck*, NC4 set off from Chatham, in the teeth of bad weather, with all four engines running roughly, including the two new ones. Repairs were effected at Halifax, Nova Scotia, but a few minutes after taking off, the engines were cutting out and Read had to alight again, this time with a blocked fuel line.

Read chugged on, but now ice began to form and the pilots were half-frozen in the open cockpit. Just before reaching Trepassey Bay, Read spotted what looked like a huge silver balloon bouncing over the iceflows —the American reserve for the water jump, airship C5, torn from her moorings by the gale, setting off alone and unmanned to disappear for ever over the Atlantic.

Meanwhile, all this American activity a few miles south of them had galvanised the British in the Cochrane Hotel. Suspicious of each other, they became united in national pride through this threat from America. Hawker and Grieve, Raynham and Morgan had cleared their respective landing strips and were making frantic preparations to take off before the Americans could make it to the other side.

NC1 and NC3 had already attempted to take off for the Azores and failed. Mindful of the British competition, maintenance men worked all night putting in a new untested engine in NC4. Just at dusk on 16th May, bucking a strong crosswind, in a flurry of foaming wakes, side by side the three Nancies thundered across Trepassey inner harbour, began bouncing on the crests of the waves, finally lifted off the water, dodged the icebergs and set course east at eighty-five miles an hour, into the Atlantic night.

And this time, the *Lame Duck* was already way in front.

*      *      *

The British government had made few preparations for their sons to be the first to do the water jump. It now became evident that the Americans had made too many.

Instead of keeping their sights on their final destination in the Azores fourteen hundred miles away, the American navigators became obsessed with finding each fifty-mile stepping stone of a ship. They worried if they could not find the vessels. If they were not in the expected position, whose navigation was wrong, the aircraft's or the ship's? A firework display of searchlights and green and white star shells was all very well, but Towers in NC3 was nearly brought down when a star shell exploded just under his wing. His navigation lights had been doused by salt

**The bridge of boats: Newfoundland–Azores.**

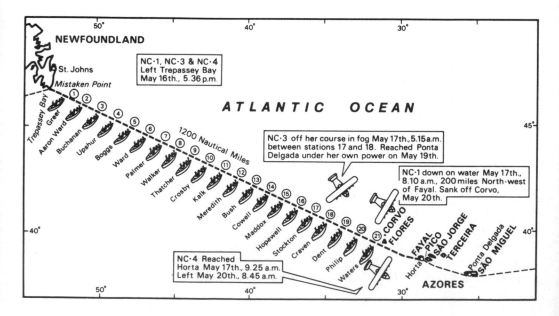

spray, and in the misty moonlight his crew just managed to avoid a collision with NC1 by flashing a pocket torch as a warning.

Then the weather worsened. By dawn, the Atlantic was one gigantic cloud, pockmarked by tiny breaks. Towers caught sight of a ship to his south, which he took to be Number 15, and altered course accordingly.

He was wrong.

And now the Atlantic showed its treacherous nature. Unforecast and totally unexpected, thick fog enveloped NC3, followed by heavy rain squalls and high winds. The flying boat tossed and bucked in the violent air. NC4's pilot lost control in thick cloud, but just in time the sun re-appeared. Tired out, cold and soaked through in the open cockpits, the pilots took thirty-minute turns to fly blind on the primitive instruments, struggling to keep NC3 from turning over on her back and spinning in. The new bubble sextant invented by Byrd, which was to become standard throughout the world, now being used on the Atlantic for the first time, could not cope in such turbulence. Within minutes they were totally lost.

NC1 was faring worse. The aircraft was flying oddly and the strength of both pilots was needed to keep her on an even keel. The flying boat had been forced down to seventy-five feet. In the thick fog, the captain-navigator, Bellinger, had become fearful of running into the volcanic island of Pico that rises 7600 feet clear up from the ocean. No ship could be raised on the radio. A decision was taken to alight and take stock. But in the heavy swell and high waves, NC1 lurched into a trough and the lower part of her tail was carried away. A frantic series of SOS-calls were sent, as for five hours the seasick crew bailed water out of the rolling, pitching hull. Then a Greek ship, the *Ionia*, loomed out of the fog, and tried to take the flying boat in tow. But in the gale the wire rope snapped, and NC1 became the first aeroplane to go to the bottom of the Atlantic.

Meanwhile, Towers had also decided, after fifteen hours flying, to stop and take stock. Still totally lost, he signalled his pilots to alight. From 500 feet the surface did not look too bad, but just before touching the water, through the darkness Towers saw the huge swell. It was too late. The pilot hit the crest, ricocheted off a wave, shot up into the air again and then plunged into the sea. The hull was split, the controls were gone. On the radio, though the destroyers could be heard, NC3 could not get through. They were only 45 miles from Flores, but they were south while the ships were searching west. The flying boat began to sink under the weight of water collected in the canvas wings, and the crew had to hack holes in the fabric to let the water out.

Nevertheless they were afloat, and Towers decided to taxi, while a crew man hung on the tip of the starboard wing for nearly twenty four hours, as a counterbalance to keep the port wing out of the water. Dawn had broken, and Pico could clearly be seen forty miles away. But Towers decided to sail towards Ponte Delgada. All that day, the crew survived on rusty water from the radiators and seawater-soaked sandwiches.

Finally, after two and a half days on the water they sighted Ponte Delgada, lowered the distress signal, hoisted the Stars and Stripes, sailed stern first into the harbour and moored unassisted.

Of the three Nancies, only the *Lame Duck* was still in the race. Read in NC4 did not miss a ship station, till suddenly he, too, ran into fog—and he missed Number 17. Wary of Pico, he had altered course south. And then, close on 09.30, through a gap in the cloud, to one side of the grey sea, Read caught sight of a darker colour—brown. They were the cliffs of the island of Flores. Spiralling down through the overcast, the *Lame Duck* levelled off over Horta harbour, and alighted fifteen hours and eighteen minutes after leaving Trepassey.

The first part of the water jump had been successfully completed.

*       *       *

Meanwhile, an unconfirmed report had reached the Cochrane Hotel that all three Nancies had safely reached the Azores. Hawker with his Sopwith Atlantic and Raynham with his Martinsyde were the furthest

Maintenance crew working on the NC-4. Note the navigator's position in the nose, the two-pilot position (closed in) just in front of the wing.     (U.S. Navy)

The Sopwith *Atlantic* in Newfoundland. The fabric covering was left unpainted to save weight.

advanced of the British in their preparations. Both were similar machines, and some tension had built up between them till they agreed to give each other notice of taking off. When the news came through that morning, in Hawker's own words, 'There was only one thing to do, namely get as much sleep as we could, for we didn't intend to have any the following night. We meant to have something more interesting on hand.'

The Australian Hawker was a typical extrovert pilot, red-faced and jovial. His navigator, Lt-Commander Mackenzie-Grieve, was a scholarly-looking man with high cheekbones, often dressed in a butterfly collar and tie. Between them, they had all the human qualities and skills that were necessary for the attempt. Grieve described Hawker as, 'an ideal pilot, with unlimited pluck, unfailingly good judgment, and what is equally to the point, an inexhaustible supply of good spirits.'

On 29th March they had arrived by ship with their Sopwith Atlantic in crates to find Newfoundland under deep snow. While the plane was being assembled—the fuselage was fabric-covered over a metal skeleton —they rushed round in an old car trying to find somewhere to take off. Each competitor had located his own private preserve where he made his secret preparations. Raynham had sportingly offered Hawker the use of his field, but Hawker had declined. All that could be found for the Sopwith was an L-shaped field that skirted a steep-sided hill two hundred feet high. Hawker and Grieve helped assemble their machine and practised their drills, including testing their life-saving suits in the detachable dinghy that formed the aft end of the Sopwith, on an ice-filled lake. Their entertainments—prohibition was in force with the resultant alcohol drought—had consisted of playing cards with the other competitors, visiting the meteorological station, gossiping over any bits of news about the Nancy flying boat plans, and eating ices at Mr Pettigrew's, the local drug-store.

On the confirmation of the news that the *Lame Duck* had reached the Azores, the Sopwith was refuelled and made ready to go. A biplane with a 350 hp Rolls Royce Eagle engine, and an all-up weight of only 5000 lb, it had the then fast cruising speed of 118 mph, well above the Nancies. After a short rest, the two men climbed on board, Hawker turned into a twenty-mile-an-hour north-east wind, charged diagonally across the field, missed a ditch at the bottom by inches and scraped up into the sky. Turning east, he jettisoned his wheels—it had already been worked out what a drag the undercarriage was, but many years were to go by before the mechanism for retracting it was perfected—and set off above a thick blanket of the usual Newfoundland fog at 105 mph indicated airspeed. Grieve got a good drift from his primitive indicator, and there was a clear horizon for him to use his marine-type sextant.

Then the Atlantic weather showed signs of worsening. 'About ten o'clock,' Hawker wrote, 'the blue in the sky had turned to purple, the warm glint of the sun had faded from the polished edges of the struts,

**Hawker and Grieve climbing, after the *Atlantic* took off from Glendenning's Farm, 18 May 1919.**                    **(Associated Newspapers)**

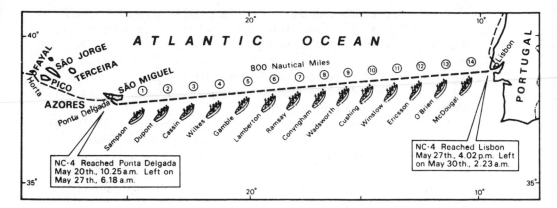

The bridge of boats: Azores–Lisbon.

and the clouds below us had become dull and patchy and grey, only giving us very infrequently a sight of the ocean beneath them.'

The Sopwith droned on eastwards into a thick cave of continuous cloud. And then, six hundred miles out, Hawker noticed the thermometer of the water-cooled engine rising. He opened the cooling shutters, but half an hour later the temperature had climbed to 176°F. If it went much higher there was a risk that the water would boil away completely, and then the engine would seize. Now seven hundred miles out, in an effort to cool it, Hawker switched off the engine and went into a long dive. Just above the tops of the waves, he switched on again, and was relieved to see the needle on the gauge now well down.

Then slowly it started to rise again. Inching up, it passed 190, then 200 and began touching 212°.

It was now night. Like a little geyser, steam was spouting out of a tiny hole in the engine, condensing into water, running down over the lower wing and solidifying into ice. Ahead was 'a bank of black clouds as solid as a range of mountains and rearing themselves up in fantastic and menacing formations'.

Up and up went the Sopwith, but her ceiling was only 13,000 feet, and she was soon engulfed in violent darkness. The only blind-flying instruments Hawker had were an airspeed indicator, altimeter, a compass that was rotating wildly and a primitive spirit-gauge attitude indicator. It was then not adequately understood that without a visible horizon, or equivalent instrument, man does not know whether he is upside down or sideways. The myth had grown in the war that the sign of a good pilot was his ability to fly by the seat of his pants in thick cloud—and had sent hundreds of airmen spinning in to their deaths.

Wisely, Hawker throttled back and managed to get under the base of the cloud. But when he pushed the throttles forward again, there was no response. The engine had stopped dead. Hawker yelled to Grieve to pump petrol into the carburettor. But when he did, nothing happened. The Sopwith continued to glide downwind towards a very rough sea. Ten feet above the waves, Hawker clumped Grieve on the back and shouted that he was going to ditch.

At that moment, the navigator's pumping produced results. The engine caught. The glide flattened. The Sopwith roared away up to 10,000 feet, managing to get between layers of cloud. But the climb had made the engine boil again and they had to descend again to just above the sea. It was only a matter of minutes now, and there would be no water left. In Hawker's words 'if only we could have slung a bucket overboard and picked up a few gallons as we went along!'

They were now almost exactly half way across the water jump. Against the deafening clatter of the engine, they shouted to each other— trying to work out what to do.

\*         \*         \*

Back in Newfoundland, Raynham was in hot pursuit. One hour after Hawker, he climbed into the Martinsyde with Morgan. Twice he tried to get airborne. On the third attempt, a side gust caught the heavily laden aircraft as it rose, and crashed it back on the ground. Raynham escaped but Morgan was hurt.

The day went by and there was no news of Hawker and Grieve. Read

**The *Raymor* in which Raynham and Morgan hoped to beat the *Atlantic*.**

was still in the Azores with NC4. Another day passed—and still no news of the fate of the Sopwith.

Its fuel would now be long exhausted. Hawker and Grieve were given up for lost. Public indignation railed against the Government for its niggardly indifference, particularly in comparison with the care and open-handedness of the Americans. King George V sent a telegram to Mrs Hawker, 'The King, fearing the worst must now be realised regarding the fate of your husband, wishes to express his deep sympathy and that of the Queen in your sudden and tragic sorrow. His Majesty feels that the nation has lost one of its most able and daring pilots, who sacrificed his life for the fame and honour of British flying.'

But Mrs Hawker steadfastly maintained that her husband was not dead. The days passed, the ship search was called off, but still she said that she was in communication with him and that she knew he was alive. She remained very calm and confident. People humoured her, saying to themselves that this was what one could expect of a grief-stricken widow who could not face the truth. It was impossible for her husband to be alive—and impossible for her to be in touch with him.

Back in Horta, bad weather grounded Read in NC4 till 20th May, when he proceeded to another Azores island, Ponte Delgada, where the Americans received a tumultuous welcome. With the Sopwith and the Martinsyde out of the race and no other Briton ready to take off from Newfoundland, the *Lame Duck* took its time. Read did not want to leave anything to chance. He had the Nancy tuned up to tip-top condition and waited for fair weather.

The *Raymor* crashes on take off.

The triumphant arrival of Read and his crew in NC-4 at Lisbon after their successful Atlantic crossing, 27 May 1919.                                                    (US Navy)

Then, on 27th May, he took off for Lisbon and after an uneventful 9 hours and 43 minutes, over a bridge of boats, alighted at Lisbon to another great ovation. Three days later, he began his last leg, again over

The crew of the NC-4 are welcomed to Plymouth by the Mayor of Plymouth at the monument which commemorates the spot where the Pilgrim Fathers embarked for America almost three hundred years before.                    (Associated Newspapers)

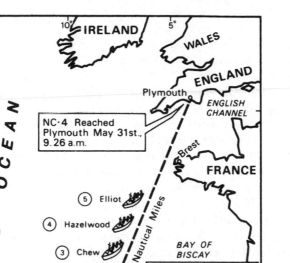

15°

10°  IRELAND

WALES

ENGLAND

Plymouth

ENGLISH
CHANNEL

-50°

ATLANTIC OCEAN

NC·4 Reached
Plymouth May 31st.,
9.26 a.m.

Brest

FRANCE

⑤ Elliot

④ Hazelwood

③ Chew

775 Nautical Miles

BAY OF
BISCAY

② Barney

Reached Ferrol
May 30th.,12.45 p.m.
Left May 31st.,2.27a.m.

① Breckinridge

Ferrol

Ⓔ Yarnell

SPAIN

Ⓓ Tarbell

Ⓒ Woolsey

Ⓑ Rathburn

Mondego
River

-40°

Ⓐ Harding

Figueira

Descended at Mondego
River near Figueira
probably about 6.40 a.m.
Left Figueira 1.28 p.m.

Lisbon

NC·4 Reached Lisbon
May 27th., 4.02 p.m.
Left May 30th., at
2.23 a.m.

PORTUGAL

10°

5°

The bridge of boats: Lisbon–Plymouth.

a bridge of American warships, stopping at Figuera and Ferrol, and alighting at Plymouth at lunchtime on 31st May. Up in London, the crew were enthusiastically fêted. It had been a magnificent flight, an epic of world history. On the steps of Parliament, the American fliers were welcomed by the Prince of Wales, Winston Churchill, Air Ministry and Foreign Office Officials.

The water jump had been done over the stepping stones of the Azores in a flying time of 53 hours and 58 minutes, spread over twenty-three days.

*     *     *

For a week there had been no news of Hawker or Grieve—and their deaths were presumed by all except Mrs Hawker who remained as calm and steadfast as ever.

Then again, the impossible occurred. On 25th May, the coastguard station at the Butt of Lewis received a message by flag signals from a tiny boat *Saved hands Sopwith aeroplane*. They interrogated *Is it Hawker?* Back came the reply *Yes*.

In fact, the plan Hawker and Grieve had decided on in mid-Atlantic was to look round for a ship. For two hours, they had zig-zagged between clouds, dodging fog banks—but there had been nothing.

Then as Hawker wrote, 'suddenly a hull loomed out of the fog and we knew that our luck, if it had been patchy, was at least good enough to stand up when the big strain came on it. I am ready to admit that I shouted for joy. Grieve says he felt like doing the same thing, but evidently the tradition of the Silent Service was too much for his voice chords. The hull belonged to the good ship *Mary* of Denmark, and she was sailing close enough for us to have touched. We flew alongside her and fired three Very light distress signals and kept close by until her crew began to appear on the decks. Then we pushed off a couple of miles

*Below:* The wreck of the Sopwith *Atlantic* half way across.        (Associated Newspapers)

*Right:* Hawker and Grieve (in white sweater) being rowed away from the *Mary* which picked them up.   (Associated Newspapers)

or so along her course, judged the wind from the wave crests, came round into it and made a cushy landing in spite of the high sea that was running.'

The *Mary* had no wireless and so could give no indication to the outside world till she reached Scotland. She carried not only the two Britons, but a bag of airmail they had hung onto from the Sopwith. This was how the very first airmail got across the water jump, appropriately baptised in the salty Atlantic.

Hawker and Grieve received a hero's welcome, a cheque for £5000 from the *Daily Mail*, as a consolation prize, and the Air Force Cross, to which neither was entitled since they were not in the RAF—the Air Ministry's gesture being to waive the regulations.

After all the celebrations and receptions were over, Hawker paid particular tribute to his navigator. Saying that the number of men in the world capable of 'navigating the trans-Atlantic aeroplane could be counted on the fingers of one hand', he added that, 'On a job of this kind, the pilot owes everything to the navigator, and I take this opportunity of publicly voicing my tremendous obligation and inexpressible admiration for Lieutenant-Commander Mackenzie-Grieve.'

More than anyone else, Hawker and Grieve gave 'belief' to doing the water jump. Two individuals had taken on the Atlantic together in a little aeroplane. They had been downed and given up for lost. But up they had bobbed again, alive and kicking, not dwelling on the dangers, praising the Sopwith and describing the engine trouble as 'a trifling mishap'. And as for the future, Hawker said, given the chance of another crack at the Atlantic, Grieve and he 'would go on a single-engined land machine as we did before'.

\*     \*     \*

The water jump had certainly been accomplished—but not in one hop.

Five days before Hawker and Grieve took off from Newfoundland, John Alcock and Arthur Whitten Brown had arrived in St John's by ship, with their big Vimy bomber—again fabric-covered over a metal frame—equipped with two of the same Rolls Royce 350 hp engines that had powered the Sopwith, packed up in crates on deck, and had booked in at the Cochrane Hotel.

In their own way, this new team was a replica of Hawker and Grieve. Alcock looked like a big and smiling farmer's boy, while the navigator Brown was studious and solemn—again the extrovert pilot and the introvert navigator, typical temperaments for these two professions throughout the years ahead. Both had served in the Royal Flying Corps. Both had been shot down and captured. While he was a prisoner, Brown, who had been badly wounded in the leg, made himself an expert in navigation, and Alcock planned to fly the Atlantic.

After being shipped from England, the Vickers Vimy is assembled in the open in Newfoundland in preparation for the Atlantic attempt. (Associated Newspapers)

While the Vickers ground staff assembled the Vimy, Alcock and Brown went on the usual thankless Newfoundland tour looking in vain for 400 yards of flat cleared ground. They tried to do a deal with Vice-Admiral Kerr, who had made an adequate aerodrome for his much larger Handley Page V1500. For the first time on the Atlantic, commercialism reared its head as Kerr demanded half the cost of the aerodrome construction, and then would only allow it to be used *after* the V1500 had taken off. Alcock refused and had to make do with a large meadow balanced on the side of a hill with a swamp at the bottom.

On 14th June 1919 they received from the meteorological officer a forecast of good weather. The Vimy was loaded with 870 gallons of fuel. Then carrying three hundred letters of mail and two stuffed black cat mascots, Twinkletoes and Lucky Jim, they climbed into the open cockpit. A crowd had assembled expecting to see them kill themselves. Alcock opened up the throttles. The Vimy lumbered up the hill in a strong crosswind, skidded round some rocks, and lurched unsteadily into the uneven air. Once airborne, the bomber immediately dropped into a valley, out of sight of the spectators who were convinced it had crashed.

Just above the ground, Alcock had allowed the Vimy to gather speed before coaxing her to 1000 feet. At 16.28 GMT they crossed the coast and

*Opposite:* John Alcock (left) and Arthur Whitten Brown in their flying suits before take off.
(Vickers)

Alcock and Brown take off in the Vimy from Lester's Field, 14 June 1919.     (Vickers)

turned onto 124° magnetic—the course for Ireland. Brown tapped out on the wireless transmitter *All well and started.*

It was the last message he sent. The tiny propeller that drove the generator for the transmitter then fell off.

Though the two men sat side by side, the noise from the engines was so great that they had to communicate by signs and notes. All round him, Brown had arranged his maps and instruments. His marine-type sextant was fitted with a spirit level to use instead of a horizon, which he expected (quite correctly) rarely to see. He had a drift bearing plate, a Mercator chart, a course and distance calculator and a stop watch.

For the next four hours, fog obscured the sea, and his log laconically recorded 'Cloud above and below. Readings impossible.'

All at once there was a rattle like machine-gun fire, and they saw a chunk of exhaust pipe had disintegrated; naked flames from the starboard engine were playing on the cross bracing wires.

They continued blindly eastwards, on dead reckoning. It was not until 20.31 that Brown managed to obtain a single shot of the sun which indicated that his position was well north. He pushed over a note to the pilot, asking him to climb. In words that have the ring of Saint-Exupéry, the navigator wrote, 'It was now quite dark. As we droned our isolated way eastward and upward, nothing could be seen outside the cockpit, except the inner struts, the engines, the red-glowing vapour through the exhaust pipes, and portions of the wing surface, which glistened faintly in the moon glimmer. I waited impatiently for the first sight of the moon, the Pole Star and other old friends of every navigator.'

But nothing appeared except more cloud. It was after midnight before Brown managed to 'shoot' Vega and the Pole Star through a gap to the north-east, which gave their first fix as 50.7° North, 31° West, indicating that they had flown 850 nautical miles at an average ground speed of 106 knots.

Further star shots were impossible, since the Vimy was now flying in 'a sea of fog'. Brown tried many times to shoot the faint and fuzzy moon —but failed. But he succeeded exactly in putting into words the feelings of thousands who were to follow him high over the North Atlantic night: 'An aura of unreality seemed to surround us as we flew onward towards the dawn and Ireland. The fantastic surroundings impinged on my alert consciousness as something extravagantly abnormal—the distorted ball of a moon, the eerie half-light, the monstrous cloud shapes, the fog below and around us, the misty indefiniteness of space, the changeless drone, drone, drone of the engines.'

And then suddenly—catastrophe. The Vimy ran into a dense cocoon of fog. Alcock could not see the nose or the wingtips, let alone the horizon. Naturally, he lost all sense of balance. The airspeed indicator shot up, giving the pilot the impression that he was diving. He pulled back on the stick. The next second, the Vimy heeled over into a scream-ing spin. The revolution counter went up. The compass needle began wildly rotating. Only the needle on the altimeter was registering reasonably accurately, rapidly unwinding anti-clockwise, 3000, 2000, 1000, 500 feet . . .

Alcock tried to centralise the controls, but with no horizon or instru-ment indications, he did not know what centre was. Brown loosened his safety belt, preparatory to ditching.

And then they left the cloud as abruptly as they had entered it. A hundred feet from the wave crests, Alcock caught sight of the horizon. Immediately he regained his sense of balance and brought the Vimy out of the spin. At full throttle, the bomber skimmed straight and level just above the sea—now pointing westwards back to Newfoundland.

Alcock swung round 180°, climbed up to 6500 feet and set course again for Ireland. Now the good weather that had been anticipated failed to materialise—another favourite trick of the North Atlantic. The cloud curtain dissolved into heavy rain, then snow, then hail. The glass face of the petrol overflow gauge on one of the centre section struts became obscured. To guard against possible trouble, Brown had to climb out on the wing in the teeth of the hail and slipstream and, balancing in the bumpy air high over the Atlantic, had to clean it and, at the same time, kick the ice off the pitot head which had rendered the airspeed indicator useless.

Not once, but again and again—out into the icy cold, hanging on to the struts to save himself from falling. Sleet had lodged in the ailerons, making lateral control almost impossible. Ice over the air intake was causing the starboard engine to pop and backfire.

The cloud continued. But now it was dawn, and at 11,000 feet Brown managed to shoot the sun which gave him a position close to the Irish coast. He wrote a note to Alcock, 'We had better go lower down, where the air is warmer, and where we might pick up a steamer.'

The pilot gently felt his way down, but it was not until 500 feet that the Vimy emerged from cloud. Brown took a drift on the sea and obtained a wind of 30 knots from 215°. This had taken the aircraft rather north, and Brown gave Alcock a southerly alteration of course.

He placed first a sandwich and some chocolate, then a drink in Alcock's left hand. The pilot's right hand had never left the stick.

Afterwards, the navigator ate and drank a little himself. Then in his own words: 'I had screwed on the lid of the thermos flask and was placing the remains of the food in the tiny cupboard behind my seat, when Alcock grabbed my shoulder, twisted me round, beamed excitedly and pointed ahead and below. His lips were moving, but whatever he said was inaudible above the roar of the engines. I followed the direction indicated by his outstretched forefinger, and barely visible through the mist, it showed me two tiny specks of—land. This happened at 8.15 a.m. on June 15.' He had been almost dead on track, unlike most of the pioneers who followed him, and his navigation log was a model of neatness and accuracy.

Brown duly noted the landfall. A few minutes later, Alcock was circling the village of Clifden in Northern Ireland, firing red flares from the Very pistol. The cloud was very low, down to 250 feet, and with the danger of high ground, the pilot decided to land. He made a perfect landing—but what he took for a field was a bog, and the Vimy turned up on its nose.

But they had flown the Atlantic in one hop lasting 16 hours and 12 minutes. Coast to coast, the average speed was 118.5 mph.

On behalf of the Royal Aero Club, who were acting as umpires for the competition, Major Mayo, a British aircraft engineer, put seals on the Vimy and checked her. A strange thing about the story of the water jump is that like Hawker and Grieve coming back alive, the same people and the same aircraft keep on turning up again and one thing always leads to another. Major Mayo reappears later as technical adviser to Imperial Airways, but on this occasion, knee deep in Irish mud, he checked the level of the tanks and was amazed to find how quickly he reached petrol. His first thought that Alcock had lots of fuel left was overshadowed by the realisation of what a strong westerly must have helped them on their way.

Now an overwhelming welcome engulfed Alcock and Brown. Kathleen Kennedy, Brown's fiancée, who had been anxiously waiting in Manchester, sent her relieved congratulations, saying that she never doubted that he would make it. At the Savoy, the *Daily Mail*'s £10,000 cheque was presented to them by Winston Churchill after a stirring speech. At Buckingham Palace, both were knighted by King George V. At Vickers Weybridge works they were cheered and chaired by the men and girls who had built the Vimy. Wherever they went, the crowds went mad. The *Sunday Evening Telegram* said, 'When the annals of flight are written in the years to come, this deed of crossing the Atlantic will be written in letters of gold and our children shall feel proud of the deeds of the men who crossed the Atlantic Ocean for the first time.'

Over on the other side of the Atlantic, Trygve Gran, the navigator of the V1500 who had been a member of Scott's ill-fated expedition to the South Pole and had found Scott and his companions frozen to death in their tent, heard about Alcock and Brown's knighthoods. Thinking that if only the Handley Page had got over first he would have been knighted, and not very good at English, he telegrammed his newly married actress wife, 'Sorry you aren't a lady.' He was unable to see what

**The Vimy on its nose in a bog at Clifden after successfully crossing the North Atlantic non-stop.** **(Associated Newspapers)**

was wrong with it—and in a sense, he was right. Even if the 1500 did get across, nobody else would be knighted.

Now the non-stop flight had been achieved, the British government would hand out no more knighthoods for the Atlantic. In their own way, those five words of Gran's prophesied the official British attitude to the water jump for the years ahead. A couple of knighthoods and some unorthodox Air Force Crosses had been dished out—and that was *that*.

\*　　\*　　\*

In the same 15th June edition of the evening newspaper that head-lined Alcock and Brown's triumph, tucked away in a corner was also announced that the airship R34 had left her shed for a final test prior to proceeding across the Atlantic, and that the trial had 'proved very satisfactory from every standpoint'.

The R34 had been built almost as a copy of the German Zeppelin L33, which had been shot down by a British fighter pilot over Norfolk after bombing London in 1916. Powered by five 250 hp engines, the airship's lift load was thirty tons and her cruising speed was 45 miles an hour.

Almost unnoticed, with typical British reticence, on 2nd July 1919, Major Scott, with a crew of thirty men, a stowaway and two carrier pigeons (in World War I, warplanes had carried pigeons which flew back to base to notify the squadron if the aircraft was shot down), inched R34 away from her mooring mast at East Fortune in Scotland and set course for New York.

The crossing had been carefully planned, with an Operations Room at the Air Ministry, and three warships had been provided. The real motive force was political—the President of the Aero Club of America had despatched a telegram to the Air Ministry to send an airship to a meeting of aviation groups at Atlantic City. The Air Ministry had hummed and hawed so much that the R34 had missed the meeting—but she was at least on her way.

Harry Hawker, thinking of passenger reaction to his own hair-raising experiences, wrote, 'I need hardly say that commercial aeroplanes are scarcely likely to be called upon to make non-stop flights of upwards of a thousand miles. That sort of journey can probably be better done with an airship.' But in fact R34, while faring very much better, did receive from the North Atlantic a fair quota of excitements. The fabric was ripped in a heavy gale at 45° west, and for hours crew men were balanced on the top of the balloon repairing it.

The Met Officer on board saw R34 was routed over the top of the lows to gain the help of the easterly winds—the first time a Composite track was flown.

She pitched badly, sometimes tilted 24° up by the bow. The Third Officer wrote, 'Sleep is somewhat elusive, my hammock is right over

On arrival at Mineola, the R34 and (left to right) Commander Lansdowne (US Navy),
Lt Durrant, Lt Harris, Major Pritchard, General Maitland, Lt Luck and Lt Shotter.

(Associated Newspapers)

Ford car (engine) and very near the propellor which is revolving
frantically. To add to this, the ship is behaving much after the fashion
affected by lambs in the spring, the technical term is, I think,
gambolling.'

There were thunderstorms over Nova Scotia, and Scott descended to
800 feet, where the crew could smell the pine forests scenting the morning air.

After 108 hours and 12 minutes, R34 arrived unannounced at New
York, and Major Pritchard, the second-in-command, had to descend by
parachute to take charge of landing operations.

Three days later, in the same quiet way, R34 set course for home,
minus one of the pigeons which had already left. It flopped on the deck
of an eastbound Atlantic liner, and finished the trip by sea. On this
crossing, one engine failed and another gave trouble, but with the help
of the winds (after a landfall at Clifden coincidently the same as Brown's)
they reached Pulham in Norfolk in 75 hours and 3 minutes.

Major Scott and his crew were received by King George V, who
appeared more interested in the pigeons than the R34's exploit. Scott
was awarded the CBE. Four more AFCs were produced. This totally
successful first double crossing of the water jump has gone comparatively

The statue of Alcock and Brown below the Control Tower at Heathrow Airport.
(CAA)

unsung, but in the light of all that was unknown then about North Atlantic weather and ice and turbulence and winds, it was a fantastic achievement deserving a place in history beside Read, Hawker and Grieve, and Alcock and Brown.

\*       \*       \*

You have been climbing steeply at $V^2 + 10$ airspeed—around 162 knots indicated. Through the clouds, it has been slightly bumpy, and there has been a slight noise not unlike the sea. Now you are at the top of the climb, and up front your captain has reported at 33,000 feet. Down below you can see nothing but battalions of continuous cloud marching east from the Atlantic to meet you. The statue of Alcock and Brown you first noticed from the coach coming out of the tunnel has long since disappeared.

But in the end, who *did* win the race to be first over the water jump—the British or the Americans?

The American newspapers gave the verdict to Read and his Nancy. But Hawker said of Alcock's flight, 'I am more gratified than I can say that British air supremacy has been maintained by British aviation and a British machine has made the first successful crossing.'

What was the reckoning? On the American side, there was the clear first via the stepping-stones of the Azores and Lisbon—though some would say that was the Mid-Atlantic. On the British side, as well as the magnificent failure of Hawker and Grieve, there was Alcock and Brown's single hop across the North Atlantic and Major Scott's double crossing in R34.

The British add their score up and say confidently that they were first. That statue of Alcock and Brown at London Airport proves it.

Except for one small thing that is not generally known, and which the British never mention. Lieutenant Arthur Whitten Brown of the Royal Flying Corps—the skilful solemn navigator who stands beside Alcock looking westwards towards the North Atlantic, which they flew together —came from an old-established American family and was born an American citizen.

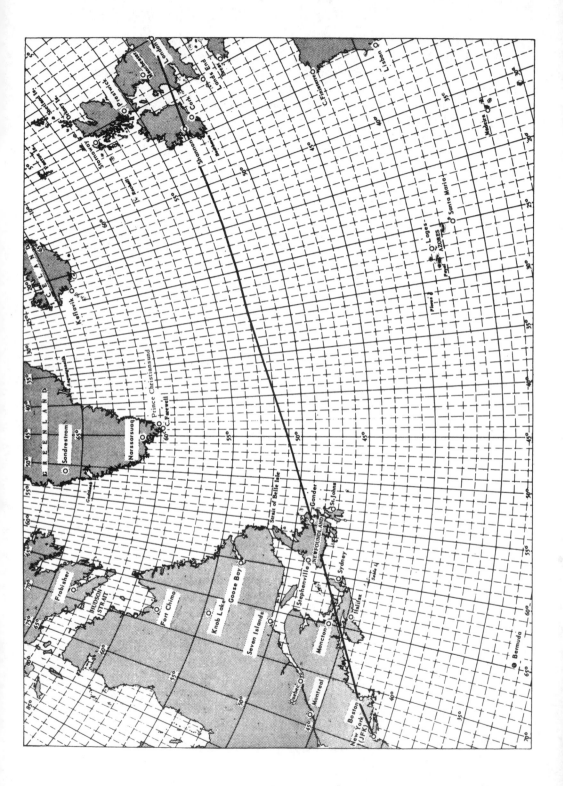

## *Two:* The Military Merry-Go-Round

If you look closely on the starboard side now, you can just see through that break in the clouds a line of cliff topped with meadowland. That is the same sort of view as Alcock and Brown must have had, and the crew of the R34—the green country of Ireland.

It was not to be seen by any more of the early pioneers for years. No champion went out to take a tilt at the North Atlantic sky—in spite of the fact that large money prizes were still being offered.

There were several reasons. First, the Atlantic *had* been conquered. Governments who controlled the money reckoned there was not enough prestige in following up the bloodless victory. The commercial possibilities had not dawned on any politicians. The US Weather Department only consisted of a few meteorologists working for the Agricultural Department, and aviation weather-forecasting was practically non-existent. Civil aviation in America was in the hands of barnstormers and aerial circus performers, who had their pick of thousands of unused warplanes for just a few dollars, in which they carried the mail. Their motto was 'The mail must go through.' Their most useful navigation instrument was a lighted cigar that indicated when it was time to land by burning their noses. The accident rate was astronomic, and the official view was that no paying passengers were ever likely to risk themselves in aeroplanes. The British government maintained that flying was for the birds. The French government was more enterprising, and so were the Germans, who had plans for the South Atlantic, using Zeppelins.

Back in Newfoundland, Admiral Kerr was told by Handley-Page to leave his exclusive airfield and take his V1500 south for the New York to London direct hop. But on the way down, the big plane broke her undercarriage, and though it was repaired, the Atlantic flight was abandoned. Instead, the V1500 became the first aerial salesman, flying round America loaded with British goods, such as ladies' frocks, tailored suits and furs. Trying to reach Cleveland, the V1500 became lost and in

[37]

*Opposite :* The route of the modern Jumbo jets.

landing on a racecourse clipped the tips of both wings off on the judge's box in the grandstand. Not even Handley-Page had any idea what to do with the wreck, and eventually ladies' bracelets were made from the longerons of the fuselage, while two of the engines were fitted to a fast rumrunner speedboat on Lake Erie.

Then one single individual had a go on his own, a West Indian pilot named Jubert Julian. He intended to fly to Ethiopia via the Azores. As a tribute to America, he set off from Roosevelt Field, New York on the Fourth of July 1924, and as a tribute to his destination he named his plane *Ethiopia I*. He thus started a trend in names of contenders for the water jump, getting away from manufacturers' numbers. Aircraft were christened for patriotic reasons *America, Old Glory, Yankee Clipper, Lithuania, Faith in Australia, American Nurse* and after cities (*Pride of Detroit, Spirit of St Louis*), and after sponsors and their families (*Sir John Carling, Winnie Mae*). Later human yearnings can be discerned in *Tail Wind* and *The Endeavour*. Certainly the strangest name of all—but appropriate to the water jump—was '*Untin' Bowler*, a Sikorsky amphibian completely financed by the *Chicago Tribune*. Unfortunately, the nearest *Ethiopia I* got to its destination was Flushing Bay a couple of minutes after take-off, but luckily the pilot was saved.

Another race now broke out—this time to be first to fly round the world—and in a fever of patriotism, preparations were hastened in a number of countries. None made them more massively and methodically than the USA, where the American Army planned to use four Douglas two-seater amphibians, named *Seattle, Boston, New Orleans* and *Chicago*. These aircraft were powered by a 420 hp Liberty engine, had an all-up weight of around 8000 lb, a speed of 100 mph, and cost just under $20,000 each. The idea was to carry floats and wheels, using whichever was appropriate to the local terrain. Once again, as with the American Navy success five years before, the organisation was immense. US warships with spares, fuel and technicians were sent out to positions all over the world.

The trip started badly. The *Seattle* crashed on a mountain peak in Alaska, but the crew walked for ten days to safety. The other three aircraft continued their adventures round the world in competition with other nationals.

The British pilot, Major MacLaren, crashed in Burma. Captain D'Oisy of France was reported to have crashed near Shanghai. Competitors from Portugal, Italy and Argentina were well on their way.

Eventually the three Douglas Cruisers reached England on 16th July 1924, where the aircraft were prepared for the water jump. In one of the many receptions, the Prince of Wales had met the Americans, told them that he was going to New York by boat in a few days, and bet them five dollars that he would be there first.

This time, the northern route of the water jump was being attempted —and almost certainly worse weather would result. Blind flying instruments were still the same—quarter moon-shaped levelling bubbles on the panel, to indicate roll, and similar instruments on the cockpit side to indicate pitch. *Boston*, *Chicago* and *New Orleans* set off from the Orkneys, in formation, straight into thick fog. *New Orleans* got into a spin but managed to pull out just above the sea and proceeded to Reykjavik. The other two returned, setting off again next morning.

This time the weather was good, but the oil pressure on *Boston* dropped to zero, and Lieutenant Wade had to alight on the water, while *Chicago* went to look for a ship. The USS *Richmond* was not far away, rescued the airmen and began towing the aircraft to the Faroes—but the sea was too rough and the *Boston* sank.

Smith and Arnold in *Chicago* and Nelson and Harding in *New Orleans* were now joined in Reykjavik by the Italian competitor, Locatelli, in a German Dornier Wal flying boat. Bad weather kept them grounded till 21st August, when all three took off for Greenland in rough formation. But thick cloud soon separated them, and though the two Americans arrived safely there was no sign of the Italian.

For three days and nights, the ubiquitous American warships looked for the Wal in heavy seas. Just on the point of giving up, the *Richmond* spotted a glint of silver among the glitter of the ice floes—the wreck of the flying boat, forced down by bad weather. Yet again, airmen were rescued by ships from the very jaws of the Atlantic.

The two Douglas aircraft took off from Greenland on 31st August for Labrador, and at the point of no return the fuel pump on *Chicago* failed. Fuel had to be hand-pumped up from the main tank for the rest of the trip, before a landing was made at Icy Tickle in Labrador. When repairs had been completed, the flight was continued via Nova Scotia.

One of the Douglas Cruisers that flew round the world, crossing the Atlantic by the northern route, August 1924. (John Underwood)

The two Douglas Cruisers *Chicago* and *New Orleans* attract the crowds after their world flight, 1924. (John Taylor)

Finally both aircraft reached New York, after being first to fly round the world in 363 hours spread over 175 days, to be greeted by a handshake from the Prince of Wales and, 'Good show, well done . . . shall we settle our bets, gentlemen?'

Now the Germans showed the world their superiority in airships. Dr Eckener flew the Zeppelin LZ126, which America had claimed as part of war reparations, from Friedrichshafen to Lakehurst, New Jersey, non-stop via the Azores in 3½ days.

The scoreboard at the end of that 1924 burst of activity was that the North Atlantic had been flown by Read in a Nancy flying boat via the stepping-stones of the Azores, by Alcock and Brown on the non-stop west to east direct flight, by Scott in the R34 direct both ways, by Smith and Arnold, Nelson and Harding in Douglas seaplanes via the west-bound Iceland–Greenland–Labrador route, and now also westbound by Eckener in the LZ126. Not one life had been lost. Ringed right round, the Atlantic looked on the point of being corralled.

But for the next two years, nobody moved.

# *Three:* **The Flying Fools**

As always, the main reason was money. Lots of prizes were on offer, including the Orteig $25,000 for non-stop either way between New York and Paris, Colonel Easterwood's $25,000 for the first successful crossing to Dallas, Texas, in under seventy-five hours, and prizes from William Randolph Hearst's newspapers, oil companies and breweries. But the rewards were for successes—nobody wanted failures. Air forces, navies and aircraft manufacturers had financed the early attempts for prestige purposes, because they had aircraft available unused in war. Now, in a climate of drastic warplane cutback and governments uninterested in civil aviation, money was much tighter. And the cost of fitting up an aeroplane to do the water jump was phonomenal—far beyond the means of aviators.

The second reason was the state of the aviation art. The early flights had conclusively demonstrated that engines were unreliable. The weather encountered (often unexpectedly), had showed both the dangers of the Atlantic sky and the difficulties, with inadequate resources and knowledge, in forecasting its moods with anything like accuracy. Then Hawker had said that the number of people in the world capable of navigating across the Atlantic could be counted on the fingers of one hand, and even six years later the science of aerial navigation was still trying to shake itself free from ship navigation and have suitable air-borne equipment made available. The pilots still did not have blind-flying instruments, and three experienced and highly trained pilots had got into a spin on the crossing. Since these early reconnaissances of the Atlantic sky had confirmed that it was one continuous cloud, what chance had the individual enthusiast?

The third was the width of the water jump—almost two thousand miles of water from Newfoundland to Ireland. That measurement mesmerised pilots, particularly as so few had any real idea of navigation. They had heard of Alcock's large fuel reserve left and of the prevailing westerly winds, but even so they could visualise, only too clearly, being lost above a desert of water or bucking impossible headwinds, so they preferred to be on the safe side and load themselves up to the gills with petrol—thus sealing their own fate. In fact, there is no positive record of anyone on the water jump, either in the early attempts or the thousands of later trans-ocean flights ever actually coming down in the Atlantic with dry tanks. What was far more dangerous was the fear of it. The West Indian Julian had shown that an aircraft overloaded with fuel ends up in Flushing Bay.

But the lesson was not learned. The first ones off on 21st September 1926, Fonck, Curtin, Islamoff and Clavier in a French attempt on the Orteig prize, flying a heavily-laden Sikorsky, crashed on take-off at New York, and Islamoff and Clavier were burned alive. Seven months later, a team full of experts—Admiral Byrd, Floyd Bennett, Noville and Fokker (who had built the trimotor aircraft)—crashed during a test flight. Four days later, Davis and Wooster failed to get airborne and drowned in their aircraft *American Legion*.

Then on 8th May 1927, Nungesser—famous as a French ace who had shot down fifty German aircraft—with Coli, tried to win the prize the hard way from Paris to New York against the westerlies. But *L'Oiseau Blanc*, with a skull, a coffin and two funeral candles painted on its side, simply disappeared.

Captain Nungesser (right) and Coli in *L'Oiseau Blanc* before their Atlantic attempt from Paris during which they disappeared, 8 May 1927. (Associated Newspapers)

The early congratulations on a bloodless victory over the Atlantic sky had been premature.

It is against this background that the achievement of Lindbergh should be viewed. He was not the first to do the water jump by a long way. But he was the first individual to conceive, organise and carry it out in the teeth of previous failures and disasters—and twelve days after the Frenchmen disappeared, he took off alone.

Wing-walker, barnstormer, ex-Army pilot, air circus parachute jumper—no wonder the crowd hero-worshipped him as 'The Flying Fool'. But the fearlessness and apparent extrovert carelessness was the front to an enigma. He looks in most of his photographs like a shy and serious young Dean of Students or a skypilot in the religious sense. 'Boss! How much you all charge foah to take me up to Heaben and leave me dah?' one Negro woman had asked him. But as an antidote, he had the same Kennedy quality of relieving this solemnity with huge

The then unknown Lindbergh standing in front of the *Spirit of St Louis* before his Atlantic flight. The original caption on this photograph described Lindbergh simply as 'a mail pilot.'                                                        (Topical Press)

boyish grins. He was not so much an introvert as a very private person, a taciturn man concealing his thoughts and feelings. A clever pilot, he also had the meticulous and scientific approach to little details of an engineer. Astute in business and public relations, he obtained the backing of the businessmen of the city of St Louis for his project, then had the Ryan Company build the *Spirit of St Louis* to his own specifications in two months for $6000. The fuselage was mostly one huge fuel tank, located behind the Wright Whirlwind 223 hp engine in front of the pilot; in order to see over the engine a submarine-type periscope was installed.

'The North Atlantic,' he was to write in a foreword for his wife's book, *Listen! The Wind*, 'is the most important, and is also the most difficult to fly, of all the oceans crossed by the trade routes of men. Distance and climate have combined to place obstacles in the path of those who wish to travel over it.' He knew the risks and he planned the crossing with painstaking thoroughness beforehand—maps, charts, everything for the 3610 miles from Roosevelt Field to Paris had been prepared. He did not take risks. He waited for the right time and the right weather—till the forecast was that 'the North Atlantic should be clear with only local storms on the coast of Europe' and 'the moon had just passed full'.

At 7.52 a.m. on 20th May 1927, Lindbergh opened the throttles of *Spirit of St Louis*. A white flag on a stick indicated the halfway mark on the runway and his intention was to abort the take-off there if he did not feel flying speed under him—the first 'V1' that jet pilots watch for today. He bumped off the ground, cleared telephone wires at the boundary by twenty feet, and set course towards Nova Scotia in excellent visibility.

A comparison with Alcock and Brown eight years before is inevitable. Lindbergh was flying between the capitals of New York and Paris, not between two sparsely inhabited regions. His route was 1650 miles longer than the shortest direct water jump. He had no radio—preferring the weight in fuel—but Alcock and Brown virtually had no radio either. He had no navigator, again preferring the fuel, being confident that even if he was 300 miles off course on the other side, he would still have the petrol to reach Paris. He hoped to position himself by the look of the terrain rather than by astro-navigation.

On the other hand, he had a comfortable cabin in comparison to the noisy freezing open cockpit of the Vimy. He knew that the Atlantic sky was navigable, and that the weather, even though rough, could be flown through, particularly at around this time of year, because others had done it.

Then he had better instruments, much better arranged on the panel in front of him—altimeter, airspeed indicator, clock, oil temperature and pressure gauge, fuel gauge, turn and bank indicator and tachometer (revolution counter). Above all, he had his attitude indicators (still spirit-level bubbles) *both* lateral and longtitudinal directly in front of him—and the reading from the earth inductor compass indicator vertically staring him back straight between the eyes, where Alcock had to peer down to the old-fashioned horizontal magnetic compass.

The earth inductor compass was first used by Byrd on his polar flights. A conducting master unit is located in the best possible position away from magnetic interference, and this cuts the earth's lines of force at different angles dependent on the heading of the aircraft. Different electromotive fields are generated on the unit and these are calibrated to read in terms of degrees. Though it was inclined to be erratic, such a compass was designed to be more accurate and, since it should not spin off course so much in turns, was more help to blind flying. Around half-way across, Lindbergh did report having difficulty with both his compasses, but at that time he was weaving in heavy turbulence, which might have been the reason.

Then for most of the time, Lindbergh had better weather—and he had carburettor heating to stop ice choking his engine.

Both Alcock and Brown's and Lindbergh's were tremendous achievements, but Lindbergh did it *alone*. No one was going to try the water jump alone again till eighteen months later, when the Englishman McDonald attempted it from Newfoundland in a Gipsy Moth. He disappeared. After McDonald, there was no solo attempt till the American Diteman in 1929. He disappeared also. In 1930, Wynne-Eaton crashed on take-off from Newfoundland. Ruth Nichols tried, but she crashed on landing in New Brunswick before starting. A year later, the American Reichers almost made it. He ditched with engine trouble only 47 miles from the Irish coast, and was picked up by the SS *President Roosevelt*. Lindbergh's successful solo water jump was not matched till, on exactly the same day but five years later, Mrs Putnam, the former Amelia Earhart, flew a Lockheed Vega from Newfoundland to Northern Ireland. Three months later, the first solo east-to-west flight was made by the British pilot Jim Mollison.

As Lindbergh approached Newfoundland in *Spirit of St Louis*, the weather thickened. Fog covered the sea, through which icebergs gleamed. Forced by gathering storms up to 10,000 feet, he noted, 'There was no moon and it was very dark. The tops of some of the storm clouds were several thousand feet above me.'

That meant blind-flying through clouds, but he weaved round them as much as possible. At one time 'sleet started to collect on the plane and I was forced to turn around and get back again into clear air'.

Then the moon appeared which made flying 'much less complicated'. But further high cloud awaited him ahead and continuously covered the sea.

Like Whitten Brown before him, he too was struck by the mystery of the Atlantic sky. 'Numerous shorelines appeared, with trees perfectly outlined against the horizon. In fact, the mirages were so natural that had I not been in mid-Atlantic and known that no land existed along my route, I would have taken them to be actual islands.'

Dawn was 1 am New York time. The temperature began rising, and there was no further danger of ice. A fog bank loomed ahead, through which he had to fly entirely blind.

Then the weather became broken, and he could see the sea below. He came right down to the tops of the waves, to get the maximum 'cushion effect' on his wings.

The constant hand-flying, often in thick cloud and storms, was desperately tiring, and he had the greatest difficulty keeping awake. At one stage when he was blind-flying, suddenly the nose went down, one wing dropped, the *Spirit of St Louis* started to dive. Another Atlantic spin appeared about to develop but, recovering his senses, Lindbergh righted the aircraft. But as he continued he felt as though he was flying in a dream. He made himself do exercises and pushed his face out into the slipstream to keep himself awake. After his ordeal, he was to write: 'I have been to eternity and back.'

The first indication that he was close to land was a fleet of fishing boats. He circled one, and saw a man's face. 'I circled again and closing the throttle as the plane passed within a few feet of the boat, I shouted, "Which way is Ireland?" '

There was no reply—but now he could see a rugged coastline on the horizon. As it curved towards the east, he had no difficulty identifying the tip of Ireland—but to make absolutely sure, in typical Lindbergh

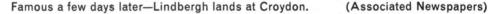

**Famous a few days later—Lindbergh lands at Croydon.**     (Associated Newspapers)

fashion, he altered course and got a pin-point actually over Cape Valentia before resuming course for southern England and Paris.

He had been almost on track. But after all that weaving and change of altitude and without radio or astro, how was that possible? Luck must have come into it. Though he carried a drift sight he did not use it, so that he can have had little idea of wind effect. His greatest worry was the cumulative extent of possible navigation errors, which he thought might put him over four hundred miles north or south of track. However, he had kept on his course, constantly turning to the left, driven by the same sort of sense of direction that many pilots have—a kind of homing instinct. Even so, he made no more oceanic flights afterwards without celestial navigation.

He wrote, 'The sun went down shortly after passing Cherbourg, and soon the beacons along the Paris–London airway became visible.'

Ahead now were the lights of Paris. Shortly afterwards he managed to identify Le Bourget by the row of hangars. Of that historic moment he simply wrote, 'I flew low over the field once, then circled around into the wind and landed.'

Alone, he had done the water jump in thirty-three and a half hours at an average speed of 107.9 miles an hour, somewhat slower than Alcock and Brown's average eight years before. Like Alcock, he had a large reserve of fuel—enough for another 850 miles. A most fantastic welcome awaited him.

He did all the right things, and said exactly the few right words that were required. He became a symbol, a phenomenon that released a mass of world emotion. He telephoned his mother. He called on Mrs Nungesser, and at the Aero Club of France said Nungesser and Coli had attempted (by the westbound against the wind) a far more difficult feat than his own. He took up a French fighter. He visited Blériot, Foch, Joffre. The Lindbergh phenomenon was, naturally enough, exploited for political reasons. 'This young man from out of the West,' as the American ambassador called him, had brought France closer to America —which indeed he had. In London, he was received by the King and Queen, and was, inevitably, decorated with the unorthodox Air Force Cross.

He took off again for France, but after thirty-eight minutes landed at Lympne. There he waited till the eight o'clock Imperial Airways Handley Page mail and passenger plane flew over, and then up he went and used the big plane as a guide to Le Bourget.

Cautious, quiet, unassuming—it is the Lindbergh legend that is remembered, not the man. This is what brought in the reported $3\frac{1}{2}$ million letters, several thousand offers of marriage, 5000 poems, 1400 gift parcels and three invitations to go to the moon in a rocket. When he was living in England to avoid further publicity of the tragic kidnapping

The Bellanca *Miss Columbia* in which Chamberlin and Levine flew the Atlantic a fortnight after Lindbergh. (Flight)

of his son, at a ball at Hever Castle, the Queen sent word to ask him to dance. He said he did not know how to—so the Queen came over and sat talking with him instead. He did many surveys for Pan American Airways, including the Greenland–Iceland and mid and south Atlantic routes. He was also the first man by years to predict the 'right' Atlantic vehicle—but few listened. The same engineer's precision and meticulous attention to detail was evident to the end of his life: when fatally ill in 1974, he gave minute details for the location and preparation of his quiet burial in his South Seas island home in Maui in the Hawaiian islands.

\*       \*       \*

Only a fortnight after Lindbergh, the pilot Chamberlin took off in a Bellanca from New York, trying for Berlin. In this same aircraft, *Miss Columbia*, with Acosta (later to fly the Atlantic with Byrd) he had established a world record by remaining airborne for over fifty-one hours. He was accompanied by his sponsor Levine who had attracted attention by being something of a clown. They had a good flight over, largely uneventful but, like Lindbergh, had come down to ground level to shout above the throttled-back engine, 'Which way to Berlin?' Flying on in the direction indicated, Chamberlin was forced by lack of fuel to land at Eisleben a few miles short of Berlin, after a record 3905 miles non-stop flight. This magnificent feat should be in the front rank with the others—but, because it was a few days after Lindbergh, is rarely remembered, though Chamberlin piloted and did almost all the navigating. Once he had handed over the piloting to Levine, in order to have a nap—only to awake and find *Miss Columbia* in a spin and Levine roaring with laughter. Chamberlin just managed to pull out in time. Levine considered that the whole thing was so easy that he wanted to turn round and fly back westwards to New York.

But Chamberlin wisely declined. So Levine, who was not a pilot, took off in his Bellanca to do it on his own, via London. He managed the take-off all right, but coming in to land at Croydon, bounced higher than the gasometers. His second attempt was no better, and now he had thoroughly frightened the people on the ground. The airport controller sent another aircraft to guide him in, and following the other pilot exactly, Levine managed to put the Bellanca down safely. But he did not proceed with his plan to do the water jump westwards.

Lindbergh and Chamberlin were the so-called 'Flying Fools'. In fact, quite apart from their aviation skill, both were astute and clever fighters of the Atlantic sky, who made their preparations carefully and wisely appreciated the strength of their opponent.

Both showed how an individual flier could organise, finance and carry out the water jump successfully—thus opening the doors to the most spectacular and the most dangerous aerial circus the world has ever known.

After their arrival in Germany—(left to right) Charles Levine, Herr Marx, the German Chancellor, Clarence Chamberlin, Herr Stresemann, the German Foreign Minister.                              (Pacific and Atlantic)

# *Four:* Those Daring Young Men on the Flying Trapeze

For the next decade, it was as though the Atlantic had been turned into an enormous circus tent, roofed by a continuous sheet of wet grey flapping canvas, possessing instead of a safety net two thousand miles of cold rough sea, over which a continuous procession of the most colourful and courageous performers balanced on the high wire while the world watched breathless and waited for them to fall.

They flew little aeroplanes dizzily painted as though in the racing colours of their sponsors, partly from panache, partly with the practical view that if they were forced down on the sea they would more easily be spotted—red, silver, black and red, snow-white, red and black, gold and white, black and white, red with green and purple stripes, orange and maroon, red, white and blue, orange and white, red and green. There was even a little Moth, piloted by the British pilot Grierson, that was painted red on one side and black on the other, appropriately named *Rouge et Noir* with its echoes of the gaming tables.

This was the era of the individuals. Out of their successes, failures and tragedies was to come the beginnings of civil aviation over the North Atlantic. It was they who brought it home to airlines and to governments and to aircraft manufacturers that it could be flown safely and that it was a real commercial proposition. It was through their example that those who called the water jump impossible gradually came to change their minds, to think that there was nothing to it.

Governments for the most part sat back with the general public and watched the circus. They were only too conscious of the expenditure of the tax-payers' money in a period of trade recession, particularly as the economic depression had now begun to bite deeply. The French and German governments backed the individual efforts of their sons with encouragement and finance. Italy backed three military airmen led by De Pinedo in a magnificent flight across the South Atlantic, and then from Newfoundland via the Azores to Lisbon in a Savoia-Marchetti flying boat in June 1927. America was uncharacteristically tight-fisted, partly because incentive prizes had, in any case, been put up by their rich citizens, partly because, at the end of the twenties, their chosen instrument for the water jump, Pan American Airways, was beginning to emerge. The British government remained true to form, facing east towards Mecca and the Empire, their backs to the Atlantic, though they had nominated Imperial Airways as *their* chosen horse if ever the water jump emerged from the circus stunt stage. Meanwhile, as casualties and attempts bordering on the crazy mounted and other governments (particularly the French) worried and began attempting to control the flights and actively to discourage them, the Air Minister in Parliament declined to intervene.

In spite of the magnificent flights of Lindbergh and Chamberlin, the prospect in front of those daring individuals who followed them looked bleak. Certainly the two Americans had shown that the way to do it was to get a rich sponsor and make the most careful preparations. But they were both highly experienced pilots, and the next New York to Paris attempt twenty-five days after Chamberlin—which really belonged to the pre-Lindbergh era in that it was Admiral Byrd's attempt in the now repaired Fokker backed by Wanamaker—was again by expert airmen, and even so, they really got into difficulties.

Byrd's generosity to other competitors in the race, including Lindbergh, in offering extensive navigation advice, in which he was so experienced, as well as the use of his runway at Roosevelt Field, had been in contrast to some British behaviour in Newfoundland before the first direct crossing.

Now with Acosta as pilot, together with Fokker test pilot Bernt Balchen (another of the immigrants to whom American aviation owes so much) and Noville as engineer and radioman, they took off into drizzle on the early morning of 29th June 1927.

Across Nova Scotia, the weather deteriorated into storm cloud, then thick fog blanketed what Byrd guessed was Newfoundland. Balchen was just reaching for chicken-in-the-basket under his seat when he was flung violently to one side. Peering up at the instrument board, he saw the bubble on the turn and bank hard over and the airspeed indicator dropping even though they were diving. Another spin had developed over the Atlantic. Balchen grabbed the controls and righted the aircraft. The Fokker had an earth inductor compass and better instruments than Alcock, but Acosta was basically a stunt pilot. He turned to Balchen and said, 'Boy! This instrument flying is one thing I don't know anything about.' Thereafter, Balchen was responsible for most of the flying, while Byrd struggled with the navigation in conditions of almost continuous cloud. Unsure of the winds, they were beginning to worry about running out of fuel.

Fortunately, the radio kept them in contact with ships, and unknown to them, they had a 30 mph tail wind. Eventually they sighted the coast of France which they identified as Brest and showed them to be well south of track.

Then the visibility deteriorated so that not even the wingtips could be seen. Le Bourget was hidden in fog. They circled what Byrd hoped was Paris, but since nothing could be seen, set course north, hoping to let down over the Channel. But when they descended on Byrd's dead-reckoning position, Balchen saw the spires of Rouen cathedral sticking up out of the mist.

Various courses were tried which in the nil visibility only confused navigation further. After 42 hours in the air, they were all tired out. Through the rain, they saw an electric sign on top of a building *Deauville.*

Byrd decided to land and threw out three carbide drift flares which ignited on the surface. Balchen hovered over the first, judged his height by the third and cut his engine over the second.

A bow wave immediately engulfed *America*. Balchen was coated with oil, and struggled for a grip as water poured on top of him. All the crew managed to struggle out into shallow water, rescuing a piece of a historic American flag and 150 lb of mail sworn in by the Post Office as the first official trans-Atlantic mail carrier. They waded ashore to find themselves near Caen, not far from what was to be the main World War II invasion beach.

The next successful crossing was that of the Americans Schlee and Brock who flew in their Stinson *Pride of Detroit* from Newfoundland to London. Unheralded, accompanied with the minimum of ballyhoo, now almost forgotten, this again was a magnificent and skilful flight that deserves far greater recognition, particularly as they then flew on by stages to Tokyo.

The Stinson *Pride of Detroit* arrives in Croydon after flying the Atlantic, 27 August 1927.                                                                    (Central News)

Schlee (left) and Brock (centre) in front of *Pride of Detroit* after their successful crossing.                                                                                    (Central News)

Much more typical of this early period and the 1920s was the attempt by Princess Lowenstein-Wertheim, who engaged two experienced British airmen, Minchin and Hamilton, to fly her in her Fokker monoplane from Salisbury Plain to Montreal. Upavon was chosen because it was one of the longest aerodromes in Britain—necessary because of the vast amount of fuel required to do the westbound trip against the headwinds. The Princess was British and had married a German prince who had been killed fighting for the Spaniards against the Americans in 1899. She was determined to be not only the first woman across, but to do the first east–west crossing before Levine or the French or the Germans did it. She was sixty. On 31st August 1927, in blustery weather, the Bishop of Cardiff christened the monoplane *St Raphael*, after the patron Saint of airmen, and off they set 'the hard way' into the teeth of the headwinds, only just managing to stagger into the air. Half-way across the water jump, their lights were spotted by an oil tanker in the night sky—and they were never seen again.

Such a colourful performance, full of panache and daring leading to tragedy, was to be repeated again and again. The fact that over three-quarters of the flights that disappeared into the Atlantic sky were flown by American, Canadian and British pilots makes one wonder whether this had something to do with national temperaments. Only one

Princess Lowenstein in full flying fig towers above her pilot after one of the earlier flights that inspired her to make her ill-fated attempt in *St Raphael* with Minchin and Hamilton, 31 August 1927.                                    (Popperfoto)

French aircraft disappeared. The Germans tackled the job extremely carefully and without bravado. The attempt of Von Huenefeld, Starke and Loose in their Junkers *Bremen* on 14th August 1927 from Dessau to New York was characteristic. After eighteen hundred miles flying, they encountered appalling weather and wisely returned. The record of the Germans on the water jump was one of methodical planning, the most careful execution and the greatest respect for the North Atlantic weather.

The British had become interested in the much dreaded northern route, and in 1930 Gino Watkin's expedition had set off to explore Greenland and live there a year to examine the possibilities of a regular air route across that particular stepping-stone to Canada. The Greenland route was in fact chosen by the Germans.

No series of Atlantic flights were carried out more quietly and successfully, one after the other, than by Von Gronau, the chief instructor at the German civil aviation school, in Dornier Wal flying boats. With Zimmer as his pilot, Hack as engineer, Albrecht as the radio operator and himself doing the navigating, he set off from Germany on 20th August 1930 via Reyjkavik, Greenland, Labrador to Halifax, Nova Scotia and landed at New York on 26th August, after 47 hours flying time.

On 8th August 1931, the same German crew set off again in a Wal, this time sponsored by Lufthansa, and again went to New York by the northern route. In July 1932 they once again flew the northern route

The crew of the Dornier *Wal*—(left to right) Albrecht, Hack, von Gronau, Zimmer—who flew the Atlantic by the northern route, August 1930. (Dornier)

Greenland's icy mountains—a view from von Gronau's Dornier *Wal*. (Dornier)

The Dornier *Wal* arrives in New York. (Dornier)

(with Von Roth as pilot instead of Zimmer)—but after landing at New York, they continued round the world.

A logical progression, sensibly surveying the route twice before going further. No German pilot disappeared or was killed on the water jump. It was the English-speaking nations who brushed aside bad Atlantic weather forecasts, ignored pleas of 'Don't go,' revved up the tiny engines of frail aircraft, smiled, waved, took-off—and vanished.

The Junkers W-33L in which the Germans, von Huenefeld and Koehl with the Irishman Fitzmaurice set off from Dublin on 12th April 1928, had much the same 'corrugated-iron' look about it that had the Ju52 troop-carrier of World War II. Years ahead of its time, an all-metal monoplane with cantilever wings, its main drawback was its small 310 hp engine. The Versailles Treaty had put restrictions on German engine capacity.

They set off Great Circle to New York just above the waves, the pilots taking three-hour stints, von Huenefeld using smoke bombs on the surface of the sea to gauge wind speed and direction. The whole of the fuselage had been coated with paraffin as an anti-icer. No radio was carried.

Early on the morning of 13th April they ran into the Newfoundland fog banks and their compasses began to behave erratically. Not knowing where they were, and worried about fuel, they suddenly saw a light. Thinking it was a ship, they circled and identified it as a lighthouse on the tip of a snow-covered island. Koehl tried a hazardous landing during which the undercarriage collapsed.

The place was Greenly Island north of Newfoundland, a thousand miles from New York. But the flight was a tremendous achievement, the first east-west crossing 'the hard way' against the prevailing west winds in 36½ hours.

The all-metal Junkers W33 in which the Germans von Huenefeld and Koehl and the Irishman Fitzmaurice completed the first east to west crossing in thirty-six and a half hours, after crashing at Greenly Island, Labrador, 13 April 1928.          (Gurra)

In the twelve months following Lindbergh, five aircraft had returned because of bad weather, three failed for mechanical reasons, one had crashed on take-off, five (two British, two Americans and one Canadian) disappeared.

Why did they go? Mainly because the Atlantic, like the mountain Everest, was *there*—and had to be thoroughly conquered. Money prizes certainly came into it and fame and scientific advancement. The wealthy Herndon said before his 1931 flight in *Miss Veedol*, 'we are doing it more for fun than anything else.' Many went for patriotic reasons. Individuals from all nations insisted on trying the water jump regardless of the dangers. On 5th August 1928 Idzikowski and Kubala took off from New York in their monoplane *Marshal Pilsudski*, but half way over had engine trouble and were forced to ditch, being rescued by the SS *Samoa*. Almost a year later off they went again, sponsored by their own government, in a grey Amiot also christened *Marshal Pilsudski*. Landing at

Graciosa in the Azores, the aircraft crashed and burst into flames in which Idzikowski died. The Portuguese brothers de Monteverde crashed taking off from New York for Lisbon in their overloaded black and white Bellanca *Magellan*. This tremendous desire of American immigrants to return to their own country in an aeroplane was a continuing great motivating force.

On 15th July 1933 Girenas and Darius set off from New York, in an orange Bellanca, to fly to their native Haunas in Lithuania, but after successfully doing the water jump and flying 5000 miles, unaccountably crashed into the Brandenburg Forest and both were killed. The Adamowicz brothers with Hoiriis continually tried to get to their native Poland, eventually in 1934 succeeding in their Bellanca *City of Warsaw*.

Waitkus, in his white and orange *Lithuania II*, did the crossing in 1935 but crashed on landing in Ireland.

Financed by their government, the Hungarians, Endresz and Magyar, attempted non-stop from Newfoundland to Budapest in their Lockheed *Justice for Hungary*, and landed with dry tanks a few miles short. In 1935, Solberg and Oscanyan in their amphibian *Eiriksson* made a successful flight via the northern route of Labrador, Greenland and Iceland to Oslo.

But the most famous and most colourful of these nationalistic enterprises was that of Corrigan, perhaps because it was so typically 'little man against the big Atlantic'. Corrigan was an Irish-American who had been a mechanic on Lindbergh's plane. Knowing he would never get clearance to fly his 165 hp Curtiss Robin across the Atlantic, he filed a flight plan from New York to Los Angeles. Twenty-one hours and thirteen minutes later, he 'mistakenly landed' in Dublin. He stoutly maintained that he had put 'red on blue' (that is, had his compass needle reversed between the lubber lines), so flying east instead of west. The authorities were not deceived, but turned a blind eye to 'Wrong Way Corrigan' as he was now known internationally.

As with Corrigan following Lindbergh, so the same names and the same dates turn up on the water jump again and again. The same aeroplanes too, under different names, and certainly the same *types* of aircraft. The honours for this era should go to the Bellancas. It was these tiny aircraft that faced most often the might of the Atlantic sky in that early era and won through—but they were closely followed by the Stinson, the larger Dornier Wal, Fokker, de Havilland, Sikorsky and later the Lockheed Vega. The record of all these aircraft on the water jump was magnificent. May 20th, the famous Lindbergh date, was chosen by several pilots to begin their own water jump (and on this date the first American 707 jet for the Atlantic was christened). The same people try the water jump, fail, and try again. Such an attitude is personified in John Grierson, who crashed in August 1933 in his DH seaplane *Rouge et Noir* taking off from Iceland, but was back again in a successful crossing a year later from London to New York in a Fox Moth called *Robert Bruce*, after the man who had watched a spider fail nine times to reach the top of a cave and succeed on the tenth attempt.

The second man successfully to complete the east-west crossing was the Australian, Kingsford-Smith, in the Fokker trimotor *Southern Cross*. So much of the expenses were borne by the Dutch (including the designer Fokker) that Kingsford-Smith chose a Dutch co-pilot, Van Dyk. Saul was the navigator and Stannage the radio operator. There was something of the eve of Waterloo about this flight. At a farewell ball in Ireland, 'the Ladies of the Curragh' presented Kingsford-Smith with a tablet inscribed in Gaelic. Storms were forecast on the Atlantic and a 25 mph headwind, but at 4.25 on 24th June 1930, the Australian opened up the three throttles and took off from the flat sands at Portmarnock,

The Australian Kingsford-Smith, who completed the east-west crossing in the Fokker *Southern Cross*, 24/25 June 1930. (Flight)

watched by a crowd of eight thousand. He was anxious to beat the Frenchmen Costes and Bellonte, who were waiting for the perfect day to make the first Paris to New York flight.

Trying to avoid blind flying, Kingsford-Smith flew below the fog bank. But Stannage was fearful of losing their long-wave aerial that trailed behind them, so he was forced to climb into the mist.

Radio first really came into its own on the water jump with this trip. It worked perfectly, and Stannage was in communication with many ships—particularly the *Transylvania* which practically navigated the *Southern Cross* over the Atlantic. Stannage would send continuous Vs (. . . —), and the various ships would take a bearing with their direction-finding loops. Knowing their own position, the ships were able to indicate the bearing of the aircraft. These bearings would then be transmitted to the *Transylvania*, acting as parent ship, which would lay off the bearings on her chart and pass Stannage the fixes obtained.

Such help was invaluable, since they never saw the sea. Kingsford-Smith tried to climb, but found such strong headwinds that his ground speed was down to 50 mph—and he was forced back into the overcast. All through the night fog enveloped the *Southern Cross*. Kingsford-Smith wrote, 'We were tired of this blind flying. It was getting on our nerves. We could see nothing, and there seemed to be no end to that opaque wall of greyness ahead of us at which we stared through the windshield.'

So down he went towards the sea—till a frantic note from Stannage *For God's sake, no lower. Aerial dragged in water twice* sent him roaring up again. The radio aerial was only 125 feet long.

Next, each of the three compasses suddenly read differently—and then there was the question of which, if any, was right. But after a climb to 3500 feet, to their relief, the needles settled down again into uniformity—and on they droned through the fog.

**The Fokker trimotor** *Southern Cross.*                    **(Pacific and Atlantic)**

Suddenly, through a rift appeared a rocky coastline which they identified as Avalon Peninsula, just south of St John's Newfoundland. They asked for a plane to come up to guide them down. Then they saw the runway at Harbour Grace, and landed after 31½ hours flying. They had completed the second—first undamaged—east-west crossing, and after refuelling continued to New York.

Two months later, the Frenchmen Costes and Bellonte in their Bréguet *Point D'Interrogation* with a 650 hp engine and carrying 1225 gallons of petrol, in a flight sponsored by Monsieur Coty, the perfume manufacturer, completed the first Paris–New York crossing in 37 hours 17 minutes. Once again, the radio worked perfectly, and they were in contact with ships—including the French weather ship *Jacques Cartier* —throughout the flight.

This era of the individual taking on the North Atlantic was the most bizarre and inspiring in the history of aviation. And the part ships played in this flying circus should not be forgotten. In the early days, the ships saw no threat in the crazy antics of the circus above their heads. The French had launched the *Ile de France* in 1926. The Germans had captured the Blue Riband of the Atlantic with the *Bremen's* record trip in 1929. So they gave the airmen free and generous help, never dreaming they were assisting in their own destruction. Ships were the stepping-stones, indispensable in providing radio bearings and weather reports, and fishing the pilots and crews out of the water. Since Wellman and his crew were spectacularly rescued by the *Trent* in 1910, there were in this early era sixteen skilful and daring rescues of airmen by seamen, often against all odds of ever finding them.

Amongst them was the British crew of a Wal flying boat under Courtney, which in 1928 had returned to the Azores because of bad weather, then set off again and one engine caught fire. After alighting on a rough ocean, an SOS was sent and the crew were rescued by SS *Minnewaska*. A Spanish attempt, in 1929, also flying a Wal, west-bound from Alcazares to New York, missed the Azores through faulty navigation and was forced to ditch. The crew were rescued by the British aircraft carrier HMS *Eagle*, only to be censured by their government, not only for incompetence but also for unpatriotically flying a German aircraft.

Perhaps the luckiest rescue was that of the Hutchinson family. Mr and Mrs Hutchinson set off in their own Sikorsky amphibian in September 1932 with three crew to fly the northern route, taking with them their two young daughters. Off Greenland, the aircraft developed a bad fuel leak. SOSs were sent, and Hutchinson put the Sikorsky down on a rough sea scattered with ice floes. Soon the amphibian was being battered to pieces by the waves. The trawler *Lord Talbot* was searching for them, when two days later a crew man saw a tiny glimmer of light.

Thinking it simply came from an Eskimo camp fire, the Captain flashed a Morse message asking whether that was the Hutchinson family. A second flash came, and the *Lord Talbot* went to investigate, rescuing all on board the Sikorsky. In fact, the first flash had come from a length of film that was being fired to attract attention from the shore—and so had the second which had been lit providentially at that exact time for the same reason.

The Germans Rody and Johanssen and the Portuguese Viega had already been given up for dead when their Junkers W33 disappeared in 1931. Nearly seven days later they were picked up off Newfoundland by the *Belmoira* from the still floating Junkers. The way these old land planes floated was extraordinary. Hawker and Grieve's Sopwith floated for five days and was picked up by the SS *Lake Charlotteville*, eventually being exhibited on the roof of Selfridge's store. No aircraft floated quite so well as Bjoerkval's red and green Bellanca, bound for Stockholm, since he had filled the wings with ping-pong balls—a wise precaution as it turned out, since the engine failed a hundred miles off Ireland, and he was rescued by a French trawler.

The rescue of Cramer and Hassell was the most dramatic. Sponsored by the Swedish population of Rockford, Illinois, and both of Scandinavian ancestry, they set off in a Stinson for Stockholm via the northern route on 16th August 1928. Aiming to land at the Greenland Expedition's base at Camp Lloyd, they lost themselves, and short of fuel, made a good landing on the ice-cap—a huge flat plateau of ice covering much of the Greenland interior.

They set off for Camp Lloyd through the snow and across crevasses, existing for the most part on what they could shoot. For twelve days in the bitter cold, their difficulties were unbelievable. Then on the thirteenth day, Cramer saw a speck on the sea and shot off a cartridge, hoping it was a boat.

In fact, it was a motorboat from the Expedition, which at that time was just about to pack up and go home. Sixteen years later, their Stinson was found by the USAAF—blown upside down now by the winds, but exactly where it had landed. But by that time, Cramer had gone. With the Canadian Paquette, he had set off via the northern route again, this time for Copenhagen in his third attempt at the water jump, on 28th July 1931.

A radio message was received from them that they had Norway in sight—then nothing. Eight months later, a Danish trawler picked up their personal papers wrapped up in an oilskin coat. But there was no clue on what had happened to them.

Gradually, the disasters and the failures got fewer. In 1927 there had been twenty-one attempts at the water jump. Four got over unscathed. One got across, but ditched in the shallows of a French beach on the

Wiley Post in front of the Lockheed Vega *Winnie Mae.* (Underwood)

other side. Ten failed, but without loss of life. Six failed fatally, either crashing on take off or disappearing. By 1931, out of eleven attempts, there were seven successful crossings. By 1935, successes were commonplace. The two biggest steps forward had been the production of reliable and more powerful engines, which by increasing speeds helped to reduce the effect of the westerly headwinds, and the fitting of Sperry gyros and artificial horizons which were fundamental to safe blind flying.

Man does not know whether he is diving, climbing or turning without a horizon; that was why there were so many spins on the Atlantic. A gyro maintains a fixed position relative to space, and through this principle, in spite of flying blind, the pilot knows his attitude. 'Trust your instruments, not yourself.' is a basic training instruction.

The first successful crossing using the artificial horizon was Post and Gatty's flight in *Winnie Mae* on 23rd June 1931 from Newfoundland to Chester in 16 hours and 17 minutes. Something of the feeling of being in heavy cloud can be gauged by Gatty's comment. At 1.30 am he had made an entry in his log book 'Flying blind.' He wrote, 'when I looked at my writing after we had landed, I was afraid somebody who was a hand-writing expert might see it and read my mood from it.'

Airmen had probed the North Atlantic sky, found out much about its make-up and temperament. The strong westerly winds were recognised as a practically permanent feature, and so was the continuous bank of cloud. The North Atlantic winter was not safe, with ice on the take-off areas and in the clouds, but the changeover periods in autumn and spring could be just as treacherous. There was a closed season for the water jump from mid-September to early April. The only people to complete the water jump outside that period were Boyd and Connor in the Bellanca *Maple Leaf*, in October of 1930. They had planned a direct flight from Montreal to England, but weather made them land at Charlottetown, and then petrol trouble forced them to land in the Scilly Isles.

Fourteen other attempts till 1935 were made out of season; two crashed, three returned for bad weather, one returned with engine trouble, two were rescued from the sea, and six disappeared. It was only with the arrival of comparatively sophisticated aircraft with gyro blind flying instruments (Waitkus in a Lockheed Vega on 21st September 1935 and Mollison in a Bellanca with a 700 hp Pratt and Whitney Wasp on 28th October 1936) that an out-of-season crossing—and only just at that—became a practical proposition. A winter crossing was still an impossibility.

*       *       *

The young women on the flying trapeze were even more daring. And the strangest attempt to fly the North Atlantic, not only out of season but in mid-winter, was tried by a woman. Once Lindbergh's non-stop New York–Paris flight had been accomplished, the passion for 'firsts' extended to other variations, such as being the first woman to do the water jump.

This race ran in two parts: first, to try to get a woman passenger or crew member across: second, for a woman to pilot herself across. It had been started by Princess Lowenstein-Wertheim, who aimed to be both the first woman *and* the first east-west across, and she had disappeared over the Atlantic in her Fokker with her crew. Then came a rich American woman, Mrs Frances Grayson, who was consumed with the same ambition to be the first woman across. In her Sikorsky amphibian *The Dawn*, she set off from New York with her pilot Stulz and navigator Goldsborough, again out of season, on 17th October 1927. But over the Atlantic, the port engine failed, and Stulz returned. Mrs Grayson was not deterred, and after repairs pressed for another attempt. But Stulz had another offer and refused. His place was taken by another experienced airman called Omdal. With Goldsborough and an engineer called

Schroeder, it was decided to try, of all times, on Christmas Eve. Gales, snow, ice and hail were forecast right across the ocean, but all warnings were ignored and Omdal took off as planned. The winter Atlantic was waiting for them. In the middle of the water jump, during the stormy night, a ship reported the sound of aircraft engines high in the sky—a strange sound in those days—followed by a loud noise. No other sound from them was ever heard again.

The wise Stulz waited till mid-season next year for another try at the first-woman-across race. On 17th June 1928 when there would be hardly any darkness on the Great Circle route, he set off from Newfoundland in a Fokker seaplane *Friendship*, powered this time by three engines, with Amelia Earhart helping with the navigation, and an engineer. The usual rain and thick clouds tossed them all over the sky, but this time could not blow the aircraft down. Twenty hours and forty minutes out of Newfoundland, they landed at Burry Port, Wales. The first part of the race had been won, and a woman was safely across.

The motives of the women to do the water jump were somewhat different from the men. Publicity certainly came into it; there were a fair sprinkling of actresses who wished to further their careers. But money as a motive had dropped out, and so had patriotism. Most of the women made the attempt because they were women and men had told them that it was impossible for a woman to do it.

Usually less well planned than the men's attempts, often reckless, sometimes zany, there was about these female flights even more dash and imagination, a kind of star tightrope turn in this aerial circus. From opposite sides of the Atlantic, out of season in early October 1927, the German Starke and three other crew were trying to get the famous Viennese actress Frau Dillenz across westwards in a Junkers seaplane, at the same time as the American Haldeman was trying to get a pretty New York show girl called Ruth Elder across eastwards in a Stinson, appropriately named *The American Girl*.

The Germans ran into bad weather, returned to Horta in the Azores and gave up the attempt. Half-way across, well south of track, the Stinson's engine seized, and Haldeman just had time to send SOS before ditching in heavy seas. The SS *Barendrecht* came to their rescue, and with the greatest difficulty managed to launch a lifeboat and pick them up. After many hours in the icy darkness of the Atlantic, drenched and bedraggled but undefeated, Ruth Elder climbed up the rope ladder to the deck, thanked the Captain, brought out a lipstick and mirror and proceeded to fix her face. She was taken to Horta where she and Frau Dillenz met and exchanged experiences.

Elsie Mackay, daughter of Lord Inchcape (then Chairman of P. and O.) and a millionairess in her own right, also wanted to be both the first woman across and also on the first east-west trip. She interested a very

*The Endeavour* stands on the snow-covered airfield at Cranwell.          (Fox)

Elsie Mackay and Captain Hinchcliffe before taking off in the *Endeavour*, 13 March 1928, for the east-west Atlantic flight during which they disappeared.

(Fox)

experienced Imperial Airways Captain called Hinchcliffe in the idea, and he left his job to become her private pilot. He went to the States, buying a Stinson Detroiter with a 200 hp engine, and shipped it back on the *Aquitania*. Again, the problem was weight, bearing in mind the fuel needed against the headwinds, but Miss Mackay pulled strings and obtained permission to use the longest RAF runway available, which was at the RAF College, Cranwell, but they had to take off within a week.

Numerous complications ensued. Miss Mackay's family heard about the attempt and came to the George Hotel, Grantham, where she and Hinchcliffe were staying, to dissuade her. The weather was appalling, with snow on the ground. The week's grace turned into a fortnight, then a telegram from the Air Ministry told them they must leave Cranwell. News also came through that a German east–west attempt was imminent.

In spite of a bad weather forecast, Hinchcliffe had little option but to go. He got into the right-hand seat, the co-pilot's seat—he had lost his left eye, in a crash during the war and preferred to fly from the co-pilot's position. On 13th March 1928, with Miss Mackay beside him and enough fuel for forty hours, he opened up the throttle of the black and gold Stinson, now called *The Endeavour* and pounded more than a mile over the snow, eventually lifting off the heavily laden aircraft into the air.

*The Endeavour* was sighted in the south-west of Ireland at 1.30 pm, having completed only 400 miles in five hours. Ships in the Atlantic reported westerly gales and mountainous seas, but none reported seeing the Stinson, which never arrived at the other side.

At the end of June 1928, an American actress–pilot called Thea Rasche crashed trying to take off from Quebec. Two and a half years were to elapse before another woman made a try—and she was a very experienced airwoman with an unlimited transport pilot's licence. With a co-pilot/navigator called MacLaren, Beryl Hart planned to fly her black and white Bellanca *Trade Wind* to Paris along the southern route, via Bermuda and the Azores. This 2000-mile trip between tiny islands is one of the most treacherous in the world, particularly liable to the appearance of unexpected headwinds, the spin-offs from hurricanes, and forming part of the notorious Bermuda Triangle, graveyard of over a hundred aircraft. (The British Tudor airliners *Star Tiger* and *Star Ariel* disappeared without trace in this area, which I flew in Constellations.)

Once again—as with Mrs Grayson—Beryl Hart's was a strange and inexplicable attempt. Certainly it was the southern route, but it is still difficult to understand why she chose mid-winter. On 3 January 1931 she set off from New York. In bumpy weather, the sextant fell on the cabin floor and broke, and within a few hours they were completely lost. In fact, their navigation was so bad that they would never have even seen Bermuda, being already three hundred miles off track, had they not turned back and landed in Virginia. As with Frances Grayson, the winter Atlantic had given them fair warning. But just like Mrs Grayson, Miss Hart chose to ignore it and off she went again—this time successfully reaching Bermuda. On 10 January, again, like Mrs Grayson, in the teeth of an adverse weather forecast, she took off and set course for the Azores. Three weeks later, the wreckage of *Trade Wind* was seen from a ship 275 miles north-west of the Azores; there was no sign of Beryl Hart or MacLaren.

Six months later, Elinor Smith wrote the undercarriage off in an aircraft appropriately called the *Question Mark*, on the way to Newfoundland to start her attempt to do it alone. She had been preceded in the same endeavour by Ruth Nichols in a very modern high-wing Lockheed Vega. Wearing a high fashion two-piece and a smart hat, she set off from New York on the first leg to St John, New Brunswick. Coming in for a landing, she bounced three times, ground-spun and crashed, ending up in hospital.

Amelia Earhart arrives in Ireland after her successful crossing in a Lockheed Vega, 20/21 May 1932.                                                                 (Lockheed)

Now came back onto the scene Mrs Putnam, formerly Amelia Earhart, who had won the race to be the first woman across with Stulz. Most women would have been content with that, particularly in the light of all the crashes and tragedies on the water jump. But of all those early women flyers, Amelia Earhart was the most dedicated and the most professional. One look at her finely chiselled face, determined chin, high forehead and bright intelligent eyes is enough to recognise that courage and singleness of purpose which illuminated her whole life. She lived to fly—and six years later, out in the Far East, she was to die flying. After her 1928 flight with Stulz, there had been snide remarks passed that she had been simply a piece of freight, the men had done it all, and that the Atlantic would certainly eat any woman who fought it on her own. It tried. In a Lockheed Vega, she set off from Newfoundland on 20 May 1932 and soon ran into bad weather. The altimeter went wrong. The engine exhaust pipe burned, allowing naked flames to play on the wings and fuselage, so that at any moment the Vega might have caught fire. But she reached the other side, landing near Londonderry, though the Vega's undercarriage was reportedly damaged in the uneven meadowland. As well as being the first woman across, now she was the first woman to have piloted and navigated herself across—and the first person, man or woman, to have done the water jump alone since Lindbergh.

That same year there was a rather different sort of flight. The American Nurses' Aviation Service had bought the Bellanca *Miss Veedol*, in which Herndon and Pangborn had completed the crossing and then flown round the world. Dr Pisculli, who had arranged the purchase, planned to use it (renamed *The American Nurse*) for scientific experiments. His pilot was called Ulrich; a nurse (who was also a pilot) called Edna Newcomer, and the doctor's pet woodchuck called 'Tailwind' were to be the subjects of tests on physical reactions in an attempt to gauge stress and fatigue. Such tests were first tried in 1783 on three animals in a balloon. Since then there have been many advances in aviation medicine—but fatigue and stress still remain something of enigmas, not yet possible to measure. (Thirty-two years later, I was part of a team investigating flight-deck workload. A series of psychological and physiological experiments on the Atlantic monitored pilots' heart-beat and showed rates of up to 150 beats a minute during stressful take-offs and landings.)

On 13 September 1932 Dr Pisculli and his subjects set off for Rome, and it was planned in addition that Edna Newcomer should drop by parachute over Florence, as a tribute to Florence Nightingale who had been born there a hundred and twelve years before. They were seen by a ship, 450 miles north of the Azores, flying east and going strong. But they never arrived at Florence or Rome—or anywhere else.

Ulrich (in flying breeches), Edna Newcomer and Dr Pisculli, before taking off from New York in the Bellanca, *The American Nurse*, 13 September 1932. (Keystone)

The next crossing in this particular race was flown by Amy Johnson and Jim Mollison, who provided for the North Atlantic its own bitter-sweet love story. Born in a strict Wesleyan Methodist family in York-shire, Amy Johnson was a clever girl who was at the same time keen on sports and interested in what were then regarded as essentially male activities. She did well at school and obtained a BA degree at Sheffield. But she fell in love with a Swiss boy. That he was foreign was bad enough, but what really made family relations strained was that he was also a Catholic and she had an open affair with him. She was expecting to marry him when in 1928 he told her in the Strand that he had just married someone else. She felt so suicidally desperate that she decided to learn to fly and have a crash.

In fact, she learned first to be an engineer. She was the first woman to receive her Ground Engineer's licence from the Air Ministry, and it has been said of her that she flew like a good engineer. Certainly she was not a born pilot. Her instructor's usual comment on her airfield approaches was, 'Woman! You'll have to go round again!' Dick Atcherley, the Schneider Trophy pilot who later had a distinguished RAF career, gave her some instruction and said, 'I was shocked to find how incapable she was of flying blind and marvelled at (and admired) her long flights, which must have put her in the most ghastly (blind) circumstances.'

But aviation was therapeutic. Thoughts of suicide disappeared. She put all her energy into flying. By 1930 she was world-famous. She had flown to Australia—and immediately became, as Lindbergh had done, a symbol that was again naturally politically exploited. 'Ambassadress of Empire', she was called and 'Australia's Sweetheart'.

It was at this moment of triumph that she left Brisbane for Sydney in an eight-passenger Avro, and went up to the cockpit where for the first time in her life she flew something larger than a Moth.

The co-pilot was Jim Mollison, an ex-boxer from Glasgow who served in the RAF before going to Australia. By the time they reached Sydney, she had promised him two dances at a ball to be given in her honour. But when he came to claim them, the Governor of Australia gave him the brush-off by telling him she was too tired.

Eventually, they met again—and married. The two things they shared were indomitable courage and a love of flying. Mollison also became world-famous through his long-distance flights—particularly the first solo flight 'the hard way' (from east to west). He set off on 18 August 1932 for New York in the Puss Moth *The Heart's Content*. But he ran into heavy headwinds and at last, safely over land and seeing a field, he lobbed down, at least expecting to be in American territory; he was greatly disappointed to find that he was in New Brunswick, close to St John.

It was natural that he and Amy would want to fly the Atlantic together, and at midnight on 22 July 1933 they set off from Pendine Sands in the DH84 Dragon *Seafarer*. For six hundred miles, they had bad weather through which they both shared the flying fifty-fifty.

**Jim Mollison says goodbye before his first solo east-west crossing in the D. H. Puss Moth, *The Heart's Content*, 18/19 August 1932.** (Flight)

Amy Johnson and Jim Mollison in front of the DH84 *Seafarer* in which they flew the Atlantic, crashing at Bridgeport on 24 July 1933. (Flight)

During her time off, Amy lay on a bed rigged under the extra petrol tanks—but neither slept for forty hours, drinking black coffee to keep them awake.

They had run into the bottom of a low and experienced heavy head-winds, and had little idea where they were. They saw icebergs which Jim reckoned were drift ice, and therefore they must be too far north. Then they saw birds— and finally the Straits of Belle Isle.

Solemnly they shook hands.

Daylight was fading as they set course for New York. Over New Brunswick, petrol was running low, and Amy wanted to land at Boston to refuel. But Jim, baulked before, was determined. Amy's last entry in the log was 'economising petrol to try to make N.Y.'

Now it was pitch dark and the petrol gauge was showing close to zero. So they decided to put down at Bridgeport.

Both were desperately tired. Mollison was particularly disappointed about New York. There might well have been a fair amount of back-seat driving, and in any case neither of them were noted for their landings. The story is that in spite of a searchlight on the windsock, Jim landed down-wind—which he denied. Anyway, just as he was holding off, in his own words 'there came a rending crash that shook old *Seafarer* and its crew as an earthquake would. We crashed ahead into knee-deep grass, turned two complete somersaults into the swamp alongside the aerodrome. With no belt to hold me in, I was flying forward through the allegedly non-splinter safety-glass windscreen that burst to let me pass and gashed me in the process. I sailed far ahead of suddenly arrested *Seafarer* and dropped head-first into sea-water and slime, where I lost all consciousness of the proceedings.'

Both of them finished up in hospital.

The Americans gave them a tumultuous welcome, but the love story was already beginning to come apart. Amy went to stay with 'that strange, charming woman, Amelia Earhart, in her Connecticut home' (Jim's words). He returned to England to get *Seafarer* rebuilt for a try at the eastbound. But when it was repaired, the undercarriage of the overloaded aircraft collapsed. In its own way, *Seafarer* symbolised their marriage. Numerous problems and tensions were developing. Amy went off to Florida for three months, Jim returned to England again.

They had one more go together on the Australian race in 1934 but at Allahabad burnt out three pistons and gave up. Afterwards, they split. Abandoning British aircraft for American, on 28 October 1936, Jim completed his third crossing by flying a Bellanca with a powerful 700 hp engine from New York to Newfoundland, and then doing the crossing to London in the world record time of 13 hours 17 minutes. The monoplane's name was *The Dorothy*.

The Atlantic love story was over. Jim Mollison flew many more North Atlantic crossings during the war as a pilot on Ferry Command. Amy joined Air Transport Auxiliary, which ferried aircraft for the RAF. Lost in heavy fog over London in 1941, flying an Oxford (the aircraft Nevil Shute helped design), Amy probably became iced up and

**Jim Mollison in the cockpit of the Bellanca *The Dorothy* just before take off, 29 October 1936.** **(Underwood)**

crashed into the Thames Estuary. The papers speculated on the report of a mystery passenger on board. Amy's body was never found.

The last flight in the women's race was the first east to west flight, the 'hard way' against the headwinds, when Beryl Markham set off from Abingdon on 4 September 1936 flying a Vega Gull called *Messenger*. Equipped with full blind flying instruments, the aircraft also was fitted with a variable pitch propeller, enabling the aircraft to fly higher and faster—but there was no radio.

Again headwinds were encountered. Again there were doubts on position. Eventually land did show up. Mrs Markham selected (as Alcock had done seventeen years before her) what she thought was a reasonable field, but which when she touched down turned out to be a bog—and *Messenger* ended up on its nose. She was near Sydney, Nova Scotia, not New York which had been her ambition, but she had done the water jump the hard way—the only woman ever to do it westbound.

**Mrs Beryl Markham in front of her Vega Gull in which she flew the Atlantic east-west, 4/5 September 1936.**                                                    **(Popperfoto)**

So ended the women-across-the-water-jump race. Clearly Amelia Earhart had won it on both counts. But Amy Johnson had done it, and so had Beryl Markham. And the women had had a far tougher ride than the men. Out of fourteen flights, one ditched, one returned for weather, three crashed and could not continue, five simply disappeared. Of the four flights that were successful, only Amelia Earhart's first, when Stulz was the pilot, escaped undamaged.

But the women had achieved their object—they had shown the men that they could do the water jump west–east, east–west *and* on their own.

\*       \*       \*

By 1938 the Atlantic had been explored in this circus by individuals of all nations. It had become a matter of national pride to do the water jump. The Americans had made thirty-eight attempts and had had twenty-one successes. The British had tried thirteen times and had five successes (three of them by Jim Mollison). Out of twelve attempts, the French had been successful four times. Out of ten attempts, the Germans had four successes. Out of four attempts, the Canadians had had two successes, and also out of four attempts the Poles had done it once.

Howard Hughes and Carl Squier, Vice President of Lockheed.       (Lockheed)

The Norwegians, the Danish, the Hungarians, the Irish, the Australians and the Italians had all had one success, while the Lithuanians had had two. Even the Russians had made one attempt in an ordinary military bomber equipped with two 850 hp engines. Kokkinaki and Gordienko had used the northern route via Iceland and Labrador. They got lost and had no idea where they were when they made a wheels-up landing, but the flashing of a lighthouse attracted them and they found out that they were on Miscou Island, New Brunswick.

Not only had the water jump been carried out many times, it had been done on every conceivable variation of route—via the northern and southern stepping-stones, direct from Newfoundland to Ireland and New York–Paris and beyond, eastwards and westwards. Now other variations were introduced into what was apparently becoming easy—the 1931 long-distance record of Boardman and Polando, from New York to Turkey, 5012 miles in 49.17 hours, was smashed by Rossi and Codos with their 5657 miles flight from New York to Rayak, for which the French government gave them a prize of a million francs. Then the commercial use of aircraft had already been tried and found very rewarding, when Merrill and Lambie on 13 May 1937, flew photographs of the coronation of George VI and Queen Elizabeth across the water jump for the New York papers. Again, there were round-the-world flights of which the water jump was only a part: Mattern's try in 1933 and Post's in July of the same year, culminating in Howard Hughes' fabulous round-the-world flight, starting from New York on 10 July 1938 in a Lockheed 14 and arriving back three days and nineteen hours later.

The Lockheed 14 was to become famous as the aircraft in which Prime Minister Chamberlain flew home from his meeting with Hitler to bring 'Peace with honour' to the British. The fact that the aircraft was American (there had been nothing British suitable) aroused acid comment, particularly as 200 had been ordered for the RAF. As Hudsons they were to be invaluable against the U-boats. The Lockheed 14 was powered by 1100 hp engines with a range of 4700 miles. It was crewed by two pilots, two navigators and a radio officer/engineer. Equipped with a modern blind-flying panel, it had also a gyrosyn compass and a gyro-controlled automatic pilot. The navigator's room was palatial and well equipped with a large chart table, a plexiglass astrodome for taking astro-sights and an optical drift indicator. Hydromatic variable pitch and fully feathering propellers were fitted, together with automatic life rafts and flotation bags, parachutes and full oxygen equipment. It had a loop aerial by which loop bearings could be taken and an automatic radio compass, of which the needle when tuned would point to any radio beacon within range. Two-stage superchargers could lift the aircraft above 16,000 feet. Hughes planned

The ultimate in the individual's aeroplane—the Lockheed 14 in which Howard Hughes flew from New York to Paris in less than half Lindbergh's time, and then continued round the world, July 1938.                    (Lockheed)

on having a fuel reserve of around 450 miles for his arrival in Paris against Lindbergh's 850 miles, showing how much confidence in navigation had grown with the latest radio aids. Hughes flew high above a solid overcast of cloud, never seeing the Atlantic, but hit all landfalls on the nose and landed right on estimate after 16 hours 35 minutes— less than half Lindbergh's time.

By 1938 the Atlantic aerial circus was beginning to look tame. The water jump had been done safely altogether too many times, and

The first Sperry directional gyro
which showed the pilot his course
accurately during a turn.   (Sperry)

The first Sperry artificial horizon, unsung
hero of the Atlantic sky which made the
commercial water jump possible.   (Sperry)

interest flagged. In any case, by now commercial proving flights had taken place. In the period 1934–8 there had been eighteen individual attempts (as apart from airlines and governments) and only two failures, neither of them fatal. What with the new radio aids to navigation (never the pioneers' strong point), the blind-flying instruments, many new concrete runways and a much more effective meteorological service, the Atlantic sky appeared to have been conquered.

But the Atlantic sky had yet to be taken on in winter. As a reminder of its still unprobed powers, as a warning that it should still be treated carefully, just as this aerial circus era had started in tragedy with overloaded aircraft crashing on take-off, so it was to end in tragedy. Four young Americans in tiny aircraft—Backman in a 90 hp Monocoupe, Smith in a 65 hp Aeronca, and Loeb and Decker in a ten-year old Ryan like Lindbergh's—took off in the spring and summer of 1939 on the water jump eastwards: all four vanished.

# *Five:* The Airlines Move to the Starting Point

The view from the windows—port, starboard, ahead, behind—is now nothing but sea and cloud. Looking at that line of horizon circling you right round, it seems impossible that land can possibly exist or that there is anything else in the world but your Jumbo jet. There is a kind of cold loneliness that not even the sunshine slanting down from the south-west can altogether burn away. Sitting with so many others, with tea and a scone and a cake on the table in front of you, with the cabin crew moving up and down, serving everyone, filtered by warmth and comfort and well-being, only a minute fragment of that feeling escapes through to you. And yet very slightly, you shiver. Along this same route at this same place at this same time flew some of the early pioneers, usually not knowing where they were, cold, hungry, deafened by noise, and often quite alone—a little cell of undiluted loneliness.

Nevertheless, one after the other, they followed each other over.

By the early nineteen-thirties, brave individuals of many countries had shown their respective governments that the Atlantic sky could be conquered and, provided reasonable precautions were taken, could be flown safely.

But it had yet to be shown that the water jump could be flown in winter, and that flights in each direction could be carried out regularly and commercially.

The most daunting factors were still the weather and the two-thousand-mile width between Ireland and Newfoundland. Governments had long since recognised the prestige potential, but the Americans and the British reckoned, particularly in a financial depression, that the political rewards now to be gained were no longer cost-effective.

Very little progress had been made during the twenties in the building of long-range civil aircraft with economic and powerful engines. Horse-power ratings had only gone up from 400 to around 600 in ten years. Cruising speeds had actually gone down (largely due to the concentration on flying boats, with their massive hulls, because of the shortage

[79]

of aerodromes) and in the late 1920s were generally around 105 mph. No commercial aircraft then existed which could stay in the air for the sixteen and a half hours flight from Ireland to Newfoundland in zero wind. Since headwinds of between forty and sixty miles an hour were common, reducing the ground speed on occasion down to perhaps as little as sixty miles an hour, the idea of producing a commercial aircraft capable of staying in the air for around thirty hours must have appeared a pipe-dream. Even if such a vehicle could be built, all its load would be fuel, and it would be so heavy it could never get off the ground except by giving it enormous wings which would cut back its speed even further. And even then there would not be an aerodrome, nor even a flying-boat harbour, long enough for it to become airborne.

Additionally, there were few radio facilities. Air navigation, as practised, was still hit-or-miss. Weather report collecting and forecasting organisation were still sketchy. An immense amount of snow fell regularly every winter over Newfoundland and there were still only primitive means of disposing of it. Ice blocked the Botwood flying-boat base from October to May. Fog still formed almost instantaneously over the cold Labrador current round the Newfoundland coast and shrouded everything on land in a damp sheet of nil visibility.

The French, the Dutch, the Belgians, the Italians and the Germans after the First World War had been interested in the possibilities and were subsidising their aviation industry. The French had constructed a most modern-looking quadruplane flying boat. The Germans had designed a similar fifty-ton craft.

The British government had recognised the international nature of air transport and aided wireless stations and meteorology, provided aerodromes and organised the licences of pilots and aircraft. But there were still no subsidies. The British privately-owned companies bravely tried to survive—and failed. When all of them faced bankruptcy in 1921, unable to compete against the subsidised European airlines, reluctantly the government helped with subsidies. But these were haphazard and very inadequate for development. Finally, the Hambling Committee (when things get too difficult for a British government, invariably a Committee is formed) recommended the amalgamation of the airlines under a £1 million subsidy spread over ten years. Even so, there were difficulties, and the Air Minister, Sir Samuel Hoare, found himself in trouble with government departments which opposed the recommendations. The Air Ministry (which had now a Department of Civil Aviation) were extremely lukewarm, and in Hoare's words, 'the Treasury did not believe in civil aviation and strongly objected to long-term commitments to companies that were obviously in financial difficulties.'

The government finally gave in, with the proviso that all aircraft and pilots must be British and could be commandeered into the RAF in a national emergency. So in 1924 Imperial Airways started with a number of indifferent aircraft (one of which was the famous G–EASI, Go Easy, a commercial version of Alcock and Brown's Vimy), and a band of skilful and experienced pilots with George Woods Humphery as general manager.

Woods Humphery was born in Glasgow and had worked his own way up through grammar school and into an engineering apprentice institute. During the First World War, he became a Major in the Royal Flying Corps, and afterwards had gone into Handley-Page, the aircraft manufacturers, eventually running their airline which was one of those which had been amalgamated under Hambling.

Woods Humphery worked himself extremely hard. He was also something of a dictator. He had started off his term of office by offering pilots a £100-a-year retainer and flying pay of 15 shillings an hour, thus initiating the first pilots' industrial dispute. He had a tendency—as the Imperial Airways Board certainly did—of treating pilots as airborne chauffeurs, not referring to them as captain till the end of the twenties, and dispensing disciplinary measures with the immediacy and suddenness of a coffee machine. Finding a man lounging in the waiting-room, whom he mistook for one of his pilots, he sacked him on the spot, only to find out that he was an Imperial Airways' passenger waiting for a late departure.

As part-time Chairman, he had the Chairman of Dunlop, Sir Eric Geddes. Sir George Beharell, also from Dunlop, was financial assistant. Backing him up was a Board over which there was a faintly feudal air. Beside him were the government politicians and government departments—the Treasury, the Air Ministry, the Foreign Office, the Dominions Office and the Colonial Office. The Post Office was also there, prosperous and powerful, interested in airmail, but on a policy of only paying for services rendered and on its own rates. The Post Office tested and licensed airline radio operators (for aircraft were airborne radio stations). The Post Office was not interested in passengers (pound for pound, mail is far more remunerative), and insisted (for many years) that mail went first. The post-horn (from the mail coach) and 'Royal Mail' painted on some British fuselages might perhaps be considered the owner's brand on the side of a steed, for it is true that the Post Office did much for the advancement of British civil aviation.

So did the American Post Office for American civil aviation. In the early 1920s, flying in the USA was largely in the hands of barnstormers and mail pilots. A private company called Aero-marine, one of whose employees was Ed Musick, later Chief Pilot of Pan American, had started a flying-boat service from Key West, and in 1921 eleven passengers and crew flew round the houses up to Toronto and Chicago and down to New Orleans. In the previous year, a passenger service had been started between Key West and Havana.

But the services could not be sustained without a subsidy. Air Mail had started in 1918, with the Army carrying it between Washington and New York as a training exercise, but the service was soon transferred to the Post Office. By mid-1924, the Post Office had blazed the way across the continent with 289 flashing beacons, together with radio installations and emergency fields. DH–4s took the mail from coast to coast in just over a day.

By that time Britain was operating extensive passenger and mail European services, but the first sustained American passenger service was still some years ahead. Juan Trippe had left the Navy, and had bought nine surplus US Navy aircraft for £100 apiece, sold six at a profit and was in the airline business, eventually as Manager of Pan American. Trippe had been to Yale where he had made a large number of rich and influential friends, amongst them the Vanderbilts, the Whitneys and the Rockefellers.

There was something of the philosopher about Juan Trippe. He was very careful of his aircrew's welfare and saw aviation as communication on a world-wide basis, as a means of travel for everyone and as the most powerful element in achieving and maintaining peace. He was also something of a visionary as well as a successful gambler. Unlike Woods Humphery, who carefully noted everything, he had no time for paperwork, and he used to deal with the mail at his desk by 'filing' it in the wastepaper basket between his knees. His best judgments, according to those who worked with him, simply came out of the top of his head. The ones he 'worked out' were rarely so good. He looked into the future and backed what he saw in his own crystal ball—always acting swiftly, moving forward systematically from the easier to the more difficult, as far as possible operating on his own, always aiming to be one jump ahead of the next man.

In all such operations, he was particularly helped by the Post Office. In 1925, Congress sponsored the Kelly Act 'to encourage commercial aviation and to authorise the Postmaster-General to contract for air mail services.' There was still no regulation and still no licensing laws, but the air mail was to be subsidised. Then followed the Morrow Board civil aviation recommendations. Early in 1926, the Post Office left the actual operation of the mail to internal airlines, and the last flight of its Air Mail Service was in September 1927.

In that same year, Trippe commenced a regular air mail service—between Key West and Havana. Not till 1928 did Pan American carry fare-paying passengers—again on the same route.

He was far behind Woods Humphery. Imperial Airways were regularly operating the main European routes. There had been survey flights to Cairo and India, and government subsidies agreed. A through service to Delhi in seven days and Calcutta in nine had been planned for years. Sir Alan Cobham had surveyed the African routes and plans for a service to the Cape, together with the establishment of aerodromes and radio stations, were being formulated.

The other European companies were also at that time ahead of the Americans. Plesman had KLM. Bouilloux-Lafont ran Aéropostale (later amalgamated into Air France). Wronsky managed Lufthansa, while Eckener directed German airship services.

It was fortunate for the future of the water jump that in its early years it was nourished and controlled by such men, most of whom kept their jobs for many years, thus ensuring stability and continuity. Of the six, in 1927 Trippe was trailing last in the race.

*        *        *

In setting up Imperial Airways, the Hambling Committee had stated that no company administered under government control was desired, but a commercial organisation run entirely on business lines and with a privileged position in regard to subsidies.

Those wise words might well have been the financial cornerstone for the setting up of Pan American Airways, not Imperial Airways. Juan Trippe saw to it that as regards his American airline this British recommendation was carried out to the letter.

Aided enormously by the flexibility of the American Post Office contract system and unhampered by government or Civil Service departments or the priority needs to serve an Empire, Juan Trippe now began a fantastic sprint. The Kelly Act was American civil aviation's Magna Carta, and provided with its air mail subsidy arrangements a near perfect basis on which to finance the tentative first steps of the airlines—far more effective than the government subsidy system which was to bedevil Imperial Airways. It was twice modified. Eighty per cent of the mail income went to the airline and when this was not enough, $2 a mile with a 300 lb capacity for foreign mail was let to Pan American. Then in 1930 it was decreed that airlines were to be paid on a space available basis; it did not matter if the space was not filled.

Trippe chose his own routes carefully for commercial and not strategic or political prestige reasons, first linking the Caribbean before widening his network. Lindbergh became his Technical Adviser, and went on surveys down to South America, over the Pacific to China and up into the Arctic. Trippe built aerodromes and flying-boat harbours, provided radio stations equipped with a full range of weather equipment, and capable of broadcasting weather as well as direction-finding information. He built up a nucleus of experienced pilots, gave them full blind-flying training, using the new Sperry gyro instruments 'under the hood', so that they could not see out. Trippe sent his agents to explore possible air mail routes and report back, sewed up the landing rights and exclusive contracts with all the countries involved, so that when it came to the awarding of the mail contract, there was no other airline able to operate but Pan American. Those companies which already held franchises and mail contracts were bought up. In this way, Trippe captured all the Caribbean and South American mail contracts, before turning his attention to the Pacific Route. Not only did he establish the friendliest of relations with the American Post Office, but he taught them all about air mail operations. The Post Office could not afford expensive research and exploration, and therefore could only award the mail contract to the operator who could do the job—when it came to international routes, this invariably meant Pan American. The partnership suited Trippe, it suited the Post Office and it suited the American government, who saw world routes blossoming with the minimum expenditure. The taxpayers' money was spent ostensibly in the form of $2 per mile for carrying the US Mail. But the US Post Office got the revenue from the inbound foreign mail, which reduced the net cost considerably.

Trippe commissioned designs for his aircraft specific to his routes, chose his own manufacturers, harried them as much as he liked—and paid for them out of his own money. He bought Sikorsky amphibians so they could operate both from sea and land.

Then he began to turn his attention to the Pacific, with its 2400-mile leg between San Francisco and Honolulu, the ideal training ground for the most difficult route in the world, the North Atlantic. (Ernest Gann calls the Pacific the female route, the Atlantic the male—the Pacific milder but treacherous, the Atlantic stronger.)

Juan Trippe's whole approach was to work out a logical development, as far as politics allowed, proceed according to plan from one stepping-stone to another—always learning, always advancing, always getting bigger.

On the other side of the Atlantic, in the late 1920s, all the European airlines were engaged in cut-throat competition between their respective capitals. On the long-range routes, Compagnie Aéropostale, for whom the novelist Saint-Exupéry flew and whose *mail must go through* philosophy he immortalised in the uncompromising manager Rivière in *Vol de Nuit*, also flew to French colonies and made great progress opening up the South Atlantic. Lufthansa ran a South American service, too, with aeroplanes and airships. KLM flew to Dutch colonies. Imperial Airways built up the Empire routes, particularly to India which at the end of the twenties could be reached in seven days for a fare of £130.

And then, on 29 November 1930, the US Post Office asked for bids for a trans-Atlantic air mail service, the contract to run for ten years from 1 June 1931. The specified load each way was 300 lb to be carried in fireproof mail compartments at the rate of $2 a mile. 'Payment for faithful performance of service will be made monthly.'

That invitation was in fact withdrawn, since no one at that time was in a position to take it up. But it pointed the way to the future. A trans-Atlantic air mail service was clearly on the horizon, and it was unthinkable that only the Americans should operate such a service. Imperial Airways, Lufthansa, Compagnie Aéropostale, KLM, the Italians, the Irish, the Canadians and numerous private organisations also wanted to be involved.

The commercial race over the water jump was on.

\*         \*         \*

But how was it to be done?

The 3500-mile London–New York route was clearly out. The depressing conclusion of the Rome Conference of Trans-Atlantic Fliers, which General Balbo of the Italian Air Force convened in 1931, was that the direct route (Ireland–Newfoundland) was impossible because of distance, the northern round-the-houses route via Iceland, Greenland, Labrador and Newfoundland was impossible because of weather. That only left the zig-zag Azores–Newfoundland route, but Portugal controlled the Azores landing rights, and in any case many people considered the Azores harbours too dangerous for flying boats.

There were no adequate aerodromes anywhere along the route, so clearly the vehicle would have to be a flying boat. The water jump was considered altogether too dangerous for fare paying passengers. That huge expanse of icy cold water weighed on everybody's mind. If a commercial aircraft came down in the Atlantic, it was considered that there would be little hope of saving anyone. 'How do you know your plane will not fall down in the middle of the Atlantic?' the Head of the British Post Office was asking the Germans in a meeting as late as 1936. 'They may not, but these things have happened. How do you know ours will not?'

No passengers: mail only, then. But a mail service that was not regularly on time was tiresome, and one that packed up in the winter, was quite insupportable.

Some compromise would have to be forthcoming, and a number of clever suggestions and inventions were proposed, particularly by the British, on how to give aircraft sufficient range to do the water jump safely, even against the winds, and at the same time carry a useful load. It is an unfortunate fact that the history of British aviation is littered with the most ingenious, advanced and useful inventions which were expensively developed, cast aside, used too late or given to the designers of other nations.

One of the first ideas was a catapult-assisted take-off. In 1918, the British had used a catapult to launch an aeroplane by a high-pressure compressed cylinder. In his first novel *Stephen Morris* published six years later, Nevil Shute had written 'Suppose we could start a mail service to America that only took five days instead of seven, and suppose we were able to run that service with, say, eighty percent regularity. Do you see how we should improve our position with America? Look at the pull that would give us over every other country in Europe.' The plot concerns a catapult service operating from a ship half-way across the Atlantic—similar in fact to the service the French and Germans were later to carry out in 1929/30, the French using the *Ile de France*, and the Germans using the *Europa* and *Bremen*. Mail time was reduced by twenty-four hours with this method. The idea of the British using catapults was considered by the Sassoon Committee of 1936, but the view was that the 'high acceleration necessary would not be tolerated by passengers' and warned that a mail service only was unacceptable in that 'America was known to be preparing a combined passenger and mail service'.

Another idea was seadromes. When I was at school, I used to read Percy F. Westerman's (the right name for a writer on the Atlantic) stories about aeroplanes flying and fighting from immense floating runways, and like many others enjoyed seeing Conrad Veidt in the film *Flying Platform 1*. An American called Armstrong actually designed such seadromes, and produced coloured brochures, which he distributed to governments. In 1933 America made plans for platforms 1000 ft by 300 ft, raised 100 ft above the sea. They were to be supported by buoyancy tanks stationed just below the surface, and were to have, apart from a runway, refuelling facilities, wireless stations, repair shops, even an hotel. The estimated cost of each one was £6 million. The French flirted with the idea for a long time, and produced the refinement of building them actually on the ocean bed, where the lost continent of Atlantis was supposed to lie submerged. They believed there were four shallows there at depths of around seventy metres. The British did not believe in Atlantis and were never enthusiastic. The Civil Air Development Committee in 1935 stated that public apprehension and political considerations would preclude the use of landplanes for passenger transport over long ocean stretches, and necessitate the rejection of anything less than a chain of five seadromes. After a careful analysis of running costs (the British have never been niggardly when it comes to paperwork on aviation matters), the expense was declared prohibitive. Imperial Airways contributed a patriotic reminder to the Sassoon Committee that 'artificial islands will deprive us of the value of our own islands within the Empire' (i.e. Newfoundland and Bermuda).

Another possibility was airships. The British had already achieved a magnificent trans-Atlantic success in the flight of the R34. In the way the British have, government interest then flagged, only to be revived again, and the massive Burney airship programme, building the R100 and R101, was started. The Germans continued with their very successful Zeppelin programme, launching and operating the *Graf Zeppelin*.

Another ingenious idea was refuelling in flight, which had first been carried out by Smith and Richter at San Diego in 1923. It was then taken up by many contenders for the world's endurance record, pushing it higher and higher over the years, until Schlieper and Carroll stayed up a full month over California.

In 1932 Sir Alan Cobham began to make further experiments and saw the commercial possibilities of a tanker refuelling another aeroplane in flight. Since the two big problems were take-off and an adequate load and range, the proposal was that a trans-Atlantic aircraft could take off comparatively light from London and be refuelled in the air off Ireland and Newfoundland, thereby operating direct to Montreal or New York. Experiments at the Royal Aircraft Establishment at Farnborough had shown that such refuelling by means of a hose connecting two aircraft flying in formation was perfectly possible, but not surprisingly indicated many difficulties, particularly in bad weather. Nothing daunted, Cobham founded Flight Refuelling Limited.

Another idea of getting over the problems of the long take-off of a trans-Atlantic aircraft heavily weighted with fuel, was a pick-a-back aircraft. Such an idea had first been carried out by Commander Porte in 1916, when he took off in a flying boat with a fighter held in place on its upper centre section by crutches and a quick-release toggle. The fighter rose 'like a dove from a roof'. Major Mayo, who had dipped Alcock's fuel tanks after the first direct crossing and was now Technical Manager of Imperial Airways, developed the idea further in the early 1930s.

A small fully loaded four-engined floatplane of advanced design was attached to a lightly loaded large flying boat. The combined power of their eight engines managed to lift the pair of them into the air, after which the mailplane disengaged from the flying boat and carried out a trans-Atlantic crossing. It was clearly not the ultimate answer, but at the time it was conceived the idea was a tremendous step forward. The Imperial Airways submission to the Sassoon Committee took the view that the Short-Mayo Composite was an improvement on the catapult and flight refuelling, and the Committee's Report stated that it 'seemed realistic in the circumstances'.

High-altitude flying was considered as a means of increasing range, in that density of the air decreases rapidly with height, thus producing far less drag, but the problem was to get adequate superchargers, since the power of piston engines also decreases enormously with height.

The reduction of weight in airmails by photographed letters (air-graphs) was also proposed, but was not to be really taken up till the war.

Each of these expedients was considered by the airlines during the early 1930s, each country having their own particular favourites and concentrating on them. But these were only interim measures in the Atlantic commercial race. Even the airship was considered altogether too slow; a three-day crossing was not a sufficient improvement on the five and a half day crossings of the liners. What was needed was a commercial vehicle specifically designed for the North Atlantic, conceived and built after much the same idea as Lindbergh had built the *Spirit of St Louis*.

There was much also to find out about the North Atlantic, apart from the right vehicle.

Who was to be allowed to fly where and when? What regulations should be imposed? What fees should be charged? What passenger and mail rates should be fixed? What were the rules of the Atlantic sky? What about weather and radio? What about landing rights? These were the days when the international organisations, the International Committee for Air Navigation (ICAN) and the International Air Traffic Association (IATA), were in their infancy, and there was no experience of administering the Atlantic sky.

As a result, endless dialogues took place between airline managers. But the most extensive dialogue of all was to be between Woods Humphery, General Manager of Imperial Airways, and Juan Trippe, founder of Pan American Airways. Both were young men in their early thirties. The game was played strenuously in a spirit of both trust and suspicion. Trippe kept his word to Woods Humphery, often in difficult circumstances, and Woods Humphery repeatedly defended Trippe. Britain has always tended to regard America affectionately as the prodigal son who made good, a bit of a wide boy but smart as two pins. Such an attitude is reflected in the vast correspondence and trans-Atlantic telephone calls between Woods Humphery and Trippe—often deposited in the wastepaper basket by Trippe, all faithfully preserved by Woods Humphery. The quotations that follow are from his record.

Problems—provided no secrets were given—were openly discussed and solutions sought from each other. Woods Humphery was worried by his British-geared engines, which were experiencing one piston failure and break-up every 200,000 engine miles. Was it the oil, he asked Trippe. Trippe asked Woods Humphery how the British government controlled rates of international air carriage of passengers and goods. Trippe provided details of American companies who came to see the British, with opinions on their viability. Salaries of pilots were compared in 1933—$600 a month plus a day for Pan Am, while Woods

Humphery wrote, 'from the date when the pilot is appointed as, what we call now, the Captain and has taken charge of services on 30,000 lb aircraft he gets a basic £400, rising by £25 annually to £750. But there are other emoluments, abroad arrangements, so that basically our Senior Captains are £1,200 a year men, our average Captains £1,000 a year men, and First Officers £500 a year men.' There was a great deal of value in this mutual exchange, from which both the British and the Americans benefited.

Nothing was organised on the Atlantic and every day was bringing out fresh problems of administration for future air services. It must have seemed to both men that the difficulties were endless. The amount of work both did was prodigious. Bearing in mind that the North Atlantic was just one of their possible routes and each was eventually operating a big air network, it is difficult to understand how they managed to get through it.

In 1929 Trippe and Woods Humphery had begun exploring the possibilities of a joint Pan Am/Imperial Airways company to operate between New York and Bermuda. Progress was slow, largely because of disagreement between Britain and Bermuda on the building of an aerodrome on the island. But Trippe and Woods Humphery had now begun to look further, towards a legalised and approved document to share exclusive services on the Atlantic as well—a politically blessed gentlemen's agreement.

And there was one thing that both the British and the Americans had insisted on—neither Pan Am nor Imperial Airways could start first.

## *Six:* The Gentlemen's Agreement

Just for a moment now, you are in high cloud. The Atlantic sky has disappeared. Nothing can be seen ahead.

That was the position of governments and airline managers at the end of the 1920s. There was no clear indication of the 'right' Atlantic vehicle, and no idea how to organise and administer the commercial water jump on an international basis. They were all in the dark trying to plan ahead, both technically and administratively, along a path where no one had been before.

Now that individuals had blazed the way, a political poker game started for the right to operate the North Atlantic. Italy, France, Germany, USA, Holland, Canada, Ireland and Britain all wanted to take part. Though no one had a commercial Atlantic aircraft, each held different cards which they proceeded to play with varying degrees of skill.

It had started dramatically in 1930, with a shut-out of Italy and Germany. A tripartite agreement, covering the North Atlantic, was entered into when three national airlines played these three cards:—

  (i) Pan American played the card that America controlled 80 per cent of the eastbound mail over the Atlantic, while Britain only controlled 25 per cent of the westbound. This seemed a strong card, but was never really examined till years later when the British Post Office did a study which showed that this conclusion was doubtful, but in any case, could not be proved. The value of the card, therefore, was unknown.

 (ii) Imperial Airways played the stepping-stones of Bermuda and Newfoundland, both under British control, two aces.

(iii) Compagnie Aéropostale played the landing facilities for 25 years in the Azores, which they had negotiated with the Portuguese. Bearing in mind that the direct route was regarded as impossible, and the northern route via Iceland extremely doubtful because of the weather, this card, at that time, was undoubtedly an ace.

Italy and Germany had no card high enough to play. Woods

Humphery, Manager of Imperial Airways, wrote to Wronsky of Lufthansa, who had objected to being left out, saying that, 'we were just all three thrown together by force of circumstances and we are indeed sorry that our old friends, the Lufthansa, were not also thrown in with us by *force majeure*.'

The rules in the game were few enough, and now, not surprisingly, the game went wildcat. Everyone wanted a foot in the door, in order to arrange matters administratively to their best future advantage.

Compagnie Aéropostale got into financial difficulties, and eventually lost its concession in the Azores for non-operation.

The game narrowed down to two—Juan Trippe of Pan American and George Woods Humphery of Imperial Airways.

The way the British and the Americans looked at the North Atlantic sky was totally different. Juan Trippe ardently believed in the commercial possibilities of the route and worked steadily to get the best advantage for his own company. The British attitude was much more complicated. They had their hands full enough with the Empire. It was in the process of being linked by air, and the British tended to regard the North Atlantic primarily as a possible aerial link with Canada, and therefore as yet another unprofitable part of the earth's surface towards which Duty and Providence beckoned them to govern. They worked towards the All-Red Route—that is, a link-up of all the Empire (the red parts on the world atlas). The big gap was the Atlantic. The other idea, which was also to dominate British thinking for the next two decades, was the Fly British policy. The final stone around Woods Humphery's neck was the Treasury's attitude—very lukewarm about the financial viability of flying, and when money was forthcoming, it came in a weird mixture of subsidy and company earnings which was to produce headaches for the next thirty years.

The American attitude was to go for hard cash. The British attitude was political and basically imperial. They wanted the sovereignty of the North Atlantic sky. By *force majeure*—a favourite Imperial Airway's phrase—they would probably have to share it with the Americans, but at least they were 'cousins' and spoke English.

For the next few years, Juan Trippe and Woods Humphery worked towards an agreement between the two companies on the North Atlantic sky. Endless correspondence between them followed, usually done by trans-Atlantic telephone—all faithfully written down and preserved by Woods Humphery.

They had their problems with the players on the fringes of the game. There had been that conference held by the Italians on the North Atlantic in Rome, which Woods Humphery identified to Trippe as 'a move by the Italians somehow or other to get a footing on the Atlantic business'.

On the Atlantic, Canada's geographical position was pivotal. She was alarmed by the apparent 'determination of the United States to at least enter, if not actually control the situation', and wrote to Imperial Airways seeking their cooperation to build a Canadian airline and a Canadian aircraft manufacturing business. Imperial Airways replied that they would like to cooperate, but were committed to the tripartite agreement. However, the door had been left open for Canada to join.

Ireland was also in a strong geographical position as the nearest land to Newfoundland. A Committee was appointed to consider trans-Atlantic air services. Surveys were made of the west coast of Ireland for a suitable site for a flying-boat station.

France had always realised the North Atlantic possibilities, but she had now lost the Azores monopoly, and had her hands full operating services to her African colonies and pioneering the South Atlantic.

Germany was playing a lone game, concentrating first on airships and South America, and then gradually working into the North Atlantic.

Pan American and Imperial Airways were aiming for an official exclusive agreement on the New York–England and the New York–Bermuda routes valid for fifteen years, laying down two services a week by each company, the splitting of eastbound and westbound mail, and the sharing of landing rights and facilities.

Progress was made. Pan American obtained a concession from Iceland, and Imperial Airways applied for a similar one. Both companies applied to Newfoundland for the necessary operating permits, but before this became law, the Canadian government intervened, stating that it wanted to participate. There were problems in Newfoundland, and the British government changed the status of Newfoundland and put it under a commission of government. As a result, Newfoundland could no longer grant the rights to air traffic in its own name. Imperial Airways requested from the British government an exclusive right to operate from Newfoundland for fifty years. The Canadian government and Pan Am objected to this, and it was changed so that Imperial Airways should also get the right to sublet the franchise to one Canadian and one American company. It was specifically understood that Pan Am could use the facilities in Bermuda when they were completed.

In July 1932 the Director of Civil Aviation, Sir Francis Shelmerdine, had gone to Canada, amongst other matters to reassure the Canadians. The brief prepared by Woods Humphery stated that the Canadians need not fear the activities of Pan American in the Maritimes 'since Imperial Airways are on friendly terms with the American Company and are in a position to see that Canada receives fair treatment'. A wry postscript added 'it is little use grieving over the United States' aerial invasion of Canada whilst the United States is prepared to spend so much money on the development of commercial aviation and the British Empire is not'.

Private companies were also knocking on the door. The British Secretary of State was approached by a company that called itself 'The New York–London–Moscow Air Lines Incorporated'. In a letter beginning 'Honorable Sir: In contemplation of future aeronautical progress, I beg to present to you a gigantic aerial transportation programme,' they requested permission to fly mail and freight from the USA to the UK.

At the end of 1934 Wesley Smith, a well-known pilot with extensive experience, came to see Burchall, Imperial Airways Commercial Manager, to try for a tie-up with Imperial Airways. Burchall reported him as saying 'that the United States already had equipment capable of flying the Atlantic regularly on a mail service,' and prophesying that aircraft would do the water jump 'at 20,000 feet and within the day'.

This was confirmation of other indications from America that Trippe's hand was getting stronger every day. While the American plans for aircraft were proceeding logically towards a North Atlantic vehicle, British aircraft plans were dominated by Empire thinking, and they were no further forward towards a 'right' Atlantic vehicle.

Trippe had no wish to make the Atlantic sky exclusive to the two nations. Though he obviously wanted to avoid competition from other American airlines, the more foreign operators who wanted to fly to New York, the more cards he had in his hands for operating reciprocal services. But the British clung to the policy of the All-Red Route, and if the Azores route could not be exclusive (though with Bermuda, they still hoped) at least they were determined that the northern route via Newfoundland would be totally controlled.

On such delicate political issues—though they were frank with each other on most other matters—both Trippe and Woods Humphery kept their cards close to their chests.

Woods Humphery kept particularly silent about his own aircraft situation. When the idea of the agreement was born, Imperial Airways had far more experience and expertise, but by 1935 Pan Am had drawn many lengths ahead.

From the beginning, it had been agreed that neither Pan Am nor Imperial Airways would start before the other. This understanding was to prove paramount—and particularly frustrating to the Americans. With his own Atlantic aircraft plans forging ahead, Trippe wanted to begin operations as soon as possible. Already, he had the Atlantic route explored and tied up. A deal had been arranged with Denmark for an air service between Europe and America via Greenland. In 1933, Lindbergh had explored the northern route and gone to Portugal and the Azores, surveying the possibilities of both the northern and the southern routes. He had come up with the view that the weather and the operational difficulties of the northern route were by no means impossible. Trippe had built up the first complete weather map of the North

Atlantic, established a meteorological and radio station at Port Washington and positioned meteorologists in Newfoundland and Ireland, where British and Canadian meteorologists were also stationed.

The agreement between Pan Am and Imperial Airways was still in draft when difficulties arose. The original intention had been that it would be a government agreement, but for constitutional reasons, Trippe reported, the US were not able to enter into an airmail agreement for a *future* service. This difficulty appeared to be circumvented by Trippe and Woods Humphery agreeing to an inter-company agreement, sharing the trans-Atlantic mail between them.

Now the game hotted up. Other European nations wanted a similar agreement with America, and began to arrive in America with that intention.

On 1st April 1935 a meeting was held at the Air Ministry to discuss French participation on the North Atlantic, at which the Colonial Office, Dominions Office, Foreign Office and the Post Office were present. Burchall represented Imperial Airways and pointed out that if the USA made a similar agreement with France 'it would give them two American flights to every one flight by any other State, the more European nations participating in the service on this basis the greater would be the number of American flights as compared with those of any one other nation.' The conclusion of the meeting was that, 'the French could not establish a trans-Atlantic service without coming to us for facilities', and it was agreed that the French should be allowed to land at Bermuda when the base was completed.

Now another complication ensued. Shelmerdine made a visit to Ireland in July 1935 to look into the establishment of a trans-Atlantic base. He also reported that the Irish wanted to come in on the Imperial Airways–Pan American agreement on a one-third basis.

This was considered unrealistic, but bearing in mind Canada's anxiety to participate and the policy of the All-Red Route, the idea of an Atlantic Company was born, Britain having 51 per cent and Canada and Ireland having 24½ per cent each. This was approved by Warren Fisher at the Treasury, and in the autumn of 1935, Shelmerdine and Sir Donald Banks, Head of the Post Office, and an Irish delegation crossed the Atlantic for discussions with the Canadians in Montreal. Bank's view was that the point of the visit should be to found a trans-Atlantic service between the UK and Canada—the participation of the Americans was really extraneous.

Trippe was understandably concerned at the emergence of this new company, particularly as the Pan Am–Imperial Airways agreement had not yet been signed and there were further complications. Trippe was assured that he would not be excluded from the Atlantic company. But he insisted that the American government would not wear this new development. He went on telling Woods Humphery that the US Government had absolutely no power to enter a postal agreement at the present time, that it could not give a contract even to an American company until that company was in a position immediately to carry out the service. He warned that the Italians, the Germans and other Europeans would be vociferous if exclusive rights were given to one foreign company. Woods Humphery quoted him as saying that, 'No Minister, not even the President, could agree to any such proposal.'

But Woods Humphery took a sanguine view, which was shared by Banks and Shelmerdine, that Trippe was overstating the risks. 'The atmosphere is distinctly friendly,' he wrote from New York, 'and from what Trippe told me of Wronsky's [Lufthansa], and Plesman's [KLM] disappointment over their efforts here, which of course you must take at its face value, I imagine they [Pan Am] realise the balance of advantage for them lies with cleaning up their arrangements with us.' On 2nd December 1935 agreement was reached in Montreal on the North Atlantic Company. This Company of Ireland, Canada and Great Britain was to be the chosen instrument of the British government to operate the North Atlantic. All eastbound and westbound aircraft were to stop at an Irish airport, subject to *force majeure*. The UK would establish radio facilities and help build the Newfoundland airport. Meteorological arrangements were also initiated, and officers posted on both sides of the Atlantic. There were immediate strong notes from France and Germany, protesting that they were being excluded.

On the same day as agreement was reached on the Atlantic Company, Judge Moore had held a preliminary meeting to consider the arrival in Washington of Banks and Shelmerdine for further discussion of the Pan Am–Imperial Airways Atlantic service.

The Americans had been informed confidentially that the Canadians wanted the trans-Atlantic line to pass through Montreal. They also knew of the British ambition for the All-Red Route.

There was a possibility that the British would make a bid for an exclusive arrangement with Pan Am by playing their two trumps, Newfoundland and Bermuda. If this ploy succeeded, it would in effect mean that on the North Atlantic, New York would be the branch line connection to the All-Red Route. In any case, the Germans, the French and the Dutch were all trying to make arrangements with the USA, so that an exclusive arrangement was not really politically possible, even if America were willing to have one. The Americans also thought it possible that Britain might ask for 50 per cent of the airmail business. This was again not really possible as the same price could not be paid to a foreign company as might be paid to an American company—the inflexibility in an otherwise flexible system—due to the subsidy element for the development of American aviation in the airmail contract.

The totally different British system had been ruefully explained by Woods Humphery in 1933: 'We carry at a pre-arranged bulk contract rate, but with no guarantee of minimum loads, such airmails as the Post Office gives us. Moreover, the Post Office fixes the rates to be paid by the public, and so the entire commercial risk rests with the air carrier.'

The Washington meeting was particularly vital for the British because of the emergence of the new Empire Air Mail Scheme, conceived by Dismore, Secretary of Imperial Airways, and worked out by Woods Humphery and Geddes. The government financing proposed in 1934 had been particularly generous. For three half-pence (less than three-quarters of today's penny) for half an ounce, mail could be sent between any two points in the Empire. Politically orientated though it certainly was, nevertheless it was a bold and imaginative scheme and had led to the ordering of the modern Empire (unfortunately not Atlantic) flying boats. Banks was naturally extremely keen to bring in Canada, where a trans-continental service to Vancouver was planned. There were also hopes to continue the All-Red Route across the Pan Am preserve of the Pacific to Australia and New Zealand to complete the red circle round the globe—though in the event these were blocked by American control of the Hawaii stepping-stone.

The Washington meeting duly commenced on 5th December 1935, in the International Committee on Civil International Aviation under the chairmanship of Judge Moore. Woods Humphery was present, but most of the talking was done by Banks. It was probably the first long-range aviation bilateral rights meeting, and discussed both the Atlantic and the New York–Bermuda service, which Banks described as 'the first link' in the Atlantic. Trippe re-applied for authority for two round trips a week on the Bermuda run, and also asked for permits 'to land in Great Britain, the Irish Free State, Newfoundland, Bermuda and Canada with respect to a scheduled trans-Atlantic service', again for two round trips a week. Mr Branch, who represented the US Post Office Department, said that they could not give contracts to Imperial Airways to carry mail. The point was whether it would be necessary to ask for further legislative measures. There were other points for experts, and the Chairman suggested that Pan Am and Imperial Airways should go into 'a huddle' ('We call it scrum', said Banks).

A further meeting was held on 12th December. Letters from Imperial Airways to the US Department of Commerce were read out asking for two Atlantic services a week carrying passengers, cargo and mail 'via Canada, the Irish Free State and Newfoundland or Bermuda' for 15 years from 1st May 1936. The Department's reply was also read out approving the applications to land in the States 'while engaging in foreign air commerce' between London and America, provided reciprocal rights were granted by the British. Mail was not specifically mentioned.

Branch again pointed out that the letter did not imply any obligations on the part of the US Post Office to give a mail contract to any particular airline. Banks said that he realised there was no commitment on the mail, but added, 'I think that the rest will follow afterwards.' The British had 'the fullest liberty with regard to the placing of a mail contract'. He went on to speak of how in Liverpool at the commencement of their journey, the British had been joined by the Irish, and on board they began to 'hammer out across the Atlantic, across that waste of sea' a first span, UK to Ireland. Then they passed Newfoundland and got that government's acceptance of the second pier. They had an enthusiastic reception in Canada to a pier there, and they felt confident when they came to the US that 'the final link would not fail'. He gave the benediction to the meeting: 'The Book says "Blessèd are the peacemakers." Let us hope that with those can be combined the bridgebuilders.'

Perhaps the British hoped for some changes in American law to accommodate the Atlantic agreement. The Postmaster General is reported as promising to ask Congress for funds for a trans-Atlantic airmail service, and the British were certainly banking on the Bermuda and Newfoundland aces to persuade the Americans to join their bridge. But it was to the US interest to have as many bilateral agreements with European countries as possible.

On 17th December 1935 Captain Rickenbacker (another of the pilot-administrators to whom American aviation owes so much, later of Eastern) visited Croydon and told the British that his idea 'of running the Atlantic service was for everybody to cooperate'. It was becoming clear that other American airlines as well as Pan American were interested.

Other governments now stepped up the pressure to get in on the game. A French delegation, headed by Baron de la Grange and Monsieur Couhé, arrived in Britain preparatory to going over to America to negotiate reciprocal rights. A meeting was held on 10th January 1936, with Shelmerdine in the chair, The Post Office, the Foreign Office, the Dominions Office, the Air Ministry and the Treasury were present, but there was no one from Imperial Airways.

The French had a six-engined flying boat, the *Lieutenant de Vaisseau Paris*, which they wanted to operate on the Azores route. They were confident they could win back the Azores landing-rights which Aéropostale had lost, provided the Portuguese government could be assured that the terminus would be Lisbon. But it would be expensive to build an aerodrome there; it would be necessary to split the cost between France, America and Britain. That was generally agreed, but de la Grange asked 'Supposing Lufthansa or the Dutch wanted to come in with us?'

The British recommended 'much better to keep the control of the Azores between ourselves,' charging other people for the use of facilities.

De la Grange also asked, 'You consider that the northern route will remain merely British?'

Shelmerdine answered, 'At any rate at the early stages.'

De la Grange went on, 'Now that other route [via the Azores] may be and probably will be international. You have no objection?'

Banks of the Post Office said, 'We ought to reserve that. I personally have not quite subscribed to your theory of opening the Atlantic to everybody. You have put this proposition to us, and I think we ought to think it over.'

Couhé said, 'This is an American proposition.'

Shelmerdine then asked, 'What do you mean by "international"? '

De la Grange replied, 'First of all, an American–French–British route.'

'Oh well,' said Banks, 'I won't react so quickly.'

The French attitude was that if the Germans wanted to come in later, they could use the facilities. Shelmerdine's view was, 'we cannot keep Germany out', to which De la Grange retorted, 'I do not think they will ask anybody's permission.'

Over on the other side, Trippe was requesting clearance to operate through Ireland on the same terms as Imperial Airways under the Atlantic Company agreement. The Pan Am–Imperial Airways agreement was still unsigned, and problems had arisen on the clause which split the mail fifty-fifty. On the file, an Imperial Airways official scribbled in pencil *'legal posit very difficult.'* However, on 15th January 1936, Shelmerdine wrote to Woods Humphery, 'We are all, I think, agreed that it is most desirable that the Agreement should be initialled before the French Delegation reaches Washington. According to my present information, their intention is to sail by the *Ile de France* on 22nd instant.'

The Pan Am–Imperial Airways Agreement was duly signed on 25th January 1936. But now there was trouble with the permits which had to be issued prior to operations, and in March 1936 Trippe wanted these cleaned up, particularly the mail clause. Clearly he feared what Woods Humphery called 'exclusivity'. He had heard that there had been leakages in Canada and perhaps at the London Post Office, and according to Woods Humphery's account of the telephone conversation, he feared that, 'the whole thing might get into a mess.' He now had the Norwegians in New York and, in Woods Humphery's own words, 'The more people who came over, the more awkward it became so long as the permits were not issued. He reminded me that Wronsky [Lufthansa] had got his experimental permits, and he thought he could not over-estimate the time element.'

Later in March, Trippe wanted the mail clause left out but Woods Humphery said 'there would be insuperable difficulties' at his end. In

Trippe's view, that was a pity because of difficulties he was having in Washington.

The difficulties came to light in April. There was pressure to obtain an Atlantic airway which *any* American company approved by the US government would be permitted to fly. Which of course Woods Humphery pointed out 'was entirely contrary to the Pan Am–Imperial Airways Agreement'.

In June 1936 a German mission arrived in Britain. As with the French mission, Shelmerdine was in the chair, and representatives of the same Departments were present. No representatives of Imperial Airways attended, but Shelmerdine had invited Woods Humphery to an informal luncheon given by the Air Ministry for the Germans at the Savoy— appropriately in the 'Patience Room'.

The Germans had nothing to offer the British, but boldly took the initiative by asking for permission to use British facilities via the Azores for twelve experimental flights across the Atlantic, carrying both mail and goods. Shelmerdine objected that such an operation was not experimental but 'really the inauguration of a regular service'.

The Germans conceded: no goods.

Banks objected to mail being carried.

The Germans cannily explained this would simply be for philatelists, but Banks was sceptical.

The Germans produced the card that they had American approval for their flights, but they wanted British acceptance, in principle, for a regular service, otherwise there was no point in carrying out the experiment. Shelmerdine pointed out that before that could be agreed, the British would have to consult their many partners, but added, 'Let us proceed on the assumption that it will be possible to operate this route for a regular service.'

By now, the Germans had more than a foot in the door. They now 'offered an experimental stage for one year', the implication being that Britain was altogether too slow. Pushing a little harder, they tried to get permission to use Newfoundland as an alternative 'but only in the event of bad weather'.

Eventually the twelve experimental flights were allowed, after which there would be a final agreement about commencement of a regular service. As regards mail, experimental mail could be carried if the British could also carry it. No equivalent British service was planned on that route, and Banks did say 'I think you are pressing us rather hard.' Nevertheless it was agreed that the facilities at Bermuda could be used when available, but before that Lufthansa could operate at their own risk. After April 1937, the carriage of mail would be looked at formally. The use of Newfoundland, due to stress of bad weather, would be permitted.

The Germans now produced their ace. They announced they were ready to start next week with Dornier 18 flying boats, catapulted from the *Westfalen* stationed beyond the Azores. This would have been a severe prestige blow to Imperial Airways. The initiative was now with the Germans. They said that they would be willing to postpone till August or September, in spite of Bermuda storms at that time, 'but no longer' because that would be a postponement that they could not explain to their superiors.

The final agreed date for starting the experimental service was 1st September 1936.

Shelmerdine, perhaps searching for at least some *quid pro quo*, suggested that there was no point in duplicating costs and Britain might cooperate on 'this catapulting business'. The German leader swiftly said they would 'be delighted to put the catapult at your disposal'.

The French and German discussions were the fore-runners of the many bilateral discussions on the exchange of air facilities that were to take place in the years ahead. For little yet had been organised administratively on the Atlantic. One-upmanship was the order of the day, but largely for political reasons. The only nation that appeared to have cottoned on to the immense commercial possibilities were the Americans, though the Germans were rapidly learning.

In New York, Trippe was still having problems. The Canadians did not want New York to be the Atlantic terminus. The Americans wanted to operate via Shediac in New Brunswick. He reported the American Government unwilling to issue permits to the British government before being satisfied with the Irish Free State and Canadian permits.

On 17th February 1937, Trippe was 'very much exercised owing to some opposition being levelled against the interchange of permits by certain groups of people who were anxious to push the interest of airships'.

On 11th March he reported that the press campaign was 'getting worse and worse', and on the same date Reuters issued a report saying that 'Negotiations on a trans-Atlantic service have reached deadlock, according to the *New York Times*.' The chief difficulty was whether Montreal or New York should be the trans-Atlantic terminal. Reuters went on, 'Both the Canadian Authorities and the British Air Ministry are represented as holding the view that an "all Empire" route via Newfoundland, with an extension across Canada to Vancouver, with New York as a branch line, is the most logical trans-Atlantic route.'

Trippe's fears of over a year ago that 'the whole thing might get into a mess' were being realised. He had aircrews ocean-trained on the Pacific route. He had aircraft that could do the water jump. The mid-Atlantic route had been opened up by Portuguese agreement to Pan Am and Imperial Airways using the Azores, and now was the time to get away from words and get down to action. Trippe could not by the agreement operate on his own, and he did not want to violate the understanding with Imperial Airways by beginning first.

In any case, the British now wanted to 'show' the Americans. So it was in much the same sort of way as some of the early pioneers were practically forced into the air by competition and circumstances, that both sides began to make preparations to go. Imperial Airways arranged with the Shell Oil Company for refuelling in Newfoundland, and it was agreed that their boats should be moored to the Shell barge. They began further training of their crews in ocean flying. Both companies over-hauled what aircraft they possessed conceivably capable of doing the water jump.

The first commercial proving flights across the Atlantic were about to begin.

## *Seven:* The Race for the Right Vehicle

All the time the political and administrative poker game was going on, the vital technical question of how to establish the right commercial service on the North Atlantic remained unsolved. Would it be airships? Would it be seadromes? Would it be catapults? Would it be flight refuelling? Would it be pick-a-back composites? Would it be flying boats?

The first and last were the favourites. Alone from the early 1930s onwards, Lindbergh had been calling for landplanes on the water jump. In an extraordinarily prophetic letter to Woods Humphery on 1st December 1936, Lindbergh had written, 'I believe that the use of flying boats will be temporary and will be discontinued as soon as suitable types of land planes can be constructed. I consider a hull will be a liability rather than an asset in the future. Our trans-oceanic passengers should be carried in supercharged cabins above storm levels and out of reach of icing conditions. Supercharging [pressurisation] can be incorporated much more easily in the cabin of a land plane than in the hull of a flying boat. From the standpoint of safety, I believe we can reduce accidents more by developing airworthiness than by emergency facilities for forced landings. A land plane is not affected by floating ice or by freezing spray, and its use reduces from three to two the elements with which an operating company must contend.' Years before in 1919, Hawker had shown the way in a land plane, jettisoning his undercarriage —now preserved in St John's museum—because it produced too much drag. Lindbergh wrote that letter from Ireland where he was one of a technical group that included Trippe and Woods Humphery to endorse the selection of Rineanna—the Marshy Point—on the banks of the Shannon as the base for the Irish Atlantic flying-boat station. The land airport was to be close and was called Shannon. The aerodrome became famous for its part in the story of the water jump. But by the time Rineanna was completed, flying boats had left the Atlantic and it was never used.

The huge Caproni triplane flying boat which would accommodate 100 passengers was really a flying test bed from which it was hoped to design an Italian Atlantic vehicle. It had a brief but eventful career in 1921. (General)

The Dornier 18 flying boat, the type that was catapulted from the Westfalen. (Dornier)

Germany had started the race and showed the world—with airships. After his flight in 1924 to deliver the LZ126, Eckener concentrated on the *Graf Zepplin*, and on 11th October 1928 set off again in this 771 foot giant with its five 570 hp reversible engines, carrying mail and twenty passengers, all of whom were accommodated in luxury with cabins, lounge and dining saloon. The crossing was made via Madeira.

Half way across, the airship ran into storms which dangerously ripped the port horizontal fin. Eckener's son and other volunteers climbed out on the fin girders, and in the teeth of the gale, balanced precariously above the Atlantic, patched up the rip with blankets. But the passage was completed safely and on 15th October, escorted by aeroplanes to Lakehurst, she was moored beside her sister ship, now christened *Los Angeles*.

In spite of fog and storms round Newfoundland, the return crossing was completed in 71 hours. Next year, Eckener flew *Graf Zeppelin* round the world. Then a regular luxury commercial service was established, and the giant airship was to make 144 trans-Atlantic flights during the course of her career.

The *Graf Zeppelin* is welcomed by cheering German schoolgirls after her maiden flight of nine and a half hours. (Popperfoto)

The first British gambit for the commercial water jump was also an airship—and it was on airships at the end of the 1920s that they spent most of their scarce civil aviation resources. They had already achieved a magnificent trans-Atlantic success in the flight of the R34. In the way the British have, government interest then flagged, only to be revived again. As Nevil Shute wrote, 'It was generally agreed in 1924 that the aeroplane would never be a very suitable vehicle for carrying passengers across the ocean, and that airships would operate all the long-distance routes of the future. We were all quite wrong, of course, but at the time it seemed reasonable.' He helped Barnes Wallis design the private-enterprise airship R100 on a geodetic or girder-like framework. Side by side, a government airship, the R101, was constructed—and a feud began. The acrimony and bitterness that resulted is described in Shute's *Slide Rule*. As a reflection of the different costs between private enterprise and nationalisation, R100 cost £411,113 and R101 £717,165. The government officials behaved, according to Shute's account, with quite unbelievable childishness and stupidity. The whole

The British R100 just before leaving Cardington for Montreal, 29 July 1930.
(Associated Newspapers)

The dining-room of the R 100 resembled an olde-worlde English teashop.
(Associated Newspapers)

idea arose out of the same Imperial Conference of 1926 which had first declared the policy of the All-Red Route, concentrating on airships and flying boats, and Canada agreed to put up a mooring tower at St Hubert near Montreal, complete with elevators to transport passengers up to the landing platform. A race developed between R100 and R101.

On 29th July 1930, the R100 set off under the command of Squadron Leader Booth from Cardington with 34½ tons of fuel to do the water jump. Nevil Shute was on board, and 'slept splendidly in pyjamas, sheet, sleeping bag and blanket'. Johnston, probably the most experienced navigator in the RAF, was one of the crew, as was a top-flight meteorological expert. Scott, the commander of R34, was also on board.

Apart from a torn fin, the crossing was uneventful. Then suddenly on 1 August through the darkness ahead was sighted an enormous fiery cross—the cross on the top of Mount Royal. Someone said, 'That's not Montreal. That's the New Jerusalem.'

A million sightseers looked over the R100 before her uneventful trip home twelve days later.

On 4th October, the R101 rose for her maiden flight to India, with Major Scott again on board and Johnston and others from the R100. The Secretary of State for Air had been repeatedly warned that the airship was totally unairworthy and strongly advised not to go. Sir Sefton Brancker, Director of civil aviation, tramped Whitehall corridors, pleading with Ministers and politicians to stop the flight. But a big political success was needed. A triumphal airship arrival in India was the requirement.

The crew were reluctant to fly, but could hardly refuse in the circumstances. The weather report was bad. The R101 took off. Soon after crossing the Channel, it was leaking and uncontrollable. The airship crashed in northern France, killing the Secretary of State, Sefton Brancker, Major Scott and forty-four others. The official accident report bluntly stated, 'It is impossible to avoid the conclusion that the R101 would not have started for India on the evening of 4th October if it had not been that reasons of public policy were considered as making it highly desirable for her to do so.' Prestige and 'public policy' were repeatedly to dog British civil aviation's progress.

The 210 ft tower at St Hubert stood hopefully for another eight years, awaiting R100's second arrival. But none came. Colonel Shelmerdine succeeded Sefton Brancker as Director of Civil Aviation.

Germany meanwhile produced the Do–X—a most extraordinary vehicle of Victorian appearance that looked more like a boat than a flying machine. Twelve engines were arranged in pairs on a platform wing, lifting a weight of 100,000 lb on take off and cruising at 110 mph. Inside, accommodation for 66 trans-Atlantic passengers was on the same luxurious scale as the German airships—cabins, bar, restaurant, lounge—while the flight deck with its huge round steering wheel, its engine room, separate navigation and radio offices, resembled the bridge of a ship. Built in 1929, it immediately captured the world record for passenger-carrying with a load of 170. Once again, the Germans had been careful and thorough. No dashing off to the ends of the earth, but short proving flights within Europe, gradually extending to Africa, then to South America and finally in May 1932, an epic flight across the South Atlantic and then up to New York. The return was made via Newfoundland and the Azores to Lisbon and then to a triumphant welcome in Berlin.

**The Prince of Wales, later King Edward VIII (collar turned up), boards the DO-X for a flight round the Solent, during which he took the controls.**
**(Dornier)**

Though the trip for such a large aircraft was certainly well in advance of its time, there had been a number of troubles and delays. The twelve engines were thirsty and the mammoth flying boat huge. It was no accident that the route was eastbound over the North Atlantic to get the help of the winds. The range was small and even Newfoundland–Azores was a tight squeeze. So the Do–X, after victoriously circling Manhattan, disappeared from the North Atlantic sky because it was not a commercial proposition.

By that time, the British had abandoned airships. Woods Humphery had told his Chairman that on his proposal the Air Ministry were going to put two experimental planes under construction for the trans-Atlantic service via the Azores. The Chairman wrote that 'he would like to be sure that these planes are being built in close consultation with us [Imperial Airways] and in keeping with the plans of our American and French friends.' Woods Humphery replied that, 'I am afraid this is rather vague because I have not yet got down to "brass tacks" with Bullock and Danreuther [Air Ministry] as they in turn have not yet received the authority of the Secretary of State to go ahead and cooperate with us on the plans of the Atlantic Service in case it comes off.'

A meeting was then held at the Air Ministry to discuss with the Directorate of Civil Aviation and the Directorate of Technical Development requirements for a trans-Atlantic mail-carrying aircraft. Imperial Airways requested a four-engined monoplane flying boat, with a crew of three, a speed of 150 mph, and a range of 2200 miles against a 30 mph headwind, refuelling in the air permitted.

On 22 September 1931 Trippe had written to Woods Humphery giving him all the details of Pan American's new Sikorsky flying boat, the S40, which while not an Atlantic aircraft was along the same lines, Woods Humphery noted with satisfaction, as Imperial Airways' own ideas. Throughout their long relationship, Trippe kept Woods Humphery informed of Pan American technical developments.

But the Air Ministry were not happy. They told Imperial Airways that the cruising speed for their proposed four-engined flying boat could not be met. In any case, the payload that could be carried was so small that such a trans-Atlantic aircraft was not practicable. They saw

**The DO-X over the Statue of Liberty before its trip across the Atlantic via the Azores, 21/22 May 1932.**                                                                    **(Dornier)**

The DO-X on her first trials in 1930 is compared to the model of the Vickers flying boat which never flew.                                          (Pacific and Atlantic)

no hope of such a plane being included in their experimental programme for new types. There was in any case a Vickers six-engined monoplane flying boat actively being considered. So Major Mayo, Imperial Airways' Technical Manager, on 26th October 1931 proposed a much smaller aircraft, and sent to Woods Humphery two draft letters for him to send on to the Air Ministry, minuting that these letters 'are intended to emphasise in fairly strong terms the importance of immediate action on the part of the Air Ministry'.

There was considerable speculation in the Press. On 29th December 1931 the *Morning Post* described great 35-ton flying boats and Air Ministry plans for 60-ton monsters to carry 100 passengers over 2500 miles.

At the same time, Pan American announced its first profit (of $105,452) for 1931, and followed that up in 1932 with a profit of $698,526. Imperial Airways' profits for these two years were £10,186 and £52,894.

Already the British had fallen behind. Geddes was complaining in the *Daily Mail* that France had 269 aircraft employed in regular air transport, Germany 177 and Britain 32. Pan American's fleet had already reached 121, and the *Daily Telegraph* reported in December 1932 that Pan American would operate the North Atlantic via Bermuda in winter and Newfoundland in summer with flying boats capable of carrying 50 passengers and several tons of mail; 'The keels of the two air leviathans have been laid in great secrecy in factories at Bridgeport, Connecticut and Baltimore, Maryland.'

These were the improvements on the Sikorsky S40—the Sikorsky 42B and the Martin 130. America was steadily progressing towards a suitable Atlantic vehicle. Airships, flight refuelling and catapults were in the process of being dismissed for the civil crossing, though seadromes were under active consideration.

France was concentrating on the South Atlantic—where again Germany was active. They were also still considering seadromes, and along with the Germans were actively interested in catapults. Early in 1932, the British government cancelled all work on the Vickers six-engined flying boats.

The Depression was, of course, still on, but the decision was really taken because the government regarded the Atlantic problem politically and strategically, not commercially. That there might be liquid gold in all that expanse of very salty water never appeared to cross their minds. Civil aviation was still a lame duck for which the Treasury had little time and less money. What small sums could be squeezed from the Air Ministry (and this was the era of the great and redoubtable Trenchard, who fought for every available penny to build up the RAF) was concentrated on the Empire Routes. The advice of independent experienced airmen who had flown the Atlantic was rarely sought. The Civil Service prided itself on being amateur. It had been built up from the sons of noble lords and gentlemen and the graduates of Oxford and Cambridge. Somehow, professionals were tradesmen, below the salt. As in the game of cricket, there were the Gentlemen (amateurs) and the Players (professionals), and when it came to a combined English side the captain was always a Gentleman. Civil aviation was only another of the Civil Service's myriad activities, which needed to be juggled into some sort of existence. A number of new files had been added which would be tossed to officials for information—for again it was a maxim that everything could be learned from papers. In this way, an Empire had for many years been successfully administered. In fact, the civil aviation side of the Air Ministry were extremely keen, but their numbers were tiny and the Civil Servants' technical knowledge very limited.

Now Italy showed her hand in the technical field. In 1930, the Italian Air Minister, General Balbo, had successfully led a formation of ten big Savoia-Marchetti S–55X flying boats across the South Atlantic. These twin-hulled aircraft with one pusher and one puller engines mounted one behind the other were designed for torpedo dropping and bombing,

Formation flights both east-west and west-east across the Atlantic were made by Balbo and his Italian pilots, July/August 1933.                                  (Taylor)

not for civil aviation. But since the North Atlantic sky was still in its politics-and-prestige stage, Balbo's next mass formation flight of twenty-four Savioa-Marchettis across the water jump made an electric impression. The formation took off on 1st July 1933 and proceeded via Holland, Ireland, Iceland, Labrador and Shediac, New Brunswick, to Montreal, Chicago and New York.

In spite of bad weather and fog, during which formation flying with so many aircraft must have been a nightmare, the Atlantic crossing was successful. Unfortunately, there had been one accident in Holland, but as an example of engine reliability and crew discipline and training this flight was unique. Balbo's ebullient and likeable personality also made a lasting impression, and as a public relations exercise as well as a technical achievement the mass water jump had been a success. On the return flight, No. 13 turned turtle taking off from the Azores for Lisbon, and sadly there was one fatality. At Rome, Mussolini welcomed the flying boats back with full (and deserved) pomp and circumstance.

Meanwhile, the Americans were moving. Lamplugh, the father of aviation insurance, told Imperial Airways that the Sikorsky 42's useful load was 1400 lb at a speed of 160 mph, but the Assistant General

Manager, Burchall, wrote that 'Mayo doesn't believe performances will be achieved, in fact, nowhere near achieved.'

Burchall had visited America in August 1933, and wrote to Mayo pointing out that the range of the two new American flying boats would presumably permit of the trans-Atlantic service straightaway. He pointed out that if the figure were anywhere near achieved, the USA would be ready very much earlier than Britain to operate the trans-Atlantic service, and suggested that 'we ought to get busy on a machine of equivalent performance.'

Mayo replied that the claims could not possibly be achieved in the case of either aircraft, saying that in his view the ranges on the North Atlantic would be considerably less than half those claimed, even with a payload of 400 lb. He said 'it might perhaps be admitted that American aircraft designers are ahead of British designers in certain classes of aircraft, but I very much doubt whether this is the case in regard to flying boats. Of course, I agree they are lucky with their Pratt and Whitney engines.' Mayo put the range of the Martin at 1360 miles against a 40 mph wind and the Sikorsky ar 1240 under similar conditions.

By this time, the germ of the idea of the Short Empire flying boats had been conceived, in which Mayo had played a considerable part, and as a British mail carrier, naturally he had in mind the Short-Mayo Composite, planned in 1932.

By 1934 Pan American had 133 aircraft, flying to 165 airports and stations and a magnificent combined aerodrome and flying-boat base at Miami.

A book called *Through Atlantic Clouds* published that year issued a warning: 'Wake up, England! Time and again our pilots have proved that English machines and English aeroplanes are second to none in the world. The opportunity awaits us now of making our aircraft as familiar over future Atlantic flying routes as our merchant vessels are upon its waves at the present day.'

The red signal calling for a Committee was flashing in Whitehall and Westminster. On 21st November 1934, in the Lords, the Secretary of State pointed out that the US Post Office subsidy had been £4,750,000 in 1933, adding, 'The United States government expenditure on the development of civil aviation in the seven years from 1927 to 1933 inclusive revealed, if we add the other items of expenditure to the amount of the subsidies, the staggering total of £25,000,000.' In comparison, Imperial Airways' subsidy had been negligible. He demanded that special arrangements *must* be made with aircraft manufacturers to build aircraft suitable for the Atlantic.

A row was brewing, and Imperial Airways in a memorandum pointed out Woods Humphery's efforts in this direction, quoting an Imperial Airways letter of 27th January 1931 to the Air Ministry, which stated that the future development of the Atlantic air service was considered to be of the utmost importance, and asking for radio and meteorological services in Newfoundland and Bermuda 'at the earliest possible moment'.

On 13th February 1935 the Director General of Civil Aviation, Colonel Shelmerdine, held a meeting in the Air Ministry with Woods Humphery and Mayo 'to clarify the situation in regard to aircraft for the North Atlantic'. He asked Air Commandore Verney of the Air Ministry technical staff his opinion of the feasibility of operating a regular air service across the Atlantic with reasonable payload, utilising the Sikorsky and Martin flying boats. Verney had recently visited America, and stated that the development of flying boats was more advanced there. The Americans were ahead in design, manufacture and power-to-weight ratios. Sikorsky and Martin had spent three years in external design and development. The minutes state that Verney 'considered that the long-range claims for the Sikorsky and Martin flying boats would be realised. It was agreed that on published claims no British flying boat had been designed to equal the Sikorsky and that we were further still behind the Martin.'

Shelmerdine pointed out that 'the Air Ministry were aware two years ago that the contracts for the Sikorsky and Martin flying boats had been placed and that as a result of examination in the Department the claims made for these aircraft were thought to be grossly exaggerated . . . After much consideration we had decided in favour of a composite aircraft (the Short-Mayo) which, when available in two years from now, must still be regarded as experimental from an operational standpoint.' Shelmerdine considered it 'significant that the USA appeared to display some aloofness in regard to the Atlantic seadrome project and he thought it would be extremely unwise to assume that the claims made for the Martin boat could not be substantially fulfilled. It was agreed that it was unthinkable that the Air Ministry should sit back and take no action on the assumption that the American claims were fantastic.'

Shelmerdine then gave the apologies for all of them—that they had rather been concerned with the Empire Air Mail Scheme, not the Atlantic.

Woods Humphery wanted specifications drawn up on the basis of the Martin 130. Shelmerdine was toying with the idea of a flying boat for mails only. Verney 'was rather averse from ruling out passenger accommodation entirely, but he did not press the view. He was also of the opinion that the possibility of a multi-engine land plane should not be disregarded.' He agreed to collaborate with Imperial Airways on specifications for a trans-Atlantic aircraft 'so long as there was no feeling that there was any attempt, on the part of service interest, to exert an influence opposed to the true interests of civil aviation.'

The aircraft decided on was a flying boat of Martin 130 design, and 'in case no response was forthcoming from the trade', a flying boat for mails only or a land plane equivalent.

In spite of the meeting, Woods Humphery wrote to Shelmerdine two days later that his invesitigations 'indicate that Short's design for our new boats was right up-to-date in every way, and indeed ahead of any-thing else, including Martin and Sikorsky'. He added the information from the New York manager that the Martin flying boat, according to rumour, was difficult to land and there was a strong opinion that the Sikorsky was better and would be preferred. The rumour was incorrect. The Martin was in fact easier to handle than the S–42, and had the advantage of being able to carry a payload on the Pacific.

The new boats referred to were the Empire boats for the Empire Air Mail Scheme, twenty-eight of which had been ordered boldly off the drawing board at a cost of £41,000 each for the Empire airmail service. Equipped with four Pegasus 1000 hp engines, their all-up weight was 44,999 lb. They were in every way modern and beautiful-looking aircraft with two decks, a restaurant, cabins, a bar and a promenade deck. Sturdily built to combat turbulent weather, they could take off quickly from small harbours. They had a comparatively high speed (for a flying boat) of 125 knots, but had a short commercial range of around 800 miles—all that was necessary on the Eastern routes for which they were designed.

In comparison, the Sikorsky 42B looked its age. Nevertheless on 16th April 1935, the Sikorsky *Pan-American Clipper* left San Francisco and covered the 2400 miles to Hawaii in 18 hours, arriving one minute behind schedule. Next day, it flew back.

Something clearly had to be done. Shelmerdine promised £10,000 towards the design of three trans-Atlantic flying boats, to which again the Air Ministry would contribute. He told Woods Humphery that 'we should negotiate—probably with Short's—a design contract for a very much larger flying boat for ocean flying, something on the lines of the 130 ton boat described by Mr Gouge [designer of the Empire boat] in his lecture to the North-East Coast Shipbuilding Federation.'

Then came further problems. Shelmerdine said that the engines visualised for these aircraft could not possibly be developed under about eight years. Air Commodore Verney said that the Air Ministry Technical Department did not disagree with the specification but they labelled it '1966 and all that'.

Shelmerdine then came up with what Lord Thomas, Chairman of BOAC from 1949 to 1956, calls 'Buggin's Turn'. This practice, which is bred out of Civil Service fairness and the Treasury view that employ-ment and the nation's economy as a whole should always be considered before commercial interests and technical specialisation, continued throughout the history of British aviation, reaching its crowning achievement in the late 1950s, when three small orders for three V-bombers of similar performance were given to three different aircraft manufacturers. The difficulties over spares and paperwork and training can be imagined. As has been seen, aircraft manufacturers were regarded rather like ironmongers. Between them and the users of their wares, the airlines, was the screen of the Civil Service. Since the British government was almost the sole buyer of their products, for too long a time the manufacturers were forced into the role of men knocking at the door of the tradesmen's entrance, pencil in hand, waiting M'Lady's pleasure. They could not argue—the customer is always right especially if she is almost your only customer. No one would wish to criticise. In return for such obeisance, they all got a share of the orders and no one is left out in the cold. At the same time, no one is allowed to get too many orders. That wouldn't be fair to the next man. It should be Buggin's Turn. Now Shelmerdine stated that the order should not go to Short's, who were certainly the most up-to-date flying-boat manufacturers in the country, but (perhaps mindful of the cancellation of the six-engined flying boats) to Vickers.

There was, of course, a good side to it. Somehow or other in the lean years, the aircraft manufacturers managed not to go broke. As a result, when World War II broke out, they had their design teams together and were in a position to carry out a magnificent production of first-class warplanes. But it hampered British airplanes in their highly competitive field. Both 'Buggin's Turn' and the curious screen between civil aircraft builders and users remained a feature of British airlines, till Lord Thomas broke it down in the early 1950s by more direct contact when he was BOAC Chairman. In comparison, Pan Am had been fortunate from the beginning in ordering such aircraft as they wanted and dealing direct with manufacturers. Their legendary Chief Engineer, Priester, who had a passion for safe maintenance and low fuel consumption, had no hesitation in harrying his suppliers with his much-feared epithet 'Confidence is out!'

As always in a crisis, up came another Committee—this time the Sassoon Committee, set up, in its own words, because Pan American were 'clearly making such progress that the early inauguration of the trans-Atlantic service will be seen to be in prospect. It is, unfortunately, not yet possible to point to corresponding developments in this country where preparations have not yet been specifically formulated.'

In a memorandum to the Committee in June 1935 Imperial Airways stated, 'The crux of the problem was finance.' Certainly the financing of Imperial Airways—part private company, part government-subsidised instrument—was a hybrid increasingly difficult to operate. Imperial Airways did not have the free choice of their routes or of the aircraft

The Martin 130 *China Clipper* left San Francisco to inaugurate the first pacific air/mail service on 22 November 1935. (Pan American World Airways)

necessary to operate them. But behind and beyond the finance there was something else. The name *Imperial* Airways (Woods Humphery's suggestion) was no accident, nor was the name *Empire* flying boat.

The Sassoon Committee, coming like the airline from a maritime and imperial nation, again chose a huge-hulled flying boat for its chosen airborne instrument. The reason given was that there were no land aerodromes in the Azores or Bermuda. It might be possible to construct a suitable one in Newfoundland. The Report stated, 'a forced landing in the sea with a land plane would necessitate the restriction of the service to mail-carrying only.' At the same time, they proposed the building of an experimental land plane, at a cost 'not exceeding £40,000.' On the building of an Atlantic aircraft, it was recognised that 'a vast step forward is involved, but it appears to the Committee essential to face the problem. We must build *now* on a basis which will enable us to compete with the Americans.'

The arguments recommenced. Again the question of where the money was coming from was uppermost. The paperwork continued. On 22nd November 1935 the Pan American Martin 130 *China Clipper* inaugurated the first Pacific airmail service by flying the 2400 miles from San Francisco to Honolulu in 21 hours, carrying seven crew and 1837 lb of mail, and then continuing to Manila in the Philippines, via Midway, Wake and Guam.

\*　　　\*　　　\*

Mayo was in a sense right—neither the Sikorsky 42B nor the Martin 130 were commercial Atlantic aeroplanes, and both gave trouble with maintenance.

But the long Pacific flights gave credibility to similar Atlantic services. And by inventing cruise control, whereby the engine revolutions were carefully adjusted for maximum range as the aircraft grew lighter through fuel consumption during the trip, by increasing the all-up weight and taking on more fuel, by variable-pitch propellers and other new inventions, the Americans had stretched their flying boats sufficiently to do the crossing with passengers. Moreover, the flying boats—particularly the Martin 130—were beautifully equipped inside with a restaurant, a galley, a bar, lounges, cabins and a promenade deck, offering a luxury equivalent to first class on a liner.

Apart from the 42B and the Martin, Pan American had other aircraft in mind for the North Atlantic. In 1936 they placed a tentative order

The German catapult ship *Westfalen* with a Dornier 18 on the catapult was stationed off the Azores.                                                    (Dornier)

The Blohm und Voss seaplane *Nordmeer*—last refinement of the German catapult aircraft across the Atlantic, which took over from the Dornier 18s. (Unknown)

for a new four-engined land plane, the DC4. And in March 1937 they had ordered three revolutionary snub-nosed Boeing Stratoliners, the first commercial aircraft to have pressurised cabins.

Keeping her hand close to her chest, Germany had also advanced in the Atlantic race and was making further plans. Her safe airship service for passengers in the *Graf Zeppelin* was unrivalled, and now the *Hindenburg* was nearing completion. To carry the mail, Germany had concentrated on catapults, converting an old cargo boat, the *Westfalen*, at a cost of only £18,100, as a mother ship for refuelling the Dornier Do18 flying boats, *Aeolus* and *Zephyr*. The necessary permission having been obtained from the British at the meeting already described, four proving flights were made in 1936 via Lisbon, Azores and Bermuda to New York. A year later Lufthansa also fitted out the *Schwabenland*, this time for the fast four-engined Blohm and Voss Ha 139 seaplane *Nordmeer*. These parent ships dragged behind them a large canvas apron. The seaplane would land on the water, taxi as far as possible over the apron, and would then be lifted on board by a crane. The apron stopped aircraft being tossed, and flattened the water to allow them to make good landings. Oil was also poured on the sea to calm it. When the seaplane had refuelled, it was shot into the air, using either compressed air or cordite. They received weather and direction-finding assistance from the French weather ship *Carimare* half way between the Azores and Bermuda, and came into New York on the radio guard of Pan American Airways. By this means a fast trans-Atlantic air mail service was operated, even though spasmodically.

At the end of 1936, a high-powered committee met in Ireland to endorse the choice of Shannon for the landplane Atlantic aerodrome and Rineanna for the flying boat base. Here they picnic on the banks of the Shannon. On the right, Juan Trippe munching sandwiches on his right, Woods Humphery holds a bottle to his lips. Between them and behind stands Lindbergh.      (25 Club)

The end of the German airship hopes on the North Atlantic—the *Hindenburg* bursts into flames, 6 May 1937. (Associated Press)

The service was one which required the utmost skill on the part of the German pilots. Down the 110 foot catapult they went, accelerating from zero to 95 mph in two seconds at $4\frac{1}{2}$G. Loaded up, the seaplanes had only marginal range, and in order to obtain the maximum lift from the compression effect of the air sandwiched between their wings and the ocean, on the crossing they flew for sixteen hours or more a few feet above the waves. The *Nordmeer* avoided Bermuda just to show that a British stepping-stone was not needed.

By her two-pronged policy of catapult seaplanes for mail and airships for passengers, Germany was forging ahead in the commercial race when on 6th May 1937, while mooring at Lakehurst, New Jersey, the *Hindenburg* had caught fire and was destroyed with the loss of thirty-six lives. That accident sealed the doom of airships as an Atlantic vehicle at that time. The *Graf Zeppelin* was withdrawn from service, although it had a spotless safety record.

Air France Transatlantique were making plans to operate Atlantic proving flights with their six-engined flying boat *Lieutenant de Vaisseau Paris*.

The six-engined flying boat *Lieutenant de Vaisseau Paris*—French contender for the Atlantic Route. (Associated Newspapers)

The British were experimenting with their usual assortment of alternatives. They planned an experimental Atlantic land-plane service with the Albatross, built by De Havilland to carry 1000 lb for 2500 miles against a headwind of 40 knots—a beautiful aeroplane with a modern look and a striking resemblance to the much later Constellation. In January 1936 the Air Ministry ordered two at a cost of £28,500 each. But the engines were underpowered, the aircraft was built of wood, and it proved to have insufficient range. When one broke its back, the Albatross was relegated mainly to the London–Paris run and the British Atlantic land-plane ambitions were dropped. There was still the pick-a-back Mayo Composite to try.

At least, the inter-company agreement had borne some fruit on the first link, the New York–Bermuda run. The Empire boat *Cavalier* had arrived in packing cases in Bermuda and in June 1937 with Pan Am's *Bermuda Clipper* had inaugurated the Bermuda–New York service.

Empire boats were also all that Imperial Airways possessed to 'make a show' on the Atlantic—stripped to the bone, stuffed with fuel, and carrying no load. To match them, the Americans played their old Sikorsky 42Bs.

A party taking place in Bermuda to celebrate the inauguration of the New York–Bermuda service in June 1937. The Pan American S-42B provides the background. Imperial Airways operated the service with the Empire boat *Cavalier*.

(Pan American World Airways)

# *Eight:* The Proving Flights

On 5th July 1937, at Foynes, Captain Wilcockson of Imperial Airways said goodbye to Mr de Valera, President of Eire, and boarded the Empire flying boat *Caledonia*, stuffed with 2320 gallons of petrol. In his report he wrote, 'I slipped moorings at 18.42 GMT. It was raining, with low cloud and a fresh westerly wind of 30 mph approximately, causing an appreciable chop on the river. I taxied round the western end of Foynes Island and took off diagonally across the river. The take-off was good and I put the aircraft direct on course for Loop Head and Bot-wood. We passed Loop Head at 19.14 flying at 500 feet in moderate rain.'

It had been pouring with rain when Wilcockson had arrived on the jetty. 'Not at all the sort of night,' he said, 'that one would choose for a jaunt of this description.'

Captain Gray and six crew had taken off in a Sikorsky 42B from Port Washington for Botwood, there to set course also on 5th July (faithful to the agreement that both Pan Am and Imperial Airways would start at the same time) for the crossing to Foynes and Southampton. This crew had two years long-range ocean experience in the Pacific on these same boats.

At long last the North Atlantic was going to be flown, not quite commercially, because there was no load on either of the flying boats, but at least by commercial airline companies in commercial-type aircraft.

Now professional airline pilots flew the North Atlantic, and they went about it in very much the same way as the early pioneers. Gray flew either between layers or in cloud much of the way at 10,000 feet. Wilcockson and his crew had no long-range ocean experience. Watchful of ice formation on the Empire boat, they flew at 1000 feet in rougher conditions. For navigation, they still relied on flame floats to obtain drifts and on the sun or the stars (when they could see them) for position lines. There were now better weather facilities and radio bearings

(QTEs) and courses to steer (QDMs) were available from stations on both sides of the Atlantic. Even so, in those first early commercial trips, the pilots still put a heavy reliance on ships as stepping-stones, and ships gave generous and unfailing assistance. An hour and a half after take off, Wilcockson was in contact with SS *New York City* and obtained a position. Forty-five minutes later, he was in contact with SS *Alaunic*, two hours after that with SS *Beaverdale*, then SS *Black Hawk*. Half-way across, *Caledonia* was watching SS *Empress of Britain*. A sight of Jupiter and Arcturus obtained shortly afterwards put *Caledonia* thirty-three miles south of track, before continuous rain enveloped them. The North Atlantic weather had not changed since Alcock and Brown's days, and it was not till 06.45 that Wilcockson could write, 'We came out over the fog at 2500 feet and saw the sun rise over the cloud layers.'

They were now closing on the Newfoundland coast. 'At 08.40 I altered course to come in on a bearing of 65°T from Botwood and at 08.56 received a QTE of 66°, showing me on correct track to make my landfall at Funk Island. At 09.10, I asked for another QTE as I had

The British Empire flying boat—the type which Imperial Airways first put on the Atlantic.                                              (British Airways)

reckoned on passing Funk Island at 09.00. The QTE now given me was 74° and some way south of Funk. I asked for another and received 73°. I altered course on these bearings at 09.12 and passed the mainland at Cobbler's Island at 09.27, not having seen Funk Island. I found out afterwards that the DF at Botwood is Bellini Tosi—not Adcock. The bearings, therefore, around 60° were in error due to dawn effect and my alteration of course put me south of my track.' Radio could be a peril in those early days as well as an aid.

Wilcockson alighted at 10.08, being met by the Governor of Newfoundland, fifteen hours and twenty-six minutes after slipping moorings. While he was in Newfoundland, he met the Captain of the SS *Geraldine May*, 'a vessel belonging to the Newfoundland Development Corporation, who had been running into Botwood for 12 years. He states that Botwood itself is practically fog-free, although fog is, ironically, encountered off the coast at varying distances from it.'

This boded badly for the positioning of the new airport at Hattie's Camp (later known as Gander) on which the Air Ministry had decided in 1936. There had been controversy on this—where should it go. The Canadian meteorologists, who were building up an excellent service, favoured Botwood for its fog-free record as well as for its potential dual-purpose role as land-plane and flying-boat base. In later years, Gander was to become practically synonymous with fog.

Wilcockson proceeded to Montreal, receiving in the air a message of congratulation from Mackenzie King, Premier of Canada. In his own words, 'I circled Quebec at 18.40 and arrived over Montreal at 20.00; several circuits were made of the city and one at St Hubert. We landed at Boucherville at 20.08 and were moored at 20.15. Our welcome was marvellous. All vessels on the river had dressed ship and were using their sirens to good effect. The Harbour Master was careful to point out that the foreign craft were making as much noise as our own. From the docks we were driven in decorated cars and accompanied by police escort to the Town Hall, where we were welcomed by the Mayor and signed the Golden Book.' *Caledonia* then flew on to New York.

Captain Gray had had a similarly successful flight, having made the Atlantic crossing in 12 hours and 30 minutes. His arrival at Foynes was described by one Irish onlooker as being 'like a messenger boy arriving on a bicycle'. He also received a great welcome from the British. Both flights had been painstakingly planned and immaculately executed, and Captain Wilcockson wrote, 'Everything had run to schedule and except for minor troubles in the aircraft, the trip from Ireland had been from all aspects 100% successful.'

His return flight was a similar success under difficult navigational conditions, again going from ship to ship for position. The usual continuous curtain of cloud covered the Atlantic. Wilcockson wrote, ' Jupiter

Captain Wilcockson in the Empire flying boat *Caledonia* arrives over Manhattan.
(British Airways)

appeared for two minutes, but we were unable to take a sight.' Gray took four hours longer on the westbound crossing.

Captain Powell flew the next Imperial Airways proving flight, alternating with Wilcockson. Five return Atlantic proving flights were made by Imperial Airways in 1937 and three by Pan American, one of which was via the new landing concession in the Azores. All of them were successful, and now it was proved beyond doubt that large commercial aircraft could fly the Atlantic, and though there had been delays, these had not been serious. The average time taken for the crossings by both types of boats was around that of *Caledonia*'s first trip—15.26 hours from Foynes to Botwood westbound and 12.15 hours eastbound.

In spite of their success, the proving flights uncovered a number of problem areas and difficulties. In the solution of these, Imperial Airways and Pan American crews and ground crews cooperated wholeheartedly and generously. Wilcockson was motivated not by politics nor prestige but by the desire to run a safe and efficient Atlantic commercial service. He had no false pride about borrowing from the Americans. In his excellent and painstaking report of the proving flights, which can be considered the cornerstone of British North

Atlantic commercial operations, he wrote, 'I attach forms used by Pan American for reporting ships' positions and think they might be adopted on our side . . . in America, I had a chat with some of the Pan American people and find they are using Pioneer Octants. They like the bubble better and it is faster than Busch and Lomb and gets better results . . . the American view is interesting as they are speaking from an experience of two years practical work.' He attached a copy of the Canadian meteorological report form which to his mind had several good ideas. And referring to the American Pacific flights, he wrote, 'Every opportunity should be taken to find out about ideas that are being taken up *now* by Pan American, as they are two years of practical work ahead of us in this field.'

There were possible dangers as well as difficulties. There was as yet no full understanding of the fickle North Atlantic weather. On the third westbound, Wilcockson wrote, 'the weather encountered on the crossing was certainly worse than expected as we ran from 07.00 to 16.00 with low cloud, fog and continuous rain for practically the whole of 9 hours flying. Wind speed must have averaged at least 35 knots from 08.00 to 16.00 GMT. This is too high a wind on which to undertake the crossing. Several times on the crossing, the ground speed was less than 100 mph.'

Captain Gray alights on the Shannon in the S-42B Clipper III 'like a messenger boy arriving on a bicycle', 6 July 1937.                    (Keystone)

Ice was a particular hazard. On the last eastbound on 21 September, Wilcockson wrote, 'at approximately 4000 feet, ice started to form fairly rapidly. We were flying in cloud with a temperature of 27°F. The ice formed fairly thickly on the windscreen, and the fixed aerial lead-in became a ball of ice. The tuning of the wireless set was altered and a bad falling off in signal strength occurred, making it difficult to contact Botwood across the width of Newfoundland. Patches of white ice were also observed on the wings.' The air speed indicator iced up in clear weather conditions and at a temperature thought at that time too low below freezing for ice to form.

Wilcockson reported that a 'dead' area for radio existed in the vicinity of Newfoundland 300 to 500 miles from the coast, insisted on by wireless operators and ships' officers—which should be borne in mind and 'any research which can be made in regard to this phenomenon may be very valuable when regular flights are contemplated.' He noted that an 8° error in the compass occurred when the dashboard lights were turned on (perhaps one of the reasons for the perennial compass problems experienced by the pioneers). He added that the two pilots were fully occupied, one with the flying and the other with the navigation, so that an engineer was 'very necessary'.

Twenty years later, Captains Gray and Wilcockson examine a plaque bearing the signatures of the two flying boat crews who flew the first proving flights. Behind them are the aircraft that provided the writing on the wall for the luxury liners—the DC7Cs.
**(Pan American)**

Bit by bit, gained by experience or borrowed, begged or stolen, a lore was being built up on operating the water jump. Wilcockson wrote 'it is a promising fact for future flights that two planes can take off in different directions and both fly to schedule.'

The first part of the commercial race had clearly been a dead-heat. But there were other parts that had yet to be run. Who would be the first to operate with a commercial load? Who would be the first to carry passengers? Who would operate a regular service, winter and summer?

The Atlantic sky was still a long way from being conquered. And there was still no commercial aeroplane adequate for the route. The British had too many routes already, the Empire operating a mileage of 80,000 by the end of 1937, well ahead of the Americans, and twice as much as France and Germany. It was adequate aircraft that they lacked.

*       *       *

The proving flights had been carried out efficiently by both British and American aircrews. Trippe telephoned Woods Humphery and proposed that the commercial service proper should begin next year. He had entered into negotiations with the French, the Germans, the Spanish, the Danes and the Norwegians. He had landing concessions from Britain and Canada in Bermuda, Canada and Newfoundland, and from Portugal in the Azores. The route was practically tied up.

But there was a need to move fast. Hard on his heels, Trippe had not only other American airlines, but the shipping companies, previously so helpful to aircraft, had now begun to see competition looming. The Economic Survey of American Merchant Marine pointed out on 10th November 1937, that the liner required four or five times more horsepower per passenger than the flying boat, and proposed that 'in view of the fact that aircraft had a definite place in overseas trade, and in view of the fact that there is a close relationship between shipping and over-water flying, it is recommended that responsibility for the economic development of this new form of transport be lodged in the Maritime Commission.' The Maritime Commission had calculated that 20,000 passengers were crossing the Atlantic, each paying £90, and guessed that 4000 of these might go by air if there was a service. They warned that 'large flying boats of 100,000 to 250,000 lb and capable of carrying up to 150 passengers may well supersede highly expensive super-liners of the *Queen Mary* and *Normandie* class.'

Congress had passed a new law aimed at helping the American Merchant Marine, and the American Export steamship line had been encouraged to add aircraft to their fleet. This competitor to Pan Am began negotiating agreements with France, Germany, Italy, Spain and the Zeppelin Corporation, and were reported as having flying boats capable of flying the North Atlantic non-stop.

And now the lawyers came in. They told Trippe that parts of the inter-company agreement might violate the Sherman Act. The Sherman Act's purpose is to prohibit any trust, combination or agreement which is in 'restraint of trade', and which tends to eliminate competition. The lawyers warned of the wording: 'the intention that Pan American and Imperial will cooperate to the fullest extent that they may legally and properly do so and that each shall have a square deal in the sense that this expression is interpreted by fair and reasonable-minded men.'

Trippe now proposed a number of amendments, including getting rid of the proposed passenger and freight pool.

Things were moving towards a climax. A number of American operators, as Trippe had warned, were ganging up on him. There was strong pressure on the US government that civil aviation should pass from the jurisdiction of the Department of Commerce to an organisation analogous to the US Maritime Commission—eventually the Civil Aviation Authority. But the Maritime Commission also wanted a part.

In March 1938, there was a special hearing by the Committee on Merchant Marine and Fisheries of the House of Representatives, in which there was a feeling that the whole thing should be settled by having a reciprocal agreement available to any British or American Company. A tremendous propaganda wave burst against the British, who were reported as having no intention of establishing a passenger air service on the Atlantic and had tied Pan Am up by the arrangement that one company should not start before the other, so that all passengers could be carried by the *Queen Mary*.

Pan American tried to hold the tide by compromising with American Export and suggesting that they should take up stock in Pan American. The 1937 survey flights carried out by Imperial Airways were criticised by the *New York Times* on 21st March 1938: 'while little was said about it at the time, the British learned that their "Empire Boats", for which so much was claimed, did not have the range for the 1900-mile jump between Newfoundland and Ireland with a payload. Pan American, on the other hand, although flying a Clipper which the operator regarded as obsolescent, carried a mail load sufficient to defray a good deal of the cost of the service, it was said.'

Imperial Airways' own American lawyer sent them this clipping saying that, 'It was his understanding it was not a fact, and it was advisable that the true condition should be made known so that this misconception, with its possible injurious effect, would cease to exist.'

The lawyer's plea went unanswered for the very good reason that it *was* a fact that the Empire boat (and the Clipper for that matter) did not nearly have Atlantic range with a payload. Before the 1937 Imperial Airways' flights, an official from the Irish Department of Industry and Commerce named Leydon, who had attended the Ottawa Conference that fixed up the Atlantic Company, had written to Woods Humphery asking for a passage with the first flying boat over the Atlantic for himself and a few friends. Woods Humphery had sent him a terse negative, saying there was no passenger accommodation, and Leydon had come back on 31st March 1937, writing that he was 'sorry that you could not see your way to allow a few of my colleagues and myself the pleasure of a flight in *Caledonia*. I was, of course, aware that there was no cabin accommodation and anybody taking this flight would have been quite prepared to stand up, or sit on the floor!' Even more tersely, Woods Humphery replied that there was no floor. The boats that flew those survey flights were stripped to the bone so that their tanks could be filled with the maximum fuel, which even then was not really sufficient.

In adversity, neither flap nor fury but a sort of courteous dottiness descends on the British, and it was so on this occasion. Sir Donald Banks, now in charge of civil aviation, telephoned Woods Humphery about the Sherman Act problem and said that he was 'in a difficulty because he was unable to get his Ministers before Easter.' On 12th April 1938, again Banks rang up at 7.30 pm and said he was 'sorry that I had had a little difficulty in getting in touch with him. On my side, I apologised for troubling him.' On 13th April Woods Humphery wrote to Banks, 'Please forgive me worrying you again about this Pan American–Imperial Airways Atlantic Agreement, but I have had another SOS from Trippe, in which he told me that he has further embarrassments looming ahead of him.' Banks told him to see the Treasury Solicitor. On 14th April Woods Humphery was with the Treasury Solicitor at Storey's Gate: 'I saw Sir Thomas Barnes and he asked me what it was I wanted to see him about. I said I imagined he knew. Sir Thomas said he knew nothing about it at all. I then described my conversation with Sir Donald Banks when he told me that "the legal people" had had no objection to the renunciation clause and the "Square Deal" clause ... Sir Thomas Barnes then called Mr Corderoy, who also said he had heard nothing about the matter, and Sir Thomas, therefore, said that the Treasury Solicitor's Department was not consulted at all and heard nothing about it until a quarter of an hour before I arrived, when Sir Donald Banks said I was coming to see him [Sir Thomas] about something or other. Sir Thomas said that this kind of thing was happening all the time in the Air Ministry.'

Woods Humphery remained loyal to Pan American. He told the Air Ministry that he could not leave them in the present position of being open to prosecution. He added that he had 'not found Pan American guilty of a breach of faith so far, and I have been working with them for ten years.' The Air Ministry was much more concerned over its position as possible accomplice, and wanted the whole thing quickly and quietly buried.

It was the beginning of the end for the Gentlemen's Agreement. By using each other's stepping-stones of the Azores, Bermuda and New-foundland, it should have been possible, according to Burchall, the Commercial Manager of Imperial Airways, to arrange matters so that 'no other British or American Companies could, therefore, operate across the Atlantic'. But the inter-company agreement was rejected as *ultra vires* in that it contravened the Anti-Trust Laws. Pan American voluntarily surrendered its Azores monopoly. Mail exchange arrangements were eliminated, and the US Government decreed that every service operated to the US by a European operator would be matched by a US service to Europe.

As regards Atlantic services, the inter-company agreement was now almost valueless to the UK. The US had freedom to operate any number of services to Europe, so long as they did not touch British stepping-stones. The US retained a right to two services a week to the UK via Bermuda or Newfoundland. The British had the right to two Atlantic services a week into New York.

The Atlantic Company stagnated on paper for a while, till it was over-come by the events of the start of the Second World War and the formation of BOAC.

Administratively, on the Atlantic services, the Americans had won. On the Atlantic route into New York, Britain was now largely on the same footing as other European countries. Her two aces, Newfoundland and Bermuda, might have been played more effectively if they had had aerodromes. At last, one was now being constructed in Newfoundland. But it was not until the war that Bermuda got her aerodrome—Kindley Field, built by the Americans under Lend-Lease.

# *Nine:* The Commercial Race is Won

While the Pan Am–Imperial Airways inter-company agreement fizzled towards an early death, the race to run the first commercial service across the Atlantic intensified. Rumours circulated that Pan American had settled on a trans-Atlantic flying-boat design. In answer, the British were busy with a stretched version of the Empire boat called the Short G.

Woods Humphery had been stressing to the Air Ministry the necessity to get back to the good relationship that Imperial Airways had enjoyed with Pan American in the past. But instead of asking Trippe point-blank about the performance of his new aircraft or actually going to the American manufacturers, Imperial Airways appeared to rely for their information on the aeronautical press, noting with satisfaction that 'US Air Services' had brought the cruising speed and payload of the new flying boats well down on what was quoted in the *Aeroplane*.

However, the prototype Short-Mayo Composite had now been built— the upper component being a long-range seaplane called *Mercury* powered by four 380 hp Rapier engines. The lower component was a modified Empire boat valled *Maia*. Joined together, the combined power of their eight engines lifted them both into the air. At altitude, the seaplane, heavily loaded with fuel, disengaged from the mother flying boat, and now having both flying speed and height, had enough range to do the water jump. There were a vast number of maintenance problems, but it could be got to work.

On 20th July 1938, *Maia* commanded by Captain Wilcockson with Captain Frost as First Officer, and *Mercury*, commanded by Captain D. C. T. Bennett (later Air Vice Marshal Bennett who organised and commanded the RAF Pathfinders, and after the war became Manager of British South American Airways), rose together from the Shannon river. Both pilots controlled the unlocking mechanism, which worked without a hitch. Two minutes later, Captain Bennett was on his way to Montreal with 1000 lb of mail, newsreels and freight. After a smooth and

[133]

**The Short-Mayo Composite—Captain Bennett flying the _Mercury_ separates from Captain Wilcockson flying the _Maia_.** (British Airways)

uneventful 20 hour flight, impeccably navigated, he landed in Montreal —the first aircraft ever to carry a commercial load across the Atlantic— before continuing to Port Washington, New York. The return flight was made via Botwood, the Azores and Lisbon.

It was, in fact, a considerable British achievement which should have received more acclaim and attention. Britain could have been the first country to establish a regular mail service across the water jump. But this success was never followed up on the Atlantic. The Air Ministry, having given a great deal of money for the research, now would not proceed. They were against an exclusive mail carrier, now wanting an aircraft that could carry passengers as well, and intimated that the Composite idea was already out of date.

Then at 19.53 on 10th August 1938, the Germans startled the world. A four-engined landplane under the command of Captain Henke took off from Berlin with very little publicity and set off on a Great Circle to New York.

This was the Focke-Wulf Condor, a sharp-nosed all-metal aircraft that looked like a bigger Albatross. At 39,000 lb all up weight, it could cruise at 220 mph at 12,000 feet—a big advance on the far slower British and American flying boats, and (apart from its tail wheel) clearly showed the shape of things to come on the Atlantic. It had a most modern flight deck, similar to that of a Constellation, and could carry 26 passengers over 1000-mile distances and nine passangers for 2500 miles.

On this occasion, the Condor was loaded with fuel and made the 3800-mile non-stop hop to New York without incident against the prevailing westerlies in just under 21 hours. Three days later, Henke calmly flew back again with the same lack of trouble.

The double crossing was a tremendous achievement, not only because of the modern design of the aircraft, but because in the era of the flying boat, not in words but in metal, the Condor pointed to the four-engined landplane as being the long-sought-after right Atlantic vehicle. It did what the British had intended the Albatross to do, and it did it on its own without any devices to help it.

The Germans had turned to landplanes. The French had also been converted. Paul Codos, Head of Air France Transatlantique, was experimenting with high-altitude landplanes for the water jump. Later, Lindbergh was to write in his diary on 15th January 1940 that he had spoken on that day with Pan Am top officials, 'of trans-oceanic routes and equipment. It seems that they have eventually come round to the

**The beautiful D. H. Albatross had a marked similarity to the Condor and to the later Constellation. Unfortunately at a time when every American manufacturer was making all-metal airliners, It was made of wood and the intention to use it on the Atlantic run was never fulfilled.** **(Flight)**

**The Focke-Wulf Condor which flew non-stop from Berlin to New York in just under twenty-five hours on 10 August 1938.**                                  (Gurra)

ideas I have been advocating for so many years, in regard to using land-planes for the North Atlantic route.' There was a certain political naivety about Lindbergh, but his despair at British airlines' and British aircraft manufacturers' methods in comparison to German, his view that Englishmen could not be told anything, they always know, his confidence that they would be defeated in the Second World War, perhaps

**Captain Henke (second from the right) and his crew being welcomed in Berlin after flying the Condor back from New York on 14 August 1938, in nineteen and a half hours.**
(Focke Wulf)

had certain of its origins in the long-drawn-out British dilettante waver-ing, like a girl with a dandelion puff, over the 'right' Atlantic aeroplane. His neat methodical mind would have missed the potential genius in the mess and muddle.

While the Condor continued its successes with flights to the Far East, the British continued with their search for the right Atlantic vehicle, no nearer solution than they had been eight years before. On 10th November 1938 Woods Humphery reported that he had got to the bottom of the DC4 position. No definite orders had been placed, though 'our Dutch friends' (KLM) were trying to place an order for four. 'At the moment', Woods Humphery added, 'the plane looks as if it is going to be quite good.' On the other hand 'the Boeing flying boats are far from right . . . in the meantime both the constructors and our friends Pan Am are feeling the financial draught on account of their delay.'

Looking at the possibilities of fleet replacement in the early summer of 1939, an Imperial Airways minute records 'British equipment is unobtainable: German equipment ought not to be considered out of the question, though its employment, particularly for passengers, might be unpopular with the public. No doubt an order would be readily accepted in that country, but deliveries might not be so good as from America unless some of the Focke-Wulf Condors are still available which were being offered to trade against oil tankers about three months ago. Is this type in any case what we want?'

The same old question. In the end, want or not, BOAC (as it had then become) obtained a Condor that had belonged to Danish airlines, flown in from Copenhagen after the German invasion in 1940 and christened G–AGAY. But not for long. Nine months later, it went to the RAF, and was later destroyed.

The Condor was not big enough or strong enough for regular com-mercial Atlantic operation, although it might perhaps have been stretched and modified but for the war.

At last, the French had managed to fly their six-engined flying boat *Lieutenant de Vaisseau Paris* across the Atlantic via the Azores on 30th August 1938. (On a flight a year later was the poet-novelist Saint-Exupéry, who had pulled every string to get on board.) They covered the 2397 miles non-stop from Horta in 22 hours and 48 minutes with no problems, and had a similarly uneventful journey home. But apart from a little courtesy mail, no real payload could be carried. A few further trips were made, both on the direct and on the Azores routes, some using tri-motor flying boats. Flight refuelling was seriously considered, but French experiments on landplanes were to be halted by the approach of war.

There had been a number of reasons for the concentration on flying boats—the shortage of land aerodromes, the 'passenger appeal' of the

**The ultimate in flying boats—the 84,000 lb Boeing 314A which could carry over thirty passengers across the Atlantic in luxury at a cruising speed of 145 mph.**

(Pan American World Airways)

luxury that could be offered. But there had also been a feeling that the North Atlantic weather was too bad except for the ruggedly constructed flying boats, and that passengers would never trust themselves over a 2000 mile expanse of water in an aircraft that could not land if things went wrong. (When I operated on Atlantic patrols, that was exactly my view. The aerodynamic performance of the Wellingtons I flew was spoiled by radar aerials, and they could not maintain height on one engine. Even so, their air-cooled Pegasus engines were much more reliable on low-level patrols than the liquid-cooled Merlins on the radar Whitleys. The first time I reported to the Operations Room at Limavady to do an anti-U-boat patrol, a Whitley was down far out in the Atlantic after reporting engine trouble. Nothing further was heard of it. Around half of the pilots who trained with me and also went on to anti-U-boat landplanes were lost in the Atlantic due to engine trouble. Eventually, when my turn came in a Whitley after the starboard engine failed, our only difficulty was remembering how to inflate the dinghy, since the shock of ditching knocked our dinghy drill clean out of our minds. As the early pioneers proved, landplanes in fact often float well. We were not far from land and were soon picked up—it is the *finding* in time that is the real difficulty in rescue from the sea.)

The rumoured big American flying boat quickly took on metal flesh. It now materialised as the Boeing 314, weighing 84,000 lb and powered by the most powerful civil aircraft engines yet, four 1500 hp Wright Cyclones. It could carry 35 passengers across the Atlantic in liner luxury: a private honeymoon suite in the rear, a 14 seat dining room, berths and cabins, seven-course meals with wines, a promenade deck, a big galley in which two stewards prepared the meals. The flight deck was palatial and carried, besides the pilots, a navigator, a radioman and an engineer. There was a cat-walk inside the wing from which the engines could be reached. In looks, the 314 bore a strong resemblance to the Empire, but it was bigger and had greater range. It had no really bad habits, but if a pilot 'dipped a wing' taxiing out of wind, on straightening, gallons of water would be decanted into the dining saloon. The only serious engine defect was sticking exhaust valves. This was very definitely the first Atlantic commercial aircraft, and Trippe naturally wanted to operate it as soon as possible.

But, tacitly, the inter-company agreement was still in force. Neither side should move before the other. The British had had extremely bad luck with their Empire boats—of the first sixteen received by mid 1937,

The Boeing flying boat 314A in dock. Note the enormous sponsons under the wings.
(Pan American World Airways)

eight had crashed or been wrecked by November 1938—and the big boats were nowhere near complete. Mindful of the successes of both *Maia-Mercury* and the Condor, and already having technically lost the race to be the first air carrier of a commercial load over the water jump, Trippe now could wait no longer. On 26th March 1939, the same Captain Gray who had carried out the first successful Sikorsky 42B proving flight, now flew the Boeing 314 *Yankee Clipper* with 21 people on board via the Azores, Lisbon, Marseilles to Southampton, covering 2750 miles in 17½ hours at a speed of 160 mph.

*     *     *

On 27th March 1939, Woods Humphery, went into the lounge of RMS *Aquitania* in mid-Atlantic and wrote a friendly letter on Cunard notepaper to the new Imperial Airways Chairman, J. C. W. Reith, beginning, 'Dear John, this flight of the *Yankee Clipper* gives me some food for thought'.

He was coming back from New York where he had discussed the North Atlantic with Trippe. At home, yet another government committee, this time under Lord Cadman, had produced a report ten months earlier that had been scathingly critical of British civil aviation, equally blaming the government and Imperial Airways. Woods Humphery had resigned as Managing Director in June 1938, but had agreed to stay on at Imperial Airways until the new management were settled in.

The row had started in Parliament on 17th November 1937, when Robert Perkins, one of the founders of the new British Air Line Pilots' Association (BALPA), had moved for a public inquiry into civil aviation with the words, 'Like the daughter of Herodias, I ask the House today to give me the head of the Secretary of State for Air on a charger.'

The Imperial Airways Board had behaved oddly, to say the least. Old shareholders received preferential treatment on an issue of new stock: a new pay policy that appeared to cut their salaries had been introduced for pilots and was never adequately explained: a dividend of 9 per cent was declared, inviting comment on whether the money was coming out of the subsidy: the directors' fees had been increased: and seven pilots, including the Chairman and Vice-Chairman of BALPA had been dismissed. Perhaps if Geddes had been alive (he had died earlier in that year) events might have been different. But his position as part-time Chairman had also been under attack.

There were further allegations that the pilots had to fly long hours on obsolete aircraft and that no adequate de-icing equipment had been provided. Rumours of all sorts of improper behaviour were circulating. The Cadman Committee investigated much *in camera* and recommended many changes.

Imperial Airways refuted many of the charges when they appeared before the Committee. The Board believed that the real reason for Cadman was to force a merger with the private company British Airways that had been formed in 1936 and was operating on European routes. A merger did take place eventually when BOAC was formed in 1940. Cadman's recommendations included the building of a pressurised landplane for the Atlantic, the specification calling for a payload of 7500 lb for 3000 miles against a 30 mph headwind. Twenty four day or twelve night passengers (in bunks) were to be carried. To their surprise, Short's got the contract and provided a beautiful four-engined design with a twin tail that looked like a cross between the Stratoliner and the Constellation, the 14/38. In spite of the rearmament programme, Short's were also to hasten the building of the 'stretched' Empire G boat specifically for the Atlantic.

Cadman had also proposed to double the British transport subsidy to £3 million, but aware that Woods Humphery basically controlled the Company, had proposed a full-time Chairman—thus the introduction of Reith, who had insisted on being both Chairman *and* Managing Director.

While praising the airline for safety and efficiency, the Cadman Report stated 'we cannot avoid the conclusion that the management of Imperial Airways has been defective in other respects. In particular, not only has it failed to cooperate fully with the Air Ministry, but it has been intolerant of suggestion and unyielding in negotiation. Internally its attitude on staff matters has left much to be desired. It appears to us that the Managing Director of the Company—presumably with the acquiescence of the Board—has taken a commercial view of his responsibilities that was too narrow.'

By an extraordinary coincidence, Woods Humphery had known Reith from the time that, as apprentice engineers, they had sat side by side in a Glasgow drawing office. The Rev. Reith officiated at the marriage of Woods Humphery and his son had been conscripted at the last minute to act as best man. The two ex-apprentices had met periodically for lunches while they both climbed different ladders to the top. Reith had just done a magnificent job in totally reorganising the BBC and giving it a firm foundation. The Imperial Airways offices at Victoria had been a furniture depository and, in Reith's view, looked it. His first decision as Chairman had been to authorise the expenditure of £238 for passengers' lavatories at Croydon aerodrome. And he had not been pleased to discover that Woods Humphery's salary was £8,500 plus £1,500 expenses—around the same as he had accepted as Chairman—and was shortly to go up further.

For a decade, Woods Humphery had played a losing game with Trippe on the North Atlantic. Now in his letter he asked for an alliance

The G Class—first British flying boat designed for the water jump, but which in the event did not go into Atlantic operation.                    (British Airways)

with his old friend and best man against the Air Ministry. Perhaps he hoped that Reith might ask him to take back his resignation so that they could work together. 'As you have now seen, we have been very badly treated by the Air Ministry for over two years, as regards inaction and indecision.' He pointed out his own efforts to get an Atlantic air-craft, and the government promise to hasten the three G-class flying boats: 'And they are still a long way off, according to plan they should have been in service last year.' He emphasised that the Atlantic 'will require millions of capital before it is established'.

He went on to point out that the Pan American 314 'intends to miss out Bermuda, and that is done intentionally to avoid British "stepping-stones". I know that they will not be able to do so very often—if at all—westbound, but the desire and perhaps the determination to do so if necessary, or eventually, is there.' He added that Imperial Airways would *have* to use Portugal and the Azores and asked for authorisation to approach Pan American to use their facilities on the islands.

For a forceful man who worked sixteen hours a day, Woods Humphery ended hesitantly, 'Perhaps these few idle thoughts of an idle man may be of use to you.' Was that sentence a hidden reference to the fact that he would soon be out of a job?

Reith's typewritten reply to 'your longhand note' was a sharp rap over the knuckles. 'Let us adopt the memorandum form in writing to each other; it is simpler and quicker—if you agree.' In numbered paragraphs, Woods Humphery was put in his place. Reith concentrated both on his superior position and his own difficulties. 'With all the power you feel Runciman and I have, which in large measure I admit, two other things are required—a really effective DG and a Secretary of State who is prepared to overrule the military side, and anyhow guarantee that civil aviation has its proper place.'

Back came Woods Humphery's reply in the prescribed form—stiff, hurt, with a bit of a dig—'I am much obliged to you for your memorandum of 14th April which is most informative and interesting.'

Nevertheless, Woods Humphery went on trying. Yet all the time, his head was actually on the charger—not Perkins' certainly since it came from his Imperial Airways friends but it amounted to the same thing He had been presented with a silver salver at a testimonial dinner after his forced resignation, which was described as 'a dirty political move'.

Woods Humphery had many excellent qualities, but a capacity for public relations was not amongst them. As soon as he took over in 1924 he had sparked off the first pilots' dispute. He had intimated his view that engineers came out of the gutter. He tended to regard aircrew like schoolboys—he was to promise the Prime Minister when he was concerned with ferrying aircraft in the war that he would not have 'a single aircraft crossing the Atlantic unless it contributed something to the war effort besides a joy-ride for the crew' (and this was the struggle to conquer the North Atlantic in winter!). He tended to lean on advisers

At a dinner in his honour after his retirement as Managing Director, George Woods Humphery receives a silver tray from his colleagues, presented by Col. Burchall, Imperial Airways Commercial Manager. Major Mayo, Imperial Airways Technical Manager, is on the left.                                    (25 Club)

rather than his own Imperial Airways people who were actually doing
the operating, and he would rarely delegate. When the Atlantic Company came up, he was opposed to its management being taken away
from him, though clearly he had far too much work to do. He tended to
be rude to Civil Service officials, and certainly did not try to understand
their problems. On top of it all, he and Geddes had sparked off a big row
by giving information to the Minister indicating that Bullock, the
Permanent Secretary at the Air Ministry, had applied to Imperial
Airways for a job. This produced another scandal amongst the whiter-
than-white mandarins, and Bullock was unfairly sacked—the first time
such a high Civil Servant had even been dismissed. It is said that Woods
Humphery preferred the company of noble Lords, for whom he had a
profound respect. Geddes had certainly protected him throughout all
their thirteen years together, and had given him pretty well a free
hand in the running of Imperial Airways. With Geddes dead, Woods
Humphery was very vulnerable, even though, because of his devoted
and endless work, he had earned the respect of those who worked for him.
He was regarded as the pillar of Imperial Airways—which, of course, he
was. When eventually the pillar fell, there were to be loud protests.

What the French saw in their crystal ball in 1938—a model interior of the projected
airliner *Rochambeau*, complete with bar and berths, a vision of the Stratocruiser which
never materialised.                                                    (Worldwide)

Meanwhile, cast in a double losing role, Woods Humphery still went on fighting. It was only in April 1939 that he heard from Reith that the Albatrosses had definitely been cancelled and he said he would be glad to know why. Hopes were now pinned on the Short 14/38 and the G-Class flying boats. But costs were rocketing. The G-Class were now to cost £86,520 and £4,750 for each engine. And they were still having trouble over uneven filling of their tanks during refuelling.

On 5th May 1939, Trippe telephoned to say that he was being urged 'by Washington' to start regular trans-Atlantic commercial services. And on 20th May, the twelfth anniversary of Lindbergh's flight, the official authority to proceed was presented to Trippe by Albert Goldman, Postmaster of New York, who said, 'I wish to express our pride—and the pride of all Americans—in the fact that American aircraft, manned by American flight captains, and carrying United States mail, are, before any other nation in the world, the first to establish a regularly scheduled air service across the Atlantic Ocean, most important of the world's trade routes, and the last frontier of world aviation.'

*Yankee Clipper*, commanded by Captain La Porte, carried out an uneventful flight via the Azores, carrying 1800 lb of mail to Marseilles. Three days later, the Under Secretary of State had to announce to the House of Commons, 'the commencement of the North Atlantic service has to be postponed for a number of reasons.'

American Export Airlines were also expected to start shortly, and according to Woods Humphery Pan Am 'is anxious to gobble up all they can before their competitors can get going with anything very serious in the way of an air service.' Trippe asked for a joint Pan Am–Imperial Airways start for the fare-paying mail and passenger service—there was again pressure from Washington.

But the British had nothing to match the 314s, and again Trippe could wait no longer. On 24th June, the first passengers went over the water jump in an American 314 to Southampton on the northern route via Newfoundland, and on 28th June *Dixie Clipper* flew the first fare-paying passengers to Marseilles, via the Azores. There were 22 passengers and the fare was $375 one way, $675 return. Thereafter, services were maintained on a weekly frequency—the northern route to Southampton and the southern to Marseilles.

A month later, the British managed to set up a new series of experimental flights on a reciprocal basis with Pan Am's 314s, using the modified Empire boats *Caribou* and *Cabot*. These aircraft had been stripped of all furnishings and had their take-off weight increased. Since they still did not have sufficient range, they would be refuelled in the air from Harrow tankers stationed at Shannon and Hattie's Camp. A grapnel was wound out of the flying boat's tail. The tanker would then fire another cable by rocket to catch the grapnel. To the flying boat's cable was connected a hose, which was then wound in from the tanker to the flying boat and connected to fuel pipes in the Empire's tail. The tanker would then fly in formation with the Empire and slightly above it, while eight hundred gallons was transferred in twelve minutes. After transfer, the hose was flushed with anti-ignition chemical, contact was broken, and the hose wound back into the tanker.

The first service carried 1000 lb of mail, and encountered strong headwinds on the Atlantic crossing which reduced the average ground speed to 89.5 knots. Fifteen successful refuelling flights were undertaken. There was one other flight which was not refuelled because the tanker was unable to locate the flying boat in bad weather. The Captains were Kelly-Rogers, Bennett and Store. The height of refuelling was usually 1000 feet. On one occasion, because of low overcast, the refuelling was done at tree-top height. On several occasions contact was prematurely broken and petrol lost. On 11th August, Bennett reported that, 'The

**A modified Empire flying boat being refuelled in mid-air from a Harrow Tanker.**

**(British Airways)**

light alloy pipe connecting the fire extinguisher to the refuelling cap fractured, and fumes of methyl bromide escaped into the aft compartment. This was vacated and the door closed.'

At the same time as these flights were going on, there was a German announcement to the effect that they were about to operate commercially with the USA, claiming that only Pan Am and Imperial Airways had prevented them doing so earlier. Woods Humphery wrote, 'no doubt they regard us as equally unfriendly. I think they may find it difficult to secure a permit from the USA. Clearly we sit tight.'

In his report on the flight-refuelled Empire boat trials, Kelly-Rogers wrote that though in the main successful on 'no fewer than five occasions has petrol been forced into the hull of the aircraft, on one occasion to such an extent that it had to be soaked up from the bilges and kept in a container until arrival at Botwood. The risk entailed in having liquid petrol in the interior of the aircraft need not be emphasised.' Kelly-Rogers concluded that 'the mechanical difficulties were not yet overcome. Flight refuelling in connection with a passenger service would be out of the question.'

The engines had behaved very satisfactorily. As regards ground services, Kelly-Rogers wrote, 'the control, wireless and meteorological services provided at the Shannon airport have been in every way satisfactory, and great credit must be given to the Eire Government and to all concerned for providing these facilities in such difficult circumstances.'

The weather itself during the flights had not been good, with much low cloud and rain, and owing to the outbreak of the Second World War meteorological information was drastically cut. This time, there was a lack of practically all ship reports and ship positions. However, Kelly-Rogers said 'all our commanders have expressed their appreciation and complete faith in the meteorological officials at both Foynes and Botwood, and this confidence has been proved by the fact that there has never been a delay over the ocean section.'

Kelly-Rogers recommended that a vessel should be stationed halfway across the North Atlantic, pointing out that the French *Carimare*, 'has a full meteorological staff and is provided with equipment to deal with most aspects of meteorology, including a study of the upper air by means of "radio sonage". The study of the surface and upper air conditions over the Atlantic is of such general international value that every endeavour should be made by all concerned to follow the lead set by the French government. Full radio equipment is also fitted, including D/F.' From that first French idea grew the complicated weather-ship network over the Atlantic, under the auspices of ICAO, that gave inestimable service to the Atlantic weather forecasting and to aircraft navigation.

Kelly-Rogers added, 'great credit must be given to the navigating personnel and crews of the aircraft for completing the series so successfully, in spite of the lack of assistance that should have been available on the ocean crossing.' With a certain pride, he compared the time-keeping with Pan Am's 314. Out of sixteen flights, only nine of Pan Am's had been on schedule, three had been 24 hours, one 48 hours, two 72 hours and one 120 hours late. Against this, fourteen Imperial Airways flights had been on schedule, and of the two that were 24 hours late, one was due to the late arrival of the mail, literally on the eve of the Second World War.

The operating heights westbound had been 1000–1500 feet, but the captains would come even lower when visibility permitted to get the lift benefit from ground effect. Kelly-Rogers considered that a better performance was needed to clear the clouds, guessing at an optimum operating height of 16,000–20,000.

Speed, he pointed out, was 'a vital necessity in the operation of a successful Atlantic service'. This was, of course, because of the strong westerly wind: the slower the aircraft, the greater the headwind effect. And Kelly-Rogers added, 'the all-round performance needed would probably be very difficult to obtain in a flying boat, and it appears that a successful service is much more likely to be operated by landplanes.' Even in regard to landing in the sea, 'it appears that a well-constructed land aircraft would probably be as safe as a flying boat.' Though, he added, there were difficulties. Snow clearance of the new aerodrome at Hattie's Camp, Newfoundland, later Gander, was one problem that might delay the opening of services till April. And secondly, in case of bad weather there was no alternate for the Newfoundland airport (which now had a Lorenz blind-landing system and contact lighting) except Moncton five hundred miles further on.

In spite of the fact that the British aircrews put up a magnificent reply to the Americans in inferior equipment, British prospects on the water jump were poor. On 11th November 1939 Reith wrote to Woods Humphery 'we are forced back to the G-Class since we really have nothing else,' and he considered they were deficient in payload. He reported that work on the Short 14/38 and the Fairey landplane 'had been stopped by order of the Ministry—very short-sighted we believe, but our pleas went unheeded.' He went on to say that 'we are fully alive to the importance of doing something on the Atlantic, and are doing what we can to meet the deplorable state of affairs, but without much success so far.'

He concluded by saying 'you will probably be interested in the organisation which is proposed for the new Corporation . . .'

This was British Overseas Airways Corporation—Reith's name for the nationalised Corporation towards which he had been working. The

**J. C. W. Reith, appointed full time Chairman and Managing Director of Imperial Airways in 1938—previously Director-General of the B.B.C., later Lord Reith.** **(British Airways)**

Editor of the *Aeroplane* commented 'I give full credit to that great Scotsman, Lord Reith, for the sardonic humour which chose the word BOA for the Corporation which swallowed it up.' It officially took over from the older companies on 1st April 1940.

Woods Humphery had not been asked to take his resignation back. At least, canny man that he was, he had seen that the severance pay for his head (£15,000) was generous. Letters of support from his former colleagues followed him. From an RAF station (blacked out because of the war) was written 'if it's anything in your life, the loyalty to you amongst the old gang's as strong if not stronger than before.' The letter added, 'I was also glad to hear that you knew of all the jiggery-pokery going on in the old firm' and that 'JCWR is not having too good a time I gather—he and I did *not* agree.'

Now the charger awaited Reith's head. Churchill found him difficult to work with, dubbed him 'Lord Wuthering Heights', and dismissed him from his position as Minister. He finished the war doing good work as a Lieutenant-Commander in the Navy.

Woods Humphery had pasted such letters and newspaper clippings in his papers, as if to preserve the end of the story. But it is doubtful if he really knew it all. He tended to blame Reith for the ills that had befallen him, believing that his best man had wanted his job in charge of Imperial Airways and had got him out.

But Reith had never wanted to exchange his supreme position in the BBC for the management of Imperial Airways. On 3rd June 1938 he had been called to 10 Downing Street and told that the Prime Minister wanted him to take on Imperial Airways immediately because of the death of Geddes. Reith wrote in his diary 'I thought this was pretty rotten—left me to get rid of the present managing director,' and insisted on seeing Baldwin. The meeting took place on 23rd June, and Reith was pleased with the interview. The next day Sir Donald Banks had pulled out all the stops to convince him of the importance of Imperial Airways. Reith's comment was 'I hope he is right.'

If Reith and Woods Humphery had managed an alliance, they would have been a formidable team. But Reith's eyes were fixed higher in the sky. In April 1939 he wrote to Warren Fisher at the Treasury 'I should like to go to the House of Lords and do not mind saying so.' He did not manage it that time, but eventually he succeeded.

Runciman was appointed Director General. Off Woods Humphery went to be assistant to the Chairman of a new department of the Canadian Pacific Railway to organise the ferrying of American-built bombers across the Atlantic.

For now the real war had come to the North Atlantic. *Cabot* and *Caribou* went into the RAF. The Blohm and Voss seaplanes that had been catapulted up into the Atlantic sky were used against coastal shipping and to hunt British submarines in the Mediterranean. (Flying a slow Wellington out to Malta in 1941, I saw one on patrol between Tunisia and Sicily, and tucked myself right down on the water, trusting to my top camouflage that he would not see me.) The French had to abandon their plans for an Atlantic commercial service.

On the North Atlantic, Pan American were left supreme—though their American monopoly of the water jump had now been strongly challenged by American Export who just before the war carried out six survey flights in Catalina flying boats. But Pan Am had been the first to establish a regular scheduled mail and passenger service—and in 1939 they also made a record profit of $1,984,438. Their 314 flying boats continued to provide the last word in airborne luxury on the water jump, though they had mechanical troubles and frequent weather delays, even operating mainly on the milder mid-Atlantic.

So the commercial race was won, and Pan American had won it. And yet in spite of all the ups and downs and disagreements and rivalries, it is perfectly clear that many other airlines and many countries, and many individuals had contributed to the establishment of this commercial service over the water jump, their very rivalry spurring them on. A vast amount of cooperation did exist, particularly among aircrews and groundcrews. The French showed the way with weatherships and ship-borne D/F. The Germans had perfected the use of catapulted aircraft, had run a first-class airship service, and had shown the way of the future with the magnificent flight of the landplane Condor. The British had shown enormous ingenuity in making do with the very little that a government that did not think big enough allowed them. Each country borrowed from each other, guarded each other on the route, provided weather information and pushed each other forward.

The next six years—as always in times of war—were to show huge strides in technical development. For there were still many aspects of the water jump—particularly the North Atlantic winter—that had yet to be conquered.

The victors of the commercial race across the water jump—Juan Trippe and John C. Leslie, Manager Pan American Atlantic Division, stand in front of a map of the Atlantic showing the Azores—Bermuda and Newfoundland routes and the times of arrival of their Boeing 314 flying boats at the terminals.

(Pan American World Airways)

# *Ten:* War Comes to the North Atlantic

Within hours of the declaration of war—on the night of 3rd September 1939 at nine pm, the liner *Athenia*, outward bound across the North Atlantic, was torpedoed by a German submarine with the loss of a hundred and twelve lives, including twenty-eight American citizens. Churchill was to say later, 'The Battle of the Atlantic was the dominating factor all through the war. Never could we forget for one moment that everything happening elsewhere on land, at sea or in the air depended ultimately on its outcome.'

While armies, navies and air forces mustered for battle, the fragile civil air link between America struggled to keep going. That first war winter was the worst weather for many years. Some of Pan American's Boeing 314 trips were delayed by as much as two weeks. Half of those begun were not completed. Backlogs of stranded Pan American passengers accumulated in Lisbon and had to be sent across by the Italian liner *Rex*.

In London, the new BOAC faced the same old problems. It still had no aircraft for the North Atlantic. And now the same battle, under new management, was resumed—this time in an effort to stop the RAF from filching what aircraft they had. The RAF had woken to the need for a Transport Command, and to the eminent suitability of the Empire flying boat for anti-submarine duties.

The new BOAC executives sent minutes to each other deploring 'this policy of erosion'. Major McCrindle, the Deputy Director-General, gloomily forecast that 'the public may wake up one day to find to their surprise and possible consternation that the airline has gone out of business.' He had taken on Woods Humphery's mantle of pressing for an Atlantic service, now in wartime clearly of more vital importance than ever before.

In this fight, BOAC collected powerful allies. On 31st March 1940 the Air Attaché at Washington wrote, 'every month or so I draft a letter which the Ambassador duly sends to the Foreign Office about civil aviation vis-à-vis this country. We here feel very strongly about the trans-Atlantic air situation and are continuously urging HMG to do something about it. I think our continued attacks on the Foreign Office and thence on the Air Ministry have brought some result with the announcement of the resumption of a sort as soon as the ice breaks. I should very much like to hear what you [the Corporation] think is the best method of attacking the FO and the AM on this subject with a view to getting something done.'

On 24th April the Secretary of State for Air was asked in Parliament whether he could make any statement with reference to the British trans-Atlantic air services for 1940.

Captain Balfour replied, 'As has already been announced, it had been hoped to reopen this important service during the present year. Recent developments here, however, made it necessary to direct the aircraft intended for use on this service to certain defence purposes for which they are particularly suited. I regret that, at the present time, defence needs must claim priority.'

BOAC had gone to war. *Cabot* and *Caribou*, which had completed the second series of Atlantic experimental flights commanded by Captain Kelly-Rogers, were now equipped with a number of machine guns, and their crew's uniforms changed to Air Force blue. They were sent off first to hunt U-boats with Coastal Command, and then to take RAF experts and Norwegian officers to set up radar stations in Norway.

But by his lightning strike on Norway, Hitler had already beaten them to it. Arriving at Bodo on a clear sunlit Sunday morning, in May 1940, the British crews heard church bells chiming across the fjord. The radar equipment had just been off-loaded when a Heinkel bomber dived. The bells had been an air-raid warning. Captain Store slipped moorings and tried to taxi *Cabot* away. The same Frost, who had been First Officer on the *Maia* flying boat part of the Short-Mayo pick-a-back, acted as fire control officer in the astrodome. The Heinkel was hit several times. Captain Long also tried to taxi *Caribou* out of danger but both flying boats had been hit, smoke was pouring out of *Cabot*'s wing roots, *Caribou*'s fuel tanks were punctured, and four of the crew were wounded. While the rest of the crew tried to repair their aircraft, the Germans attacked again with bombs and machine gun fire. *Caribou* was burned out, and though the crew of *Cabot* tried to hide her between a high cliff and an island, she was found and finished off by a Dornier Do18— ironically the same type of flying boat that had been catapulted from the Azores mother ship.

But back in England, in spite of the war, BOAC were still pressing for further Atlantic crossings. The *New York Times* had pointed out the immense propaganda value of such a service at that time. *Clare* and *Clyde*, the sister ships of the two sunk flying boats, were fitted with extra fuel tanks. Arrangements were made for the use of the positions of selected ships between Foynes and Botwood for navigation purposes.

But three weeks later, it was all back in the melting-pot, and had been referred to the Cabinet. According to a furious BOAC management, the Air Ministry 'had put a spoke in the wheel last week for the following reasons—(i) because they "just wanted it postponed" (ii) because the Prime Minister had said he wanted a boat load of his friends to go to the Congo (iii) because the Middle East wanted a service from the UK to Bathurst or Takoradi.' Their view was that 'the Air Ministry are being completely "bloody-minded".' To add fuel to the flames, news was released that the GPO were paying £240,000 a year to the USA for conveyance of airmails across the Atlantic.

This time, the airline won. Captain Kelly-Rogers flew *Clare* across the water jump on 4th August 1940, carrying mail, the morning's newspapers and three passengers, arriving in New York to a tremendous welcome and news coverage. Later, more round trips were made. But the government got every ounce out of their aircrew in instructing them by a note how also to be diplomats. 'A tribute may appropriately be paid to Pan American Airways for its remarkable achievement in maintaining alone through the past ten months a regular trans-Atlantic Air Service.' They were to thank the American people for their aircraft, engines and volunteers, assure them that the British people were '100 per cent behind the government,' an in view of German claims to have bombed London to bits—the Battle of Britain was at its height—they were to stress the relatively minor character of the damage so far inflicted.

The demand for Pan Am seats over the Atlantic was now so great that a priority system had to be introduced by the government. Mail took precedence, and then essential war cargo. The Boeing 314s were carrying enormous loads, up to a peak of 13,620 lb.

But there were problems. Pan American's plans for further North Atlantic progress were being nipped in the bud. The Sikorsky 42B and the Martin 130 (of which only three were ordered) were not commercial North Atlantic aircraft. The DC4 was running into production difficulties. Due to defence commitments, Pan American's order of 40 Lockheed Constellations, one of the Atlantic landplanes which were to supersede all their flying boats by 1946, had to be postponed indefinitely.

In America there was now more government control. The Civil Aeronautics Board had been formed with extensive powers to grant licences and alter mail rates. And competition on the Atlantic began to increase. American Export Airlines now had three Vought-Sikorsky flying boats which could carry 16 passengers non-stop across the water jump, and on 26th May 1942 the new airline flew from New York to Foynes and continued Atlantic services throughout the war.

The Lockheed night shift at Burbank, California, working on Hudsons to be flown over the Atlantic by the Ferry Service to serve as U-boat hunters with RAF Coastal Command. Note the roundels on the fuselages. (Lockheed)

The war had reversed the Fly British policy, and the Ministry of Aircraft Production was trying to buy some much needed long-range civil aircraft from America. Trippe suggested some of his Sikorsky 42Bs, but Major McCrindle of BOAC refused them. Instead, in April 1941 BOAC bought three 314As from Pan Am at a cost of $1 million each. *Bangor*, *Berwick* and *Bristol* operated a magnificent service to many points of the world from Baltimore throughout the rest of the war.

\*     \*     \*

When the Second World War started, the North Atlantic winter still remained unconquered. Those few gallant men and women who had taken on the winter crossing in aeroplanes had all either failed or disappeared. The Pan American 314 flying boat was routed in the 1939 winter via the Azores, and even that far south ran into innumerable difficulties and delays.

And then, in May 1940, Churchill came to power with an aggressive war policy. For this, he relied on shipments of American aircraft and armaments, but these were far too slow and were often sunk by German U-boats on the crossing.

# CONSOLIDATED

The Consolidated Catalina—here in RAF colours—the type that made six survey flights across the Atlantic operated by American Export Airlines.

The aircraft must therefore fly over.

The degree that the North Atlantic winter was still feared is shown by the losses expected by the British government from this course of action. Three aircraft lost out of seven was considered acceptable. Anything worse, and the aircraft would have to continue to be sent by ship. RAF Coastal Command, the British experts on oceanic flying, had already given their considered opinion that the year-round water jump could not be done.

Much was still unknown. It was estimated that few cloud tops would go up beyond 15,000 feet (30,000 feet and upwards became later not unknown). It was thought that icing could not occur below −10° centigrade (it was found subsequently at temperatures of −20° and below). Would the alcohol de-icing on the propellers be adequate? Could the carburettor heaters cope with the ice from a severe front?

Some progress had been made with aerodromes. Shelmerdine had a low opinion of the use of Newfoundland, but on the premise that it was a thousand miles out into the Atlantic and must therefore be some help, a party had seen sent out to find one flat square mile. The best site, weatherwise and operationally, according to McTaggart-Cowan, the doyen of North Atlantic weather, was close to Botwood. The party set off on their explorations in the caboose of a railway train, and perhaps therefore not surprisingly chose Hattie's Camp, a pine and spruce forest where there was a lumber distribution centre that sent split wood to St John's by rail in the total absence of roads. The Newfoundland government had voted five million dollars which the British government was going to underwrite. This was fortunate for Newfoundland, in that it is reported that the British estimate simply included the cost of cutting down the trees, it not having been realised that the roots of each one would have to be grubbed up. As a result, construction moved forward slowly and expensively. Eventually the British approached the Canadians, who finished the job. Shelmerdine took it all philosophically, saying that if they had known the right figure, they would never have started the aerodrome. Hattie's Camp, better known as Gander after the neighbouring lake, said to be so deep that it never froze, was in fact to prove of inestimable value in the war.

Now, in June 1940, Churchill put Beaverbrook in charge of a Ministry divorced from the Air Ministry—that of Aircraft Production. As such, one of Beaverbrook's responsibilities was getting the American aircraft across the water jump, and he tackled the problem with characteristic and unorthodox vigour.

Once again, private citizens came to the help of governments. Using the old-boy network, Beaverbrook contacted his old friend, Sir Edward Beatty of Canadian Pacific Railways, to organise a service called Atfero. Woods Humphery had been appointed second-in-command. The newly formed BOAC would provide the first crews and managers, including Burchall and Captain D. C. T. Bennett who had flown the *Mercury* part of the Short-Mayo Composite across the Atlantic two years previously. Also helping a great deal were eleven generous Canadian businessmen as 'dollar-a-year men', including Morris Wilson of the Royal Bank of Canada, Harold Long and J. W. McConnell.

Once again, the colourful aerial circus across the water jump started up as American and Canadian bush pilots, cowboys, ships' navigators, civilian radio operators, barnstormers, skywriters and stuntmen were recruited at 1000 dollars a month to get the aircraft over. It was said that McConnell used to see an aircraft in the sky, race to where it landed and get the crew to sign on. Most of the pilots had only a rudimentary idea of oceanic flying, and some of the navigators and radio officers had never even flown. But volunteers kept on coming over the border from the USA, some using the same route across the Great Lakes as the old bootleggers' run.

A school was set up by Bennett at St Hubert where the R100 had berthed just outside Montreal. The difficulties of obtaining the bombers (America was still neutral) was solved by having them dragged across the Canadian border by horses before being flown to St Hubert.

The BOAC pilots backing up Bennett—all volunteers (amongst them Wilcockson, Ross, Page and Cripps)—received only their usual pay plus a bonus for the Atlantic. This was the origin of North Atlantic pay that later benefited BOAC pilots like myself and was anathema to the rest of the Corporation aircrew.

The big problem was navigation. There were few radio aids—even Gander still had no range—and the recruited navigators could hardly be expected to reach the First Class Navigators' Licence standard which was required for the Atlantic crossing.

It was therefore decided that the first flights should go in formation at night (because at least the stars were there for astro), led by Bennett.

After fuel-consumption tests and compass checks, seven Hudsons flew to Gander where now there was a good and extremely wide runway, a brick building housing McTaggart-Cowan and his meteorologists, a few army huts, and two sleeping-cars and a dining-car parked in a railway siding that were the crews' quarters.

Bennett made the most careful preparations for the flight, including an anti-collision procedure in the event of the formation going into cloud. On 10 November 1940 the weather forecast was reasonable, with little cloud above 15,000 feet and a + 23-knot tail-wind component. The flight plan was 9 hours 32 minutes to Aldergrove in Northern Ireland, and there was a full moon.

Bennett decided to go.

That date was well outside the closed season for the water jump. No one had ever flown across the North Atlantic successfully in winter before. There was much that was quite unknown, particularly about ice. Only a handful of the Hudson crews had any trans-oceanic experience. And it was wartime. It is against that background that Bennett's performance should be judged.

There was thick snow on the ground. To the strains of *There'll always be an England* played by a band wearing greatcoats and lumbermen's fur hats, one after the other the Hudsons took off, easily picked up Bennett's aircraft from the extra identification light that had been fitted, and, all in formation, set course east. As they climbed, the band changed the tune to *Lead, Kindly Light*.

The weather stayed reasonable till half way across. For rations, the crews ate the sandwiches and drank the coffee provided by the Newfoundland Railway car. But already there had been problems in one aircraft with an oil leak, then the radio blew up after shorting in the antenna switchbox, and next the radio compass went unserviceable.

A front broke up the formation at 35° West. Some aircraft went up as high as 18,000 feet trying to get above the cloud. The bomb-bay tank ran dry on one, and both engines started cutting out.

Most of the formation were north of track and, after landfall, course was altered south towards Ireland.

At Aldergrove, Bennett was waiting for them. He kept watch by the window till the last aircraft was down. Then he wrote in his report 'all arrived safely, and without incident.'

In the town by the Lough to which the aircrews went, the Irish would not believe that the crossing had been made. It needed the American and Canadian accents and the wide cowboy hats to convince them that these boys really had done the water jump. Of the twenty-two men, nine were Americans, six British, six Canadians and one Australian.

The second formation of Hudsons was delayed because of snow and ice, but again successfully made it. Further flights were made without incident till the flight of 28 December, when two Hudsons out of six had to return with engine failures.

Beaverbrook was delighted with the results, but Bennett was not satisfied. He told Beaverbrook that formation flying was not satisfactory, and that each aircraft should have a navigator with flying experience. These he obtained from the Empire Training Scheme schools in Canada that had been set up to train aircrews for the RAF. He gave selected graduates three flights at night to accustom them to using astro, then off they went.

The plan worked well. B17 Fortresses and Hudsons were flown over by assorted ferry pilots. Losses were far fewer than expected—even though excitement and emergencies were perennial. One pilot wrote 'No trip was the same as another. I did sixty-four of them, one way and another, over the Atlantic ferry routes, and there wasn't one that didn't produce some sort of moment when I thought we'd had it.'

Now aircraft of all sorts in ever-increasing numbers came over. There were men to fly them—and women. Jacqueline Cochrane, already a famous American pilot, delivered a Hudson over the water jump (though her male colleagues insisted a man should take off and land).

The Lend-Lease Bill passed Congress and in March 1941 received proper Presidential assent. 'The stuff was coming,' as Churchill wrote. 'It was for us to get it over.'

For the passengers, the trips were excruciating. Until heating from the exhausts was provided, it was often icy and always draughty. Tossing about in the middle of Atlantic storms, at any moment the engines might roar up to rated power as the captain climbed to try to avoid ice. Up at twenty thousand feet, sucking oxygen for hours at a time, few passengers had much appetite for the ham and cheese sandwiches provided, even though winter westbounds to Gander across the water jump could last more than fifteen hours.

This contemporary report shows what it was like to be an Atlantic passenger in 1941: 'We entered the plane through a small opening almost in the bottom of the fuselage, the door opening downwards and bearing steps on its inner side. We found ourselves in a high compartment which is perhaps best described as the main well of the machine. To the right were steps up to the tail compartment, while to the left was a passageway to the forward part of the machine. There were also some steps up to the wireless operator's cabin. We were undecided where to go until the wireless operator told us that the captain preferred passengers to be in the bomb bay while the plane was taking off. So we moved forward into the next compartment. Our eyes were not accustomed to the darkness and we could see practically nothing. Very gingerly, I sat down on something; it turned out to be a box . . .'

On the Boeing 314s, however, which flew a trans-Atlantic VIP service via Bermuda, there was luxury.

In January 1942 Captain Kelly-Rogers flew Churchill to Bermuda in one of them, after a conference with Roosevelt. The Prime Minister was so impressed with their speed and comfort that instead of boarding the battleship that was waiting in Bermuda to take him home, he decided to return on the flying boat.

Churchill was accompanied by Martin, his private secretary, Charles Wilson, his physician, Dudley Pound, the First Sea Lord, Charles Portal, Chief of the Air Staff, Beaverbrook, Minister of Aircraft Production, and Hollis, Secretary to the Chiefs of Staff Committee.

The subsequent flight in *Berwick* has been described in some detail by Churchill in Volume III of *The Second World War*. After 'a merry dinner' he had slept soundly in 'a good broad bed in the bridal suite at the stern with large windows on either side.'

While still west of Ireland, weather at Pembroke Dock, the designated terminal, deteriorated badly and Captain Kelly-Rogers decided to divert to Plymouth which was only a little further distant. He made the necessary alterations of course to starboard, sent his Estimated Time of Arrival (ETA) as 0900 and alighted in Plymouth Sound at 0859.

It was a relieved and happy Captain Kelly-Rogers who accompanied Churchill ashore at Plymouth, but he would have been less happy if he had known the words which Churchill would use years later to conclude Volume III of his wartime memoirs. Recalling his visit to the flight deck when approaching the English coast, Churchill wrote that he sensed a feeling of anxiety around him and 'that we did not know where we were.' He goes on to say that later on he learned that if they had held their course for another five or six minutes before turning northwards 'we should have been over the German batteries in Brest.' At least four of the passengers subsequently had descriptions of the incident published, all of which drew heavily on Churchill's account.

Captain Kelly-Rogers' report, handed in after the flight, shows that the route followed to Plymouth was normal in the circumstances and his time of arrival as predicted. Had it been as suggested by Churchill, he would have arrived at least half an hour later. Furthermore, the flying boat was under radar surveillance controlled by Prestwick during the latter stages of the flight and according to the Control Officer it was 'nowhere near Brest'.

The difference between these facts and Churchill's account is difficult to understand, though it has been suggested that he liked to finish a book on a high dramatic note. At any rate, he was certainly converted to flying, and made several more Atlantic trips in the Boeing 314.

\*      \*      \*

The Ferry Service with its multi-national pilots delivered the warplanes to Britain quickly enough. But then they had to wait around for a ship's passage to take them back to the other side to fetch some more. Pilots were like gold. And deliveries were slowed up intolerably.

What was required was a return ferry service to fly the pilots back, and a suitable aircraft with which to operate it.

It is here that the Consolidated B24 built by Henry Ford (helped by Lindbergh) at Willow Run, makes its appearance in the civil saga of the Atlantic sky. It had a strange name for a bomber—Liberator. Ugly, pignosed and fat-bodied, it had a thin sword of a wing that caught the least bit of ice. It was heavy on the controls and so reluctant to leave the ground that when fully loaded it used almost all the runway before lumbering up into the air. Behind the two pilots was an engineer's panel, and an Engineer Officer now became a regular crew member. The paramount points about the aircraft were its great range and its four most reliable Pratt and Whitney Wasp engines. On 1st July 1941 the US Air Force had begun their overseas air transport services with a flight of B24s to Scotland across the water jump.

The British plan was to use a civil version of the bomber to fly eastbound over the Atlantic with mail and VIPs. On the westbound, they would then take back the pilots who had delivered their bombers to Britain.

Seven Liberators were delivered for this purpose in April 1941. By this time the ferry service, set up and efficiently run by private individuals, as so often happens, was taken over by government. For various reasons, it was felt that the military should run the show. The Air Ministry had also recognised that air forces now needed transport aircraft as well as bombers and fighters. The Atlantic Ferry Service became the first group (nevertheless called Number 45) of the now RAF Transport Command. Pilots trained under the Empire Air Training Scheme, and other RAF pilots were used to augment the ferry crews. And the Liberators were primarily used to run a service across the water jump. The main function was to fly back the ferry crews and it was therefore named the Return Ferry Service. More highly experienced

A BOAC Liberator in black night camouflage on the Return Ferry Service at Dorval.
(British Airways)

Imperial Airways/BOAC pilots came over to help run it—amongst them Jones, Messenger, Allen, Stewart, Bennett, Carroll, Buxton, Scott, Andrew and Prowse. The first eastbound service left Montreal on 4th May 1941. The westbound service carried seven returning aircrew.

As well as having to buck eighty-knot headwinds, the RFS pilots had to cope with such contingencies as a seagull crashing through the windscreen on take-off at Gander, so the Captain had to fly across the Atlantic with a −40°F hurricane in his face. An undercarriage leg refused to retract, and the aircraft made the crossing with one leg down. Clear ice coated one Liberator, slowing its speed by fifty-five knots to dangerously near stalling.

Battered by the westerly winter gales, the Liberators clanked and whined alarmingly. So alarmingly that they caused a curious incident aboard an RFS Liberator flying General Sikorski, Head of the Polish Forces, and his staff to America. Two hours out over the Atlantic a stick bomb was discovered in the Elsan toilet at the rear of the aircraft. It was assumed that this was an attempt on the General's life. In fact, according to Donald Fish, then in MI5, later BOAC's Security Superintendent, this stick bomb had come into the possession of a Polish

*Opposite:* Mass production at Burbank of the new Atlantic airliner, the Lockheed Constellation, which was diverted by the war to the USAAF.
(Lockheed)

Wing-Commander on General Sikorski's staff. For reasons of his own, this Wing-Commander had kept it quietly in his brief case—till the whines and bangs of the westbound Liberator had convinced him that his bomb was going off. He had rushed with it to the rear toilet, and put it down. He had then discovered to his dismay that the toilet was an Elsan with inadequate bomb-quenching properties and immediately reported his 'find' to a fellow passenger. The facts were eventually uncovered, and the matter dealt with by the Polish authorities.

The Lancastrian—a converted Lancaster Bomber—was used by Trans-Canada Airlines to fly the mail across the Atlantic in 1943. (Air Canada)

The Ferry Service went on throughout the winter, each trip teaching the crews more about the North Atlantic winter. Because of the war, there were few weather reports. Fortunately the Atlantic weather service had been well set up beforehand. A weather man had spent a year going to and fro across the Atlantic on the SS *Manchester Port*. In spite of being continually sea-sick, he measured temperature, pressure and cloud heights, logged speed and direction, tracked fronts, and built up weather maps. Then McTaggart-Cowan in Gander had revised the whole concept of North Atlantic weather forecasting, producing the folder that would be standard for pilots for many years of pressure chart at sea level and altitude, an often luridly crayoned cross-section of the weather to be expected by zones, and a landing and alternate forecast. In addition, two weather ships heroically kept station in spite of the risks, one being attacked by a U-boat.

In the air, there were also casualties, but far fewer than expected. One RFS Liberator, after take-off from Prestwick, crashed into Goat Fell, the highest mountain on the island of Arran. There were no survivors. Approaching Gander, Captain Eves was caught in heavy ice. The visibility was 900 yards, in drizzle, cloud base one hundred feet. Trying desperately three times to get in, he crashed on the shore of Gander Lake. All on board were killed.

Backwards and forwards went the Return Ferry Service across the Atlantic for the rest of the war. Services were increased to three a week. The crews took marmalade, jam, chocolate, cigarettes and nylons to war-rationed Britain, arriving after each eastbound like Santa Claus. The RFS pilots continued to clock up the crossings, Captain Stewart being the first to reach a hundred. They carried 2000 passengers, 140,000 lb of freight and 2,000,000 lb of mail.

As regards ferrying bombers, the American, British and Canadian pilots delivered 37,000 aircraft to Prestwick—chosen for its good weather record and built up because Aldergrove was too small—from various North American aerodromes.

Because there was so much of this wartime haphazard traffic across the Atlantic, air traffic control had to be set up. A Conference was held in Ottawa in 1942, from which originated the Trans-Atlantic Safety Service Organisation, which was to play an important part in the weather, communications and other organisation, and a volume of coordinated information on operating the North Atlantic was produced.

Many types of aircraft were ferried, but the honours of conquering the North Atlantic winter must go to that ugly duckling—the Liberator, flown by the BOAC pilots of the Return Ferry Service.

The RFS were the origin of the Atlantic Division of BOAC. Their aircraft were serviced by the Canadians at Dorval, and in 1943, due to pressure from Canadian servicemen who were not receiving their mail, a service was started in Lancastrians that was the beginning of Trans-Canada Airlines' Atlantic Service.

**Mail being loaded into a Lancastrian.**                                                 **(Air Canada)**

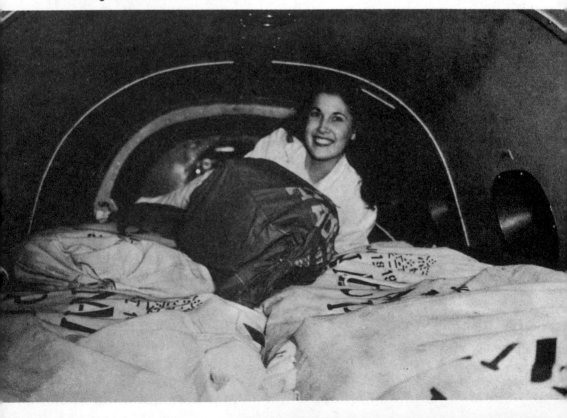

The international nature of the Ferry Service had taught the British pilots a great deal. All through the war, internal American airlines had been continuing. Range stations had been set up throughout the continent, and cities were linked by the airways formed by the spokes of their radio legs.

The Americans had complained that the British pilots did not know much about range flying. That was soon remedied—the British learned from the Americans who had objected. All through the war, American civil aircraft construction was in continual operation and expanding enormously, while the British operations were all related to the war effort and their civil aviation inevitably marked time.

By being based in Canada, over three thousand miles from their politicians and Civil Servants and all the interference with which the British operators had been plagued, right in the burgeoning heart of civil aviation, BOAC learned American methods and procedures, technical and commercial know-how, the latest ways of operating, and established excellent relationships with American airlines, aircraft manufacturers and civil aviation authorities.

It was the best break that a British airline had ever had.

*         *         *

While American Liberators flown by British crews were conquering the North Atlantic winter, down below them on the sea the Allies were losing the far bloodier Battle of the Atlantic.

**The Vought-Sikorsky VS 44 introduced by American Overseas Airlines on 26 May 1942. to operate non-stop from New York to Foynes.                    (Underwood)**

Up to the time that America entered the war at the end of 1941, four and a half million tons of shipping had been sunk. Churchill was worried that the Americans would then need all their equipment for themselves, and that it would be the end of Lend-Lease, which had been the mainstay in Britain's survival. No more, he feared, would American aircraft be flown across what he called the life-line of the Atlantic to help Britain.

The RAF anti-U-boat forces were grouped in Coastal Command. The Americans had no equivalent. I was in Coastal Command throughout the war, and we began by flying what Bomber Command did not want. Our Whitleys and Wellingtons were quite inadequate, and even the Sunderland flying boats (Empire boats modified for war) had not the real range required. We went as far as we could go from bases in Ireland into the Atlantic—four hundred miles at most. And then we would only have time for a token search of the sea before going home. The aircraft were known as 'sticklebacks' from the early airborne radar aerials sticking out of the wings and fuselage, which reduced our speed to 95 knots. The mariners wryly regarded our appearance in the same way as they regarded seagulls—the first sign that they were safely home.

Hardly anyone saw a U-boat, but now and again we saw four-engined Condors—the military version of the Condor which had so dramatically flown across the Atlantic in 1938. Now they were prowling on the sea lanes, bombing ships and reporting convoys.

Flying a Wellington on convoy patrol, I once saw a Condor suddenly push its wet gleaming nose through the clouds—an eerie sight, dead in front of me, a kind of grey ghost in the rain. This one banked sharply to port and disappeared as suddenly as it came, merging with the grey Atlantic sky. My nose gunner, highly excited, fired shot after shot of red tracers from his twin .303 Brownings into the empty air.

A year later, British bullets did connect with a shape coming out of the Atlantic mists. A night-fighter attached to the RAF closed on an aircraft near the Eddystone lighthouse. In the darkness ahead, the pilot caught sight of a four-engined aeroplane and fired. Down went the big aircraft, catching fire and spiralling into the ocean. But this was no Condor returning from convoy reconnaissance—this was Captain Humphrey Page of Imperial Airways who had done magnificent work pioneering the North Atlantic winter, returning from Cairo in a British Liberator.

It was ironic that the only service aircraft then capable of reaching the air gap half way across the ocean where most of the sinkings were taking place was the Condor.

A ring of aerodromes was needed on all the Atlantic stepping-stones, from which long-range aircraft could operate. Gander was proving invaluable. Now the Americans began to show what they could do, to

Churchill's great delight. 'American blood flowed in my veins,' he was to write in *The Second World War*, 'I thought of a remark which Edward Grey had made to me more than thirty years before—that the United States is like a "gigantic boiler. Once the fire is lighted under it there is no limit to the power it can generate." ' In double-quick time, they built Stephenville in Newfoundland, Keflavik in Iceland, Bluie West at the end of a precipitous fjord in Greenland. The Canadians had also moved fast. On the shores of Lake Melville, a hundred and fifty miles inside Labrador, with no roads and no railways and icebound most of the year, they had flown in everything necessary for an aerodrome in 7000 flights without a scratch to aircraft or freight—and had built Goose. A radio range was installed in Gander. St Hubert as the west base was too small: Hildred (later to be Director-General of the International Air Transport Association) took one look at the RCAF base at Dorval, and bought it for $1 million without consulting the Treasury. All that was needed now was an adequate aerodrome in the Azores: and, as usual in the history of the Atlantic sky, the *right* aeroplane, this time for war.

It made its appearance quietly. 'The air gap in the North Atlantic south-east of Greenland,' Churchill wrote in his memoirs 'was now closed by means of the very-long-range (VLR) Liberator squadrons based in Newfoundland and Iceland.'

The U-boats' safe and happy hunting ground in the gap was beginning to be closed. Terence Bulloch, top-scoring RAF ace with eight U-boat sinkings, later to be a BOAC Captain on the Atlantic, and Desmond Isted, both flying Liberators, sighted thirteen U-boats massing to attack convoy HX217 on the same day, and attacked eleven of them. On the resulting failure of the U-boats' attack on the convoy the official German Navy statement was that 'following an analysis of this action, Flag Officer U-boats stated that the results were poor due to the strength of the escort.' Two Liberators had made all the difference on that occasion. But there were still not enough of them. According to the Admiralty 'the Germans never came so near disrupting communications between the New World and the Old as in the first twenty days of March 1943.' In the nine months to May 1943, $3\frac{3}{4}$ million tons of shipping were sunk.

Then the Casablanca Conference declared that the defeat of the U-boats was the number one priority. Immediately, Fortresses and then Liberators came into the anti-U-boat squadrons in increasing numbers.

Towards the end of the year, the British reached an arrangement with Portugal to build an aerodrome in a narrow valley between a ridge and a mountain on the island of Terceira in the Azores. I was one of the captains of two squadrons of Fortresses who flew out. A boat-load of perforated metal strips known as 'artificial runway' had preceded us. Together with the Portuguese, aircrews and groundcrews laid the new runway in a north-westerly direction, living in tents till it was done. Apart from a certain springing effect, as though on a roller-coaster, and the fact that it always made a clanking noise when you landed, it wasn't a bad runway.

Now the air gap was closed tight. Air cover was provided right across the Atlantic. Early in 1944, six hundred miles north of the Azores, in a Fortress I attacked a U-boat previously sighted at night by a Wellington equipped with a searchlight. With the help of naval forces, U575 was sunk.

There was now no safe place for the U-boats. Total air cover—mainly provided by Liberators, coupled with the skill of the larger naval forces—had defeated them. The sinkings dropped dramatically. The Battle of the Atlantic had been won. Many ships and aircraft had, of course, shared in the victory. But one of the most outstanding contributions had certainly come from the Liberator.

First, the conquest of the North Atlantic winter. Then the Battle of the Atlantic. Ugly, uncomfortable, earthbound, ice-prone American Consolidated B24—how very right was your name of Liberator!

*       *       *

BOAC continued to fly their Liberators on the North Atlantic Return Ferry Service throughout the rest of the war. Their three Boeings, now based in Baltimore, did occasional North Atlantic trips but concentrated mainly on the southern routes. Pan American organised and carried out, with the USAAF, a vast ferry service across the mid and south Atlantic.

There is a widely held belief that during the war the Americans insisted that the British should devote their entire aircraft industry to the building of warplanes, leaving a clear field for their own civil aircraft manufacturers. It appears, however, that the British concentrated on warplanes of their own choice—perfectly understandable during that total war—and unfortunately not many were designed to profit from military experience so as to start life as an eagle and be transformed into a dove, an exercise in legerdemain at which the Americans were to show themselves past masters.

In the spring of 1941, aircraft designer Roxbee-Cox of the Royal Aircraft Establishment had written wistfully to BOAC, 'I expect you know of Pan American's specification issued to the American aircraft industry. It is a very bold and spirited affair. Also I saw in today's *Times* Glenn Martin has developed a basic design for a 125 ton aeroplane, 280 mph, cruising range 11,000 miles. I think it would be a very good thing if we made a few basic designs, even if we made nothing else.'

As regards the commercial water jump, the British were almost in the same position as they had always been years previously—they had nothing really suitable. The All-Red Route, the Fly British policy, had been overtaken by history. Much criticism for such a state of affairs has been levelled at many people. Aviation financing had been positively miserly. There had been inadequate communication between the airline operator and the aircraft manufacturer—almost always with the screen of the Air Ministry between, with no civil aviation experience and heavily biased towards the military. Eyes had been turned eastwards to the Empire routes, and aircraft had only been ordered for short stages. An almost total lack of understanding of the necessarily commercial nature of civil aviation had been shown, and far too great an emphasis had been put on its prestige potential. All that had come out of plans since 1931 for the *right* Atlantic vehicle—the Vickers six-engined flying boat, the Albatross, the Short 14/38, the Fairey land-plane and others—had come to nothing. Ingenious but expensive makeshifts to tide over range difficulties on the North Atlantic, such as the Short-Mayo Composite and flight refuelling, had taken years of Whitehall-corridor-tramping to get a hearing, even longer to put into operation, and had been suddenly dropped.

Particularly against a background of war, perennial financial stringency, and rearmament, such criticism by hindsight is easy. When one is trying to look forward from any situation, so much clouds the territory ahead. The cookie may crumble in so many ways. Certainly the British had not thought anywhere near big enough, but then they were continuously being pinched by their shrinking resources and the need for economy. Certainly they had shown far more inventiveness than any other nation, but even this rebounded against them in that they were always too busy investigating new ideas and new possibilities—evaluating them, comparing them, discarding them—to get down to the hard fact of making decisions.

Three facts, however, clearly emerge. A public funds subsidy financing system, with its need for parliamentary authority and surveillance, allocated piecemeal side by side with Company profits, is an unwieldy and unyielding instrument likely to cause endless trouble, interference and recriminations, and nowhere near as workable as the unfettered American financing system of a Post Office subsidy.

Secondly, from the administrative point of view, it is impossible to have bosses who are always changing. Imperial Airways had been lucky to have the long and unbroken partnership between Geddes and Woods Humphery, but had suffered from continual changes of Minister. Now there were not only an even greater variety of Ministers, but also of Chairmen and Chief Executives of BOAC. These sometimes brought in their own favourite sons over the heads of loyal and hard-working long-term officers. Reith certainly fought the Air Ministry for two years before being neutralised by a Ministerial appointment and then getting the sack. Runciman continued the battle that had always gone on against the anomalous situation of the airline which neither had the defined authority of the armed services, nor the responsibility for its own decisions of an independent company. Threatened with subjugation to RAF Transport Command, Chairmen and Chief Executives resigned, one after the other—Runciman, Pearson, Critchley. By the end of the war, Britain did at long last have a Minister of Civil Aviation, but no sooner had Viscount Swinton been appointed than the government changed and Lord Winster became Minister. This toing and froing in the rooms at the top was to be something that BOAC had to learn to live with in the years ahead, strikingly contrasting with Pan American where for so many years Juan Trippe had reigned supreme.

Thirdly, the resourcefulness, skill, efficiency and devotion of the individual British people who made up the airline's staff since 1924— not just the aircrew, but the administrators, engineers, traffic and engineering staff—had never been doubted. On that one point, and that point only, there had not been real criticism and never been an argument.

What had happened during the war regarding future aircraft was yet another government committee, the Brabazon Committee of 1942. Two years before, Churchill had written a minute, 'I should deprecate setting up a special committee. We are overrun with them, like the Australians were with rabbits.' British civil aviation was certainly so overrun, but in fact the Brabazon Committee was perhaps the wisest and most imaginative aviation committee that has ever sat. That it should convene in the darkest days of a total war, when defeat appeared imminent, and calmly make such excellent plans for the future of British civil aviation reflects the greatest credit on the experts, Civil Servants and airline executives, who were its representatives. Once again, British inventiveness came bubbling up to the surface. A number of large and advanced aircraft were proposed.

First, a huge flying boat called the Saunders-Roe Princess, capable of carrying eighty passengers non-stop across the Atlantic in accommodation equivalent to first-class Atlantic liners. Separate passenger cabins, a promenade deck, a large dining-room, an observation lounge, a smoking-room, a library, all were to be provided, and the galley and its capacity to produce gourmet meals (in those days of food rationing and Maconochie's stew) was lavishly and lovingly planned. Its ten Proteus turbo-prop engines, eight of them in coupled pairs, were to give it a speed of nearly 300 miles an hour.

This flying boat was twinned with a huge land-plane called the Brabazon of 290,000 all-up-weight and a wing-span of 230 feet, fully pressurised and powered by eight British Centaurus engines of 2650 hp, geared in pairs to huge contra-rotating propellers. It was to carry eighty passengers across the Atlantic, all provided with sleeping berths. The cruising speed was to be 250 mph and the aircraft would comfortably operate London–New York non-stop. It would be the first British aircraft to have a tricycle undercarriage, and there would be two decks, the upper deck forming a lounge, bar and dining-room, which would become the cinema when meals were not being served, the lower deck housing the galleys, cabins, and toilets fitted with showers. Never had such lavish crew accommodation been provided, giving each of the specialist engineer and radio crew his own room, the Captain his own separate cabin.

There were two medium-sized Empire route aircraft proposed, one with four Proteus turbo-prop engines later called the Britannia. And, most revolutionary of all, the Brabazon IV, the first jet-propelled air-liner in the world, designed to fly high above the weather at 30,000 feet—later to be famous as the Comet.

After years of lagging behind the Americans and the Germans in the building of civil aero-engines, a British Committee had proposed a huge advance over the rest of the world that might well change an impossible lagging position to commercial supremacy over the water jump. Two types of jet engines were to be built—one in which the jets would drive a propeller (turbo-prop), and the other on which there would be no propeller, but a pure jet. At the very moment when the world watched and waited for the United Kingdom to topple from its impossible position into total disaster, at a time when meetings continued under the table because bombs were falling around them, on the apparently irrelevant subject of the future of their civil aviation industry, the British had at last thought big.

## *Eleven:* The Buttercup Route

Now as you glance through the porthole, you suddenly notice that all the clouds have gone. Burnished bright yellow by the evening sun, far below you the Atlantic is as calm as a mill pond.

Peace came to the water jump almost as suddenly. By then it had been established as a viable commercial all-the-year-round operation, capable of providing a daily mail service, a considerable cargo capacity and the carriage of passengers from Europe to America against the westerly wind—though with intermediate stops—in less than twenty-four hours.

In addition, all sorts of improvements, further inventions and developments had been inherited from the war: a proper understanding of cruise control, so as to get the maximum possible range from the fuel, a very efficient meteorological service: the establishment of long-range radio navigation aids, such as Loran and Gee which could give an aircraft an accurate position way out in the Atlantic: cabins enabling aircraft to fly up to 25,000 feet yet pressurised down to 5,000, so that the passengers did not need oxygen masks: improved alcohol-spray de-icing equipment on the propellers, more efficient inflating and deflating rubber boots to break up ice along the leading edge, adequate hot-air control to prevent the carburetors icing up; sufficient aerodromes; more powerful engines; and above all, a land aircraft actually designed for the long ocean crossing.

The world's airlines now shook themselves free of their military aviation overlords, and with varying degrees of success began to prepare themselves for renewed battle on the North Atlantic front. Lufthansa were not allowed to operate. The founder of KLM had spent much of his time in preparations, making his plans for the Atlantic future of his airline, and the moment it was possible, Plesman was free to begin implementing them. The Swedes were in an excellent financial position, and France also had considerable funds available. Pan American, which in spite of having its progress drastically curtailed, had amassed valuable trans-Atlantic experience with its 314 Boeings, now got rid of all flying boats. They had wisely cashed in on the glut of military transport aircraft to buy 45 C54 landplane aircraft, which had proved themselves in war, and cost only $90,000 each. They had converted them to the DC4—unpressurised, slow, but with a trans-Atlantic capability.

Everyone rushed over from Europe—Air France, SAS, KLM—to buy the latest American aircraft, the Lockheed Constellation, which Pan Am had sacrificed to the Army four years before. This beautiful 93,000 lb aircraft clearly had its origins in the De Havilland Albatross —particularly evident in the similarity of the smooth sweeping curve of its fuselage and the shape and sit of its engines. Powered by four 2200 hp Wright engines, it could carry forty-five passengers in pressurised comfort (above the weather, it was said) at 260 mph for 3000 miles. Here at long last, was the commercially viable Atlantic landplane that the world's airlines had been looking for.

Still saddled with the Fly British policy and without the authority for foreign equipment they might consider necessary, only BOAC hesitated. The Corporation had 207 aircraft of seventeen different types —ten landplane and seven flying boat. They had no cash, but as a legacy from the Return Ferry Service, their experienced civil aircrew were amongst the finest in the world.

The situation presented its familiar difficulties—too much politics, too few adequate aircraft. The aviation industry was again in one of its government-induced upheavals. Now *three* chosen aviation instruments were set up—British European Airways for short continental routes, British South American Airways for the mid-Atlantic across the Caribbean and South America, and British Overseas Airways for the North Atlantic, Africa, Australia and the Far East, together with a Minister of Civil Aviation with a Cabinet seat to look after them. A vast number of large military aircraft were now redundant, and the Treasury was naturally anxious to use as many of these for civil aviation as possible. The York, a hybrid made out of the successful four-engined Lancaster bomber parts, could carry 24 passengers over a medium range. The Lancastrian, a straightforward Lancaster conversion, could carry nine passengers by day or six by night. Neither was pressurised and an oxygen supply was provided for each passenger. There was also the Avro Tudor, a civil long-range design again spawned by the Lancaster. This aircraft had no tricycle undercarriage but was pressurised. All these aircraft were powered by the Rolls Royce Merlin liquid-cooled engine, which had proved itself in the war as a fine high-altitude engine. The Americans had discarded the liquid-cooled engine for civil transport work in the middle 1930s, but Trans-Canada Airlines were to power their North Stars (basically DC4s) with Merlins for the Atlantic route.

The Lockheed Constellation that led the way after the war in providing speed and comfort for the Atlantic air passenger. (British Airways)

BOAC now produced a memorandum showing why, in their view, the Lancastrian and the York were unsuitable for the North Atlantic, and since neither the Tudors nor the Brabazon types were anywhere near ready, they pressed the Minister for permission to buy Constellations. As always with any foreign equipment, it was necessary to obtain Treasury agreement. The Treasury attitude is that a pound spent inside the UK is kept within the economy, while one spent overseas is lost in its entirety. Furthermore, anything British-bought will automatically advertise Britain, produce foreign technicians trained in British hardware who might well be expected to continue buying equipment with which they were familiar, and thus produce a future demand for spares. The only argument that the Treasury accepts for buying foreign is that there is no British equivalent. This policy is perfectly logical, particularly when it is borne in mind that among the Treasury's main preoccupations should be the stemming of inflation and the bolstering up of the value of the pound. There was at that time the usual shortage of dollars. The trouble is that in an environment as competitive, as changeable, and of such erratic financial fortunes as a rapidly burgeoning North Atlantic air route, unless the national aircraft industry can produce comparable and suitable equipment, the user is heavily handicapped.

Treasury and Cabinet approval to buy five Constellations at £200,000 each was not forthcoming until 15th April 1946, when the Minister wrote to Lord Knollys, BOAC Chairman, giving him the authority but adding that this was to 'meet an emergency and my main preoccupation remains to see the Tudor is brought into operation on the North Atlantic as soon as possible.'

On 3rd May 1946, Lord Knollys met the Minister to discuss future North Atlantic plans. The flying boat service over the water jump had ceased from 7th March (Pan American had stopped flying boat services, and the three British Boeing 314s were no longer economic). Only the Liberators were operating. It was hoped that a daily service could be operated by September, with two services a week calling at Prestwick. Any increase in that frequency would depend on the use of the Tudor Is, and problems had arisen with the aircraft, particularly with the oil-tank installation and the cabin pressurisation. The all-up weight had been increased to 80,000 lb and this would adversely affect its performance. The minutes of the meeting went on: 'Another difficulty arose from the fact that, in order to schedule for a large petrol reserve, to ensure

Veteran Imperial Airways and **BOAC** Captain O. P. Jones at the controls of a Constellation.                                                                                 (Private)

regularity of operation, it might only be possible to book six passengers on each trip. This rendered the aircraft exceedingly uneconomic. The Tudor I, therefore, might be a failure and never come into service. Even if it did operate it would be uneconomic and not competitive with the aircraft in use by American operators.'

Since, in BOAC's view, the introduction of Lancastrians 'would be a retrograde step', the possibility of equipping American aircraft with British gas turbine engines was discussed, but the decision that was taken for the present was that six Liberator services a week should continue to run—the only BOAC trans-Atlantic service until replaced by the daily Constellation.

The future up to 1950 was considered bleak, and the only hope of getting through it was to buy more American aircraft. It was recognised, however, that the repercussions of such an action would not be confined to the Atlantic route, but would be bound to spread to the Commonwealth routes, where considerable difficulty had already been experienced in keeping Dominion operators to the use of British aircraft.

Beyond that sticky period, however, great hopes were expressed for the Brabazon, the Princess flying boat, the Britannia, the Tudor II and above all for the pure-jet Comet (the MCA had ordered 70), the half-scale model of which was to fly in the near future. However, it was suggested 'that the aircraft might be rather small. For this reason and, as an insurance against the failure of the Comet, there should be justification for asking for tenders for a larger aircraft on the same lines.' Every now and then, going through old yellowing papers, with the infinite benefit of hindsight, one comes across a couple of sentences like these which might have changed history, if they had been implemented. One wonders who was the wise man who made that suggestion and why a course of action that might have meant a British lead of ten years over the American 707 simply disappeared into dust.

Even so, with a cautious but Micawber-like optimism that has always been a characteristic of the British government's chosen instrument, BOAC looked beyond the petty difficulties of the present to the bright future beyond, when there was every chance that at 550 miles an hour they would leave their competitors standing.

Meanwhile, they moved fast and announced that the first of their five trans-Atlantic Constellations, *Bristol II*, would leave London at 22.00 hours on 1st July 1946, under the command of Captain O. P. Jones, well known for his piercing blue eyes and torpedo beard, who had been in Imperial Airways from the beginning and was already the Grand Old Man of British Civil Aviation. The service from New York would be commanded by Captain Jim Percy, another million-miler and again one of the highly experienced stalwarts who formed the backbone of BOAC.

The fare was to be £93 single, £167 return.

*       *       *

On 5th July 1946, at Prestwick, I boarded a brilliantly polished silver Liberator, Yoke Baker and took a seat by a porthole half-way down the starboard side of the fuselage. I was on the staff of BOAC as a First Officer, and I was off to join the Atlantic Division, then stationed at Montreal.

Six years earlier, I had done my first flying from Prestwick, then a grass field, now with two wide concrete runways. Here I had had inordinate trouble with my first solo in a Tiger Moth, when I became mixed up with a flight of Battle of Britain Hurricanes doing formation take-offs and landings. Here I had made my first feeble efforts at instrument flying, using much the same basic instruments as Alcock had done to cross the Atlantic. Here I had practised forced landings after engine failure. Here I had had to steel myself to force the Tiger into a spin, rotating like an express merry-go-round—just as the big Vimy had done half way across the Atlantic—till with stick fully forward and opposite rudder I pulled out, feeling giddy and a trifle sick, just above the tops of the heather-covered hills. Here I had actually gone out of sight of the airfield, all of sixty miles to Stranraer and back on my first cross-country.

Since that time, I had flown on operations in Coastal Command and test flying, and I had now twelve other types in my log book and 2,303 hours, half of them in four-engined aircraft and over 900 hours in command of the military version of the Liberator, in which I was now sitting. The end of the war had given me three alternatives. I could go back to the university. I could accept a permanent commission in the RAF, to which I had been gazetted. Or I could take my 'B' Licence and Second Class Navigation Ticket and enter civil aviation. I chose the last, and went to London for my examination.

Even though fifteen years had passed since First Officers were called Mates, airline captains were still called Masters and a strong mercantile flavour permeated the hall in which I was examined. Dully lit, inadequately heated, the place seemed to smell of rope, tar, coal, sea-water and twist tobacco. A bearded retired Merchant Navy Captain regarded me solemnly over his spectacles and began to ask me searching questions on the lights shown by moored flying boats, tides and the rules of the sea.

It never really gets dark up north in early July, and it was still daylight when we took off from Prestwick that night and climbed on a north-westerly heading over the mountain of Goat Fell that had claimed one Liberator of the Return Ferry Service during the war. At 10,000 feet, the engines were reduced to cruising power, and we set course over the Atlantic on a Great Circle track.

The Atlantic was still the same dirty grey prison-clothing colour, flecked with the white arrows of waves breaking in the direction of the wind. Great puffs of black cloud, like enormous flak bursts, mushroomed our way ahead. Only on the northern horizon was there colour—a bright orange ribbon that never left us all night where the sun was just below the line of sight, treating us to a kind of permanent dawn.

The scene was not new to me. I had spent hundreds of hours looking for U-boats over these waters, most of the time in thick mist and rain. Just above the waves, we had searched for survivors from missing ships and aircraft, sometimes found life-boats with no one living inside them, but mostly there were just huge patches of oil scattered with flotsam. I had circled convoys of ships, smoke wafting out of their funnels.

There was nothing there now. I settled back in my seat, and the steward brought hot coffee out of a thermos flask—much better coffee than the RAF had provided. The hours droned by, the familiar Pratt and Whitney Wasps buzzing confidently—I had never had an engine failure on them and they had gone on turning, even when once filled with flak from a German destroyer. Before each one of my hundred operational trips, I had had a queasy feeling in the pit of my stomach that I might not come home. This was my first water jump, and never for one moment did I think we might not make it to the other side.

I knew nothing of the history of the route I was flying, with the exception of Lindbergh's flight. I had never heard of Alcock and Brown nor Read nor Major Scott. I knew nothing of ice—we used to do our patrols very low, in the Skaggerak at night right down to fifty feet. I knew very little of airways, cruise control of engines, range and beam flying, blind landings apart from Ground Controlled Approach. I knew very little radio telephony procedure, not much about engines. My main qualification for my job was some knowledge of navigation, including astro, and much experience in taking off and landing on this same type of aircraft at weights considerably in excess of what would now be allowed. The Atlantic, I assumed, had been conquered—as indeed it had been—by other men and women. It had been shown clearly that the water jump could be carried out, winter or summer, by the Return Ferry Service, which had completed its 2000th crossing on 10th February 1946. What aircraft I might be flying, the political and economic wrangles that might have taken place, the future possibilities of this route, did not concern me. That I was to come in on the tail end of the pioneering of the water jump—the establishment of a regular all-the-year-round scheduled commercially viable passenger, mail and cargo service across the Atlantic—never once crossed my mind. I had a new job in which I wanted to do well, and a similar attitude prevailed amongst my fellow ex-RAF officers who joined the Atlantic Division with me.

Our arrival had clearly been the subject of apprehension amongst the highly experienced million-mile civil captains, known as 'the Barons'. It had been considered that having been captains ourselves for anything up to six years, we would be antagonistic to sitting in the right-hand seat. The Training Captain, a Canadian called Charlie Pentland, introduced himself by saying that his job was 'to turn gallant young gentlemen into fussy old women'. In fact, he did much more than that. He and his fellow training captain, Bill May, who had once been a bush pilot, taught me a great deal about flying the Atlantic. Between them, they began to build the firm foundations on which BOAC's magnificent Atlantic safety record is founded. Captain Kelly-Rogers was the Manager.

On that first crossing of mine, the weather gradually deteriorated. I wrote in my diary, 'round about seven o'clock we started flying over icebergs. We crossed the rocky coast of Labrador and Goose Bay at 8.30. The sky was a magnificent raspberry colour, the air was like ice cold water, and Goose Lake was calm as glass. The Mealy Mountains to the south showed up pale and luminous against the dark background of the fir trees.' We had had a quick flight of 11 hours and 24 minutes, but now we stayed on the ground in the olive green modern reception buildings, drinking endless coffee for nine hours, delayed with an oil leak. Even so it was still light when we were overhead Montreal. The evening sun slanted a sideways searchlight beam out of a still blue sky. Looking out of the window, I saw the cross on the top of Mount Royal, the wide curve of the St Lawrence spoked by bridges. Five minutes later, doing a straight-in approach onto runway 28 (that is facing magnetic direction of 280°), we were down.

**Typical North Atlantic winter weather for the Liberator.**

The whole trip had taken 24 hours and 58 minutes, but I was much too excited to feel tired. I went to the wooden Dorval Inn that smelled faintly of pine and paint and slept in a room in which before me young pilots who had completed their training under the Empire scheme had slept before going off to do their water jump.

Like the Baines Sisters of *The Old Wives' Tale* before me, I had no inkling of my own minute place in history. There were two things I had to do next day, and these I did immediately after a quick breakfast.

The first was to get digs for myself, which I did with the Donnellys in Westmount, who welcomed me warmly as Dan had been a pilot in the RFC during World War I. The second was to go to Macy's and—fresh from six years' wartime rationing—order a steak and a double cream sundae.

*     *     *

The Liberator had lived up to its name, and had served BOAC proud. Now was the time for it to go to grass, and the service was scheduled to end in September 1946. First Officers like myself would operate in the right-hand seat of Constellations for route experience, before being trained on Tudors for a command.

KLM, Air France and Pan Am were operating Constellations and DC4s. American Airlines had got control of American Export, and as American Overseas Airlines were also operating DC4s. They had beaten Pan Am by two days in the race to put a landplane service commercially on the Atlantic by beginning their DC4 operations on 23rd October 1945. Pan American had ordered 18 DC6Bs, a stretched and pressurised version of the DC4, which could carry 100 passengers at 300 mph over the Atlantic. This 'stretching' of aircraft was to be a feature of American aviation design. Another huge new aircraft, developed from the B29 Superfortress bomber, the Boeing Stratocruiser had made its appearance. Weighing 145,800 lb it was to be the heaviest piston-engined airliner ever built. Powered by four 3500 hp 24 cylinder 'corn-cob' Pratt and Whitney engines, it provided accommodation for 61 passengers, as well as a ten-seater lounge bar down a spiral staircase on the 'ground floor'. It was designed to cruise at 275 mph at 25,000 feet—rather slow but providing super-luxury with berths and gourmet meals from a superb galley. Pan American ordered 29. KLM and Air France preferred to standardise and ordered stretched versions of the Constellation, the 1049. Back in London, BOAC peered into its crystal ball.

It had clouded up again since the Brabazon Committee days. There had been further delays on the Tudor and the Brabazon I, and the Chairman of BOAC had written to the Minister pointing out the formidable qualities of the Stratocruiser, and had obtained his permission to go on Boeing's waiting list as a precaution—a wise one as it turned out. On 5th February 1947 the Technical Director wrote to the Atlantic Division Manager, 'As a result of the tests recently carried out by the Development Flight (BOAC) on the Tudor I, it is doubtful whether this aircraft will, in the near future, be suitable for Atlantic operations and the Chairman has directed that we should assume, for next year's planning purposes, that it will not be suitable. After further modifications and development work has been carried out by the manufacturers and when the aircraft can be handed over with a stated guaranteed performance and an adequate supply of spares, the Corporation will then recommence a training programme and organise a maintenance base, set down spares and do all that is necessary to get them into service as quickly as possible. In the meantime, nothing further will be done in the way of training, provision of staff and stores and such matters.'

All this added up to 'keeping the Liberators going for a further period. I should be glad if you would go into your training programme and let me know just what effect this will have on your plans for the Liberators. Commercial Department say that provided they can be operated on regular days they will be commercially usable for the carriage of mail and freight and not, therefore, be a total debit charge against training in your Division.'

So the Liberators continued, and after local training and radio instruction, I was off on my first service across the Atlantic, as a First Officer to the same Captain who had brought me over. The most nerve-racking part was at the beginning when over the R/T I was given our airways clearance. This was a complicated route out, with heights and positions called out at breakneck speed in a Canadian accent from the Tower. It was the First Officer's duty to repeat this back word-perfect even faster than it was received.

I found it almost impossible, as did most of my fellow First Officers. It was too fast to write, too long to memorise. Unless you had a pretty good idea of what your clearance was, you were, at any rate at the beginning, likely to stumble or not understand it.

That August morning was blazing hot, and the flight deck smelled of that peculiar Liberator smell—metallic, oily, petrol-sweet. In addition there was the flowery scent of the Captain's hair cream, for he carried a bottle in his briefcase and brushed his hair regularly with it at intervals throughout the trip.

While taxiing sedately round the perimeter, the clearance came at me with the unexpectedness of an ambush by machine gun. I asked for a repeat—apparently a heinous offence. When it came at the speed of light, I repeated it back wrongly—an even more heinous offence. The Tower corrected me, and the Captain repeated it all back, immediately and word-perfect—the most heinous offence of all.

All he said to me was, 'Wait till you get to New York.'

It was six months before I did. Then I knew what he meant. In the bewildering criss-cross of airways, over the R/T came an even more bewildering assortment of accents, while the American ringmasters in their control towers spoke twice as fast as the Canadians. Your clearance came to you suddenly, a single shot embedded in shrapnel. You had to listen for and identify your own call-sign amongst myriads of others and if you did not get it immediately and repeat all your clearance back, like a naughty boy you went to the bottom of the class and had to work your way up again.

Fortunately, this agonising torture has joined the Iron Maiden in the shades of history. Leaving London, your First Officer simply receives a Brecon 22 Departure. Without the now standardised arrivals and departures over the R/T at speed would have come 'Climb ahead to intercept 263 London Radial until 7 miles DME London. Right turn onto 276 to Woodley NDB. Cross Woodley above 4, not above 5.' And that would have been an easy one.

The peculiar arrow of the Speedbird that was BOAC's trademark (inherited from Imperial Airways) was already on the dark blue crew car that picked us up, two hours before departure, in our dark blue uniforms to go out to Dorval. There the flight plan to Goose or Gander would have already been prepared by the Operations Officer on the choice of height and track with the most favourable winds. An average component eastbound of around plus 20 knots kept the trip time down. What delayed things was that some of the Barons, in our view, took an inordinate time to make a decision on the flight plan, and might require it to be done two or three times, or work it out themselves, after visiting the meteorological office and collecting the charts of surface and upper winds and a coloured cross-section of the entire route, with the weather to be expected through each zone colourfully depicted in crayon.

Nevertheless, the Barons had a high regard for punctuality, and no matter what might have gone before, there was a last-minute rush to sign the load and trim sheet and the aircraft log and be off on time. We carried a load of 4000 lb of freight and mail, with sometimes a staff passenger, a steward or sometimes the new genus of British aircrew, a stewardess, bedding themselves down on the top of the mail bags in the icy draughty fuselage. The only Liberator with seats was Yoke Baker, now the training aircraft.

At the end of the runway, the inevitable check on each of the two magnetos on each engine for a drop to show on the revolution counter—in ninety per cent of delayed flights the reason for piston-engined aircraft returning to the ramp. Then the four throttles would be advanced to 46in Manifold Pressure, the brakes released, and we would be off.

A slow climb over a different-coloured Canada—parched olive green in summer, blazing maple red in the fall, glittering white, with the St

Lawrence a vast frozen diamond vein, in winter—up to a cruising altitude usually of 9000 feet. Any higher, we would have to put on our rubber masks and suck oxygen, which nobody wanted to do unless absolutely necessary. The Engineer would set up the throttles, revolutions and mixture for the most economical cruise, and then (he also acted as steward) he would deal out the ham and cheese sandwiches and the Canadian apple cake which were invariably our rations, to the two pilots, the radio officer, the navigator and himself. Then he would pour out the coffee from a king-sized thermos jar into the little white cardboard cups called in Canada 'buttercups'.

These buttercups had another purpose. After drinking, a small amount of coffee was left at the bottom. Smoking was prohibited, and there were no ashtrays. So these buttercups became the receptacle for cigarette ends, after a surreptitious smoke. When full, they were slung out of the window, and it was said that there was no need of navigation. All you had to do was to follow the trail of buttercups and you would never get lost. So the Liberator operation was called 'the Buttercup Route'.

After eating, the Captain would usually say 'Would you like to do the first two hours?' and I would inevitably say yes, I would. Then he would push his chair right back, call for a blanket, and curl up with his head on his chest, while we flew airways on towards Gander airport.

Depending on the Captain, he would emerge two hours, three hours, four hours or just on the circuit at Gander to do the landing.

An hour at Gander for refuelling, and then off again to Prestwick, finally ending up in London.

Those long hours over the Atlantic taught me a lot. Most of the ex-Imperial Airways Captains were characters, and sometimes they would reminisce over the good old days when the Master, particularly of a flying boat, really was a king. A guard of honour of station staff saw him on board. If things were not to his satisfaction, there was hell to pay. One flying-boat Captain had turned back to his point of departure because milk for his tea had not been put on board. I learned of presents, of jewels being given to aircrew who flew eastern potentates, of magnificent soirées in their honour, of the time the captain ate the special oysters put on board for Royalty visiting Australia, and of the compliment he paid the Catering Manager on this long-overdue improvement in the flying rations.

The Liberators were now used not only as mail and cargo carriers, but to train the ex-RAF pilots in Atlantic Command, before taking over the Constellations and possibly the Tudors. One Junior Captain, as we were called after our command course, operated eastbound with another Junior Captain as First Officer. On the other side, we changed places and swapped roles for the westbound.

The schedule was a long one; eighteen and a half hours eastbound, twenty-four and a half hours westbound via Keflavik, departing in the late afternoon from Montreal and the evening from London, in order to arrive at a reasonable time in both places. Often, when the weather was bad, up we would have to go to 25,000 feet. There the heating was never adequate, the frozen staff passengers would be bedded down on the flight-deck floor, and hour after hour everyone would suck oxygen. Cannonballs of ice slung off the propellers would crash against the metal sides. Sometimes the upcurrents were so fierce that both pilots would be needed to level the wallowing wings. Mist often awaited us in London, and fog or snow was the usual Gander winter weather. Sometimes it was difficult to get in—particularly in to Keflavik. In January 1948, I wrote in my diary, 'The forecaster was giving a Low well to the east of Iceland. When I remonstrated that the landing forecast gave a south-west wind at Keflavik (thus assuming the Low to be moving in on the place) he said that was Keflavik's forecast, he himself would give a north-west. Took off from London Airport on runway 14. Cloud base 800 feet. Cleared to climb to 4000 feet on the north-east leg of the range, then out. We had flight planned at 8000, but the weather was bad and up and up we went, finishing at 22,000. Temperature off the clock. We approached Keflavik, working 126.18 mcs. We had asked for a Ground Controlled Approach, and sure enough it was a south-west wind. I heard them changing runways. Cloud base 800 feet, snowing, visibility poor. GCA took us over, but were not good. They were trying to take us round the cumulo-nimbus anvils, but let us in for a beauty. I had throttled back to 15 inches, but the speed was 180 knots and we were still climbing at 4000 feet a minute. We broke cloud at 300 feet, after a long straight run. Still snowing. GCA said the runway should be 'dead in front of you now'. I saw it, half a mile to port. I did a corkscrew but then GCA said 'Don't land yet. Lorries on the runway clearing snow.' So at fifty feet, I opened up and went round again. Circled visually, then I led in for another GCA. This time straight in, but landed with the port wheel on a cleared strip of the runway, the starboard in deep snow with no braking action. Temperature +1. We taxied and clambered out into the wet.'

But those hours on the Buttercup Route were the happiest flying hours of my life. We were given almost total independence. The little silver kingdom of the Liberator might lack many comforts, but it really *was* our world. Nobody ever questioned any decision. The mail and the cargo remained silent, and the staff passengers shivered but smiled. Every hour we would report our position, the wind and the weather. With the automatic pilot in and the four Pratt and Whitneys sweetly turning, the rest of the time was ours.

The Atlantic is different from continental routes because of the length of time the pilots spend comparatively uninterrupted. On the European and Eastern routes, they would be fidgeting around checking something or other every few minutes. And as one veteran British pilot said, 'It's the only route you fly for a very long time, and there on the other side, you find they still speak English.'

Always before I had been scanning the sea for U-boats and the sky for fighters. Now there was time to look around me, at the cloud cauldrons, at the dawns and the sunsets, at the icebergs polkadotting the sea, at the eternally changing white-flecked greys and greens and blacks of the North Atlantic. Even the storms had a grandness. Then the clouds were like dark caves which the blunt nose of the Liberator explored—sometimes setting off an avalanche of snow, or releasing a torrent of diamond hailstones, or a reservoir of rain, to come flooding down on top of us, making the engines sputter like damp matches and turning the view from the windscreen into the porthole of a bathyscape under the ocean, the Perspex covered with the phosphorescent eels of electric rain.

Those were the days best to appreciate both the dangers and the beauty of the North Atlantic sky—when you were there right in its intestines. Now at around 35,000 you are almost always above cloud, and with the evaporation of the dangers some of the beauty has gone too. You miss the big cumulo-nimbus build-ups above you. These days you are in an inverted bowl of blue with cloud far below you. You could be anywhere.

Not only did the Liberators provide the best possible training for the new generation of North Atlantic captains. They were also used for another batch of flight refuelling trials, in the hope that by this means Britain might still be the first to run a non-stop commercial service, perhaps with the jet-propelled Comet.

Months passed into years, and still the Liberators went on flying on the Buttercup Route. Another dollar crisis burst on Britain, and the Treasury cut BOAC's grant. It was pointed out that the operating cost of the Liberators was £404,586 against a revenue of £391,942. The load was 935 kilos of mail, 36 kilos of diplomatic mail, against the Constellation's 556 kilos of mail, 37 kilos of freight and 3720 kilos of passengers. Withdrawal would, therefore, save around £12,500 annually, but the Chairman said that, 'it would be unwise to grasp at a possible small saving at the expense of drastically reducing our participation in the highly competitive Atlantic passenger traffic, in which our effort is already necessarily very much restricted compared with competition.'

The withdrawal dates continued to be postponed, now due to late delivery of the Stratocruisers. Eventually, in the Spring of 1949, most of them were sold to Scottish Aviation for £1,500 each, with additional engines at £400 the set of four.

My last crossing in a Liberator was in the same Yoke Baker in which I had first gone off to join BOAC, over two and a half years previously. It was one of YB's last flights on the Corporation, landing at London at 9.55 on 28th March 1949. Not one hair of anyone's head had been touched by the Liberator's commercial service over the water jump.

Yoke Baker eventually went, re-equipped with a bar and other trimmings and as sumptuously appointed as a ceremonial elephant, to become the private aeroplane of an Eastern potentate—and then to join the other Liberators in the Valhalla of all good and faithful aircraft.

\*     \*     \*

The war had bequeathed excellent aerodromes with long concrete runways and excellent facilities all round the Atlantic. La Guardia was still being used as the American terminal, but Idlewild, with twelve runways, a capacity for 30,000 passengers a day, and every sort of shop, restaurant, night-flying facility and with a marine alighting base alongside—was being built half an hour from central New York. There were now also Santa Maria in the Azores, Kindley Field in Bermuda and Keflavik in Iceland.

At the London end, the British had been considering where to site their own main terminal airport. Money had been spent on Croydon before deciding it was too small. A proliferation of alternatives were studied: Heston was inadequate, Gatwick was flooded in the winter, Lullingstone was too expensive. Still flying-boat conscious, the authorities had looked at combined sea and land bases such as the possibility of Langstone Harbour and Portsmouth airport, which had then been dropped. Now they considered Heathrow together with the Staines reservoir, but this fell through because of the fear of pollution to London's water supply and the fog hazards from off the reservoir.

Perennially conscious of cost in civil aviation and trying to get two for the price of one, the British now considered the possibility of a combined RAF/civil aerodrome. Eventually, on a site where a Celtic temple had stood, on a heath beloved by highwaymen and cavalry regiments, back to the 1920 London terminal aerodrome went British civil aviation, and Heathrow was built in the typical RAF triangular runway pattern (though the RAF base never came) with the Control Area in the wrong place and the tunnel approach from the main road a built-in traffic limiting factor. (Further future expensive aerodrome-siting exercises, such as the abortive search for the third London Airport, loomed ahead.)

As the building proceeded at London Airport, mud was everywhere. Tents for passenger accommodation were put up. The place resembled an army encampment. The BOAC operations office for the Atlantic service was a wooden hut where the redoubtable Minnie Mann, who had been with Imperial Airways in the early days, welcomed everyone in and made their arrangements.

In spite of the advances in engines, aircraft were still slow. Twenty hours was a long time to be cooped up, particularly in unpressurised aircraft, sometimes sucking oxygen. There were many competitors for an unknown number of passengers—yet governments had to plan future facilities for aerodromes and airlines had to plan and make contracts for new airliners.

Safety across the water jump had been established by the thousands of crossings during the war. Now the vital factors were comfort, speed and cost. Cost would depend on many additional factors, such as the price of fuel, salaries and the daily available flying hours available after maintenance for each aircraft. The availability record during the war of around five or six hours a day was good, but with the vaulting cost of airliners and subsequent depreciation charges, this would have to be substantially increased. Turn-round and refuelling times would have to be improved.

According to their national characteristics and environments, the various airlines now made their guesses on priorities for the North Atlantic commercial passenger.

## *Twelve:* The Point of No Return

You are almost a thousand miles from land. This used to be called the Point of No Return, where you had to go on because you couldn't go back . . .

> And there's nothing below but the drink,
> It's then you will see the Gremlins,
> Green and gamboge and gold,
> Male and female and neuter,
> Gremlins both young and old.
> White ones will wiggle your wingtips,
> Male ones will muddle your maps,
> Green ones will guzzle your glycol,
> Females will flutter your flaps.

Round here has always been the best time to see them. Especially in the evening half-light, the violets and greys from the dying day, the perfect backcloth smudging to the mystery of the moving shadows that now fill the sky. The gremlins were invented by the RAF to explain the extraordinary and unexplainable things that used to happen to their aircraft. And extraordinary and unexplainable things do happen on the North Atlantic.

Airmen are just as superstitious as seamen. Many of the early pioneers took mascots along with them for luck. The Commander of the R34 took along a gold thumbs-up charm, the Engineer Officer carried a pair of his wife's silk stockings, and in addition there was a cat on board. Mary Pickford, the world's film-star sweetheart, gave a long-haired terrier, Tailwind II, to Mears for his Atlantic flight with Brown in August 1930 —to no avail, as they crashed at Newfoundland. Poor Hinchcliffe was superstitious: really against his will and better judgment he was more or less forced into the air on his ill-fated flight of 13th March 1928. Balbo believed women were lucky, and had his wife sit in the pilot's seat and touch all the controls of his Savoia-Marchetti before the Italian mass formation flight in 1933.

Vertically downwards now is where the lost continent of Atlantis was supposed to be. Over three hundred and fifty years ago Bacon wrote about its 'inhabitants': 'We imitate also the flight of birds . . . we have some degrees of flying in the air.' What is certainly a fact is the volcanic mountain range, a scar on the earth's crust that runs below the sea from the Antarctic up to Iceland. It is also true that in my experience on the old piston-engined aircraft this is where you listened.

The gremlins used to put the engines out of synchronisation. Or there would suddenly be a high banshee wail as a propeller 'ran away', the needle on the revolution counter going off the clock. In a BOAC Stratocruiser, the propeller on Number Four (starboard outer engine) ran away on Christmas Eve. The Captain reduced speed to try to keep the propeller revolutions within limits. Oil was pouring out of the engine. A reserve supply of oil was carried on the Stratocruiser, and this was pumped into Number Four. The indications from the gauges showed that the oil was simply going overboard. There were two possibilities: either the propeller would seize, which would make flying difficult; or the propeller would come off, possibly crashing into the aircraft. Over the R/T, the Captain reported his predicament.

There were two strange things about this incident. The first was that before leaving London the Captain had read a new instruction in Pilots' Orders on what to do if a Stratocruiser propeller ran away. The second was that a Pan American pilot heard the British pilot on the radio. This American had experienced a propeller coming off a Stratocruiser—extraordinary that this American should be there, in that there were only a few occasions when propellers came off Stratocruisers, of which a hundred and two were made, flying many millions of miles.

The American pilot now told the British pilot exactly what would happen. The propeller housing, made of magnesium, caught fire, and burnt with a brilliant white light. The four-blade propeller came off and flew well ahead of the aircraft where it looked like a giant catherine wheel, before disappearing into the Atlantic as the Stratocruiser caught it up. The British Stratocruiser continued safely on three without the drag of the useless propeller.

Here I once lost two engines on a Constellation—but a Constellation on two was comparatively easy so long as the other two kept going, which they did. The BA Wright Cyclone engine on the Constellation was marginal—there was basically insufficient oil for it—and we used to lose engines regularly. The oil pressure would drop and the oil temperature would rise—and you had then one minute to feather before it burst into flames. But the warning was sufficient, and there were few fires. All the same, just here particularly, you watched the dials and listened.

These were the early days of pressurised cabins, and another favourite trick of the gremlins was to pull the plugs on the pressurisation. Flying at 22,000 feet, all at once you would lose your pressurisation. White condensation, always mistaken for smoke in the passenger cabin and causing consternation, used to form and before the passengers became unconscious through shortage of oxygen we would have to dive steeply to ten thousand feet—always rather hair-raising—and there remain for the rest of the flight unpressurised.

The hydraulics sometimes went, or the powered control system. The Constellation had manual and hydraulically boosted controls—very heavy but just manageable on the former, easy on the latter. One aircraft half-way across the Atlantic had hydraulic trouble and the captain began to take out the boosters but they stuck between manual and boosted. The aircraft became virtually uncontrollable. It began to climb of its own accord, then stall, losing thousands of feet, before climbing up again to repeat the stalling manoeuvre. The trip to Prestwick was terrifying for everyone, but the captain managed to control the aircraft and land safely. Sometimes the auto-pilot started weaving. Or ice suddenly and inexplicably began to form. Or the aircraft used to be violently tossed around, though there was no cloud and you would be flying in clear air.

This used to be particularly frightening because there was no known reason and it could not be seen. It was only later that this was found to be caused by a jet stream, a thin corridor of air in which winds of up to 200 mph could be found, and along the wind shear would be whirlpools and turbulence now called Clear Air Turbulence.

Weird things certainly used to happen—and people would act strangely. Round here, Lindbergh suddenly became conscious of ghostly shapes coming aboard the *Spirit of St Louis*. Not far away, a First Officer, wishing to adjust the automatic pilot controls on a Liberator, inadvertently pulled the master ignition switch. All four engines immediately cut. Captain O. P. Jones was in the Engineer's position, writing up the log book. As the aircraft glided several thousands of feet towards the sea, he closed the log book, laid his pen beside it, turned to the Engineer and remarked, 'Strangely quiet, isn't it, Mr Stack?' before striding forward to remedy the mishap and bring the engines back to life again.

There is a strange quality about the Atlantic. I found, amongst most other pilots, that I developed an instinct of whether I was north or south of track. Certainly some of the early fliers, particularly Amy Johnson and Lindbergh, had this uncanny sense of direction. This gift, rather than their navigation, kept some of them in impossible conditions and after zig-zag courses more or less on track. The pigeon from the R34 was on track for Britain across the water jump from Mineola when it reached a steamer eight hundred miles out in the Atlantic. But what is this instinct, and how do humans, birds and animals get it?

The Atlantic sky has more spectacular mysteries. That shadow of the Jumbo you can see following you on the top of the clouds, ringed round with a rainbow, was first reported in 1919, framing the airship R34 in 'white, yellow, pink and dark blue circles'. It has a perfectly simple schoolroom physics explanation—the diffraction effect from the bending of rays of light round minute water drops, but it still retains the mysterious shiver of its name that comes from a German castle—the Brocken Spectre.

The following incident may also have a perfectly simple explanation—but what is it? On a routine BOAC North Atlantic flight, the Captain and the First Officer suddenly saw what appeared to be a flight of aircraft approaching on the port side. Immediate contact was made with Control who stated that there was no other traffic. It now became apparent that these were no ordinary aircraft anyway, being of a rounded shape, and the First Officer drew sketches of what they both saw, while the Captain increased power in an attempt to close. Hostile forces were suspected and Canadian fighters were scrambled, but before they arrived, the objects had faded into the horizon. Mirages? Clouds? Aircrew are amongst the people least subject to flights of fancy. This crew were highly experienced. Such a mistake was just conceivably possible for one pilot to make, but not by all the crew on that flight deck. Certainly the American authorities took the report seriously on the aircraft's arrival in New York. Could they have been flying saucers from another planet, in which many people believe? If not, what were they? No aircraft of any nationality of that shape had flown then or since.

Then every time I flew the Atlantic from Montreal via Labrador, just half-way to Goose invariably the compass started to deviate. This phenomenon had been noticed by other pilots, and a peak sticking up out of the icy desolation had been held responsible. It came to be known as the Iron Mountain or the Magic Mountain—the theory being was that it was full of metal which was attracting the magnetic compass needle. The early pioneers used to have trouble with their compasses. Though various theories were propounded the real reasons were never discovered. The needle behaved as if bewitched, and was perhaps a reason for some of the mysterious disappearances on the Atlantic.

There were so many of them. Nungesser and Coli in *L'Oiseau Blanc*, Princess Lowenstein in *St Raphael*, Medcalf and Tulley in *Sir John Carling*, Mrs Grayson and the crew of *The Dawn*, MacDonald, Kaeser and Luscher in *Jung Schweitzerland*, Diteman, Maclaren and Beryl Hart in *Trade Wind*, Cramer and Paquette, Lee and Bochkon in *Green Mountain Bay*, Edna Newcomer in *The American Nurse*—the list goes on and on. And not only the early flights, but in the later commercial days such as the two Tudors, which disappeared around this area near Bermuda in what has come to be called the Bermuda Triangle. Unexplained disappearances always send a shiver down your spine. What happened—and why?

No Atlantic disappearance was ever more mysterious than that of the ex-Captain of Imperial Airways Hinchcliffe and Lord Inchcape's daughter in *The Endeavour*, trying to do both the first east-west crossing and also to be the first to fly a woman across. A month after the aircraft had disappeared, Mrs Hinchcliffe received a letter from a medium saying that the writer had had a communication from him. Mrs Hinchcliffe did not believe in spiritualism, and did not answer the letter, but two months later she recieved another one from Sir Arthur Conan Doyle, telling her the medium who had written to her was completely trustworthy and that a second medium had told him that Mrs Hinchcliffe was not English and had children and was this true? Both were correct. The first medium also informed her of the correct address of a solicitor Hinchcliffe had consulted several years before.

Mrs Hinchcliffe went to a séance incognito, in the course of which a message was received through the medium informing her that *The Endeavour* had run into gales, one strut had broken and another cracked, and in heavy sleet and buffeting, Hinchcliffe had turned south. At three in the morning he had come down in the water north of the Azores. He and Miss Mackay had both been drowned.

Times and courses appeared to correspond and a pilot in peril half way across the Atlantic might well turn towards the nearest point of land which would be the Azores. Through the medium also came the message that Hinchcliffe was worried about his eyesight (he only had one eye) and was sure he would not be able to fly much longer. He had taken on the trip to provide for his wife and children. This was perfectly true. The pilot's name also appeared—spelt backwards. And the message 'Tell them there is no Death, but everlasting Life. Life here is but a journey and a change to different conditions.'

On 1st March 1929 Mrs Hinchcliffe received a letter from the Air Ministry, informing her that a wheel had been washed ashore in Donegal with a tyre 76168547 Goodrich Silvertown Cord Airplane 150/508, manufactured by the Goodrich Company, Akron, Ohio, USA. This tyre was identified by the company as one that was fitted to *The Endeavour*.

This discovery might well have been considered to have exploded the theory, except that the tyre was inflated and the wheel probably would float far, and the North Atlantic drift of the Gulf Stream does dip towards the Azores and then curve up towards Ireland. There were, in addition, other spirit manifestations including a spirit photograph of Hinchcliffe as a young man which his wife did not recognise but his mother did, culminating in a séance where she saw his face.

And then there was Mrs Hawker, who remained so calm and totally certain that her husband was alive, in spite of everyone telling her that what she believed was impossible. Yet after his presumed death came the news that a ship had rescued him and he was safe in Scotland. Mrs Hawker had been totally right—but how did she know? Was it what is now called Extra-Sensory Perception?

In Nevil Shute's novel *No Highway* a similar means is used to find the tail of the fictitious Atlantic aircraft Reindeer which has fallen off after 1393 hours total flying into the Labrador forests. It is vitally important to find this tail, and Mr Honey, the aircraft designer, sits his young daughter down with a planchette board. The pencil produces the words *under the foot of the Bear*. The (fictitious) Director of the Royal Aircraft Establishment tells Honey 'it's not the sort of science that usually emanates from this Establishment, and not the sort that anybody here can possibly endorse.' However a search is undertaken and the missing tail discovered a quarter of a mile due south of a lake called the Dancing Bear. The cause of the Reindeer crash is found to be 'a fatigue failure of the front spar flange of the port tail plane'.

A real-life search was undertaken for the pieces of the Comet which also broke up. Ships of the Navy clawed them up from the bottom of the Mediterranean. These pieces were fitted together on a fuselage skeleton at the Royal Aircraft Establishment. Under the brilliant organisation of the Director, Sir Arnold Hall, the cause of the Comet disaster was discovered. The water-tank tests used made a vast contribution to the testing of pressurised structures which benefited the world's aircraft manufacturers and ensured the safety of your 747's cabin. But the causes of the Comet disaster and the cause of the fictitious Reindeer crash were the same—metal fatigue. Yet the book was published in 1948 and the Comet crashed into the Mediteranean in 1954. Coincidence? Foresight? An inspired engineering prediction? Or what?

Some of the early pioneers were fortunate in *not* disappearing—and there was a mystery even in that. On 14th May 1934 the American Pond and the Italian Sabelli took off for Rome in an orange and maroon Bellanca called *Leonardo da Vinci*. Three-quarters of the way across the ocean, the engine began overheating and the oil pressure dropped alarmingly. Pond and Sabelli had to make for the nearest land, and put down in an Irish field. It is reported that an engineer checked the engines and found strips of cardboard in the oil tank, a metal bottle cap almost sealing off the oil pipe, and a stopcock to an auxiliary fuel tank turned off. In addition, two canteens of water filled by Pond before departure and untouched during the flight were now found empty. Who did it? Was it sabotage? Was this the first murder attempt over the Atlantic?

The second case of possible sabotage on the Atlantic was far more tragic. When the *Hindenburg* burst into flames at Lakehurst on 6th May 1937, thirty-six people died. Various theories were advanced on the cause of the accident. Letters warning of disaster had been received by the German Ambassador, but at that time of international tension, the Americans understandably wanted to avoid an international incident. For their part, the Nazis did not want a simple human explanation to be established as the cause for destroying a key symbol of the Third Reich. A confidential memorandum on possible sabotage by the German Technical Commission was not made public. Some evidence has come to light of bomb material collected at the site, and there was an eye-witness account by a survivor of an explosion very like that of a bomb on board. Nevertheless Goering stated that the cause was an Act of God, and the Americans settled for St Elmo's fire among 'the most probable causes'.

St Elmo's fire has always been a frequent sight on the Atlantic. Especially in the piston-engined days, a ghostly fireworks display would regularly be put on. Suddenly, the aerials and the propeller tips would be transformed into sparklers, fizzing away, sending glittering stars out into the night. It is as though the magnesium in the aeroplane is burning and you can almost smell the whiff of smoke. St Elmo's fire, named after a fictitious saint, is all very mysterious and can look quite terrifying—but it is just harmless static electricity and has never hurt anybody or anything.

Just as vivid as St Elmo's fire are the wriggling phosphorescent snakes on the windscreens during a storm, so bright you can almost read by them, caused by charged water drops exploding on the Perspex. Electric rain is also quite harmless, yet coming in from the bright passenger cabin into the darkened flight deck, the first impression is that the aircraft nose has caught alight. Kingsford-Smith, crossing in *Southern Cross* in June 1930, commented on vivid flashes that would outline the three propellers in weird blue light, flinging out blue rings of static electricity twelve inches thick, and strange lights playing up and down the leading edge.

Over on the right, you can see a mysterious white line slowly progressing across the horizon—a jet contrail. It consists of fine ice crystals. When kerosene burns one of the by-products is water which freezes at the jet's high altitude, forming the well-known trail of 'smoke'.

That bright halo made up of jewelled light over the northern horizon can be seen even better from this altitude than in the old days. The Aurora Borealis that haloes the northern rim of the Atlantic is not fully understood. It might be the reflected glitter of the snows of the Arctic, or sunspot activity, the entering into the atmosphere of sun particles, its appearance at the poles due to the deflecting action of the earth's magnetic field. One thing is certain; the brighter the aurora, the weaker the radio communication. And one winter trip when we could actually read the whole way across, so bright was the light, we could raise no one on the radio throughout the crossing. Sometimes it advances south, and in one of my books I described what happened in a Liberator south of Greenland on the way from Iceland. 'We came into a huge cone of Northern Lights, waiting for us like a gigantic cage hung on the belt of Orion. Then the ghostly door slid shut, and we were caught by thick silvery bars, imprisoned by the light that boiled and frothed and bubbled in a great crucible at the apex till it poured down triumphantly all over us in glittering blues and whites and diamonds. We stared up at the white-hot light as it danced and shimmered before our eyes, till suddenly, leaning forward to touch it, we could see it no more; fairy-like, it had gone.'

There is beauty as well as mystery about the Atlantic, defying logic and rational reasoning. The rescues particularly are noteworthy in that it was often on the point of giving up that the ship's crew saw the glint of metal. On sometimes no information at all, what chance was there of finding a tiny aircraft in the vast Atlantic? Yet again and again, it is done—the 'impossible' rescue from the 'impossible' ocean on the 'impossible' route.

As you look through the window along the darkening wings, it is no longer possible to see the gremlins. On the water jump, the whole species became extinct. The basic strength of modern aircraft design provided an unsuitable environment for them. In spite of apparent complications, the whole maintenance programme now hinges on simplicity and reliability. The state of the aeroplane can accurately be judged from data collection and data analysis systems. Faults are easily isolated by ground test equipment operating from accessible test points and there is a whole range of built-in test equipment actually on board. Of course now and again there are still faults and problems, but stuttering, back-firing, revolution dropping, pressurisation going, all those familiar gremlin tricks have become the curiosities of history. And no longer now on the Atlantic is there a Point of No Return.

Sitting here comfortably in the quiet rock-steady safety of the 747, you are convinced that everything can be explained. Everything has a reason. Gremlins, ghosts, mysteries, all have fled.

And yet, in this shadowy half-light just before you can see the stars, as you look around and see nothing at all in the inverted bottomless bowl of the Atlantic sky except the red winking of the port navigation light, you remember all those impossible rescues, the pioneers who took off and disappeared, Mrs Hawker's certainty that her husband was alive, Captain Hinchcliffe's account of how he met his death, all the impossible deeds that men and women did on this impossible route.

You begin to wonder. And then, you are . . . not quite so sure.

# Thirteen: Passengers Come to the North Atlantic

'I woke up unconscionably early with the conviction that I should certainly not go to sleep again. I must confess that I felt rather frightened. I thought of the ocean spaces, and that we should never be within a thousand miles of land until we approached the British Isles.'

Those words of Winston Churchill before he embarked at Bermuda as a passenger in the Boeing 314 flying boat to do the water jump to England on 16th January 1942 speak for millions who came after him. He went on, 'I had always regarded an Atlantic flight with awe. But the die was cast. Still, I must admit that if at breakfast, or even before luncheon, they had come to me to report that the weather had changed and we must go by sea I should have easily reconciled myself to a voyage in the splendid ship which had come all this way to fetch us.'

Now certainly thousands of safe crossings had been carried out during the war, but the passengers then were mostly people who *had* to go on urgent wartime business, and had their fares paid into the bargain.

Who would pay good money to do the water jump? None, certainly, in a Liberator. Perhaps not very many even in the 314 flying boats or the unpressurised DC4. Peace-time trans-Atlantic air passengers were still largely an unknown quantity. But they were clearly nowhere near as profitable as mail, and additionally it was clear they would be far from silent. They complained bitterly about the big marquees which were their departure and arrival lounges at the new London Airport. The flying-boat services had often been delayed in bleak places, such as Newfoundland, where passengers were rowed ashore to breakfast on a cold beach, while their aircraft was being repaired and refuelled. There was no shelter of any kind to greet them off the wallowing launches at Foynes; not even, an Imperial Airways observer noted, umbrellas. The heating was erratic, the sound-proofing inadequate. Airlines pinned their hopes on the new, fully pressurised Constellation that would fly above the weather. But then one crashed at Richmond, Virginia, and the CAB ordered them not to fly above 10,000 ft pending modifications.

[197]

Roller-coasting their way blindly through heavy turbulence, passengers were as sick as dogs. Not only that, they were frightened. An Atlantic storm still carried the punch of several atom bombs. The aircraft used to heave and toss, soar one moment, dive the next, heel over, waggle its tail. Beyond the grey wet cottonwool that fuzzed the portholes, to the tune of bottles and crockery crashing in the galley, passengers could just see the navigation lights going up and down like red and green ping-pong balls in time to the frantic waggling of the wings.

Fireworks were also provided. The cumulonimbus clouds used to be cracked open by jagged electric forks. Once, south of Greenland, I was struck by lightning. Suddenly there was an enormous magnesium flash and a noise like a land-mine going off. The whole aircraft became momentarily luminous. Every metal plate in the aircraft clanged like a hundred cymbals, the noise echoing and echoing in our ears. I could smell an acrid whiff of burning, as though we had been hit by anti-aircraft fire. Going out of synchronisation, the four propellers began to scream their heads off. Then just as suddenly, silence except for the engines as the aircraft—unruffled, undamaged—chugged onward on its way.

Intensive airline advertising was initiated. But how many passengers could be enticed away from the delights of the first-class Atlantic liners' saloons to *this*?

**The ex-RAF caravan which served as the BOAC Transport Office at London after the war. Passengers were accommodated in tents.** (British Airways)

The Pan American World Airways Worldport at Kennedy.

(Pan American World Airways)

The guessing game started.

Real competition against the luxury liners was regarded by the airlines as very difficult. The idea of actually putting them out of business would have been regarded as preposterous. The *Queen Mary* and the *Queen Elizabeth* were annually earning $50 million, badly needed dollars for Britain. France, Canada and the USA all had plans to compete with them.

Some shipping companies, particularly Cunard, were not worried by competition from the air. On the other hand, other companies, particularly Canada Steamships, showed very great interest in entering Atlantic aviation. BOAC, probably influenced by the high fare (equivalent to first-class sea travel) did not think that a great many could be weaned away from ships, but made a cautious guess of an annual figure of 40,000 air passages across the Atlantic, to be shared amongst

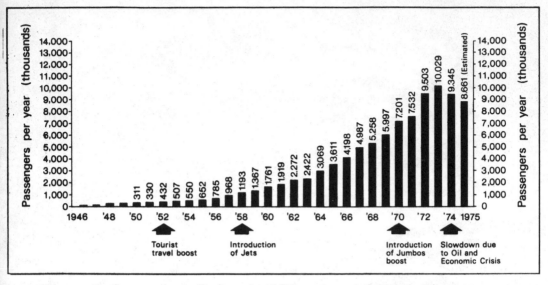

**The growth of passenger traffic flown by IATA carriers on the North Atlantic.**
*(figures obtained from IATA and CAA)*

BOAC, PAA, TWA, Air France, KLM, AOA, SAS, TCA and Sabena. They considered PAA's guess (500,000) and TWA's (575,000) purposely inflated to encourage further government support.

What did the post-war Atlantic air passenger want?

The British with comparatively low incomes (I signed on for BOAC as a fully qualified First Officer, after six years in the RAF mostly as a four-engined captain, at a starting salary of £375) still considered flying the Atlantic would be for the rich and the businessmen. Therefore, they opted for aircraft with good cabin arrangements (ample seats and lots of leg-room) and good food and cossetting, and their order was comfort, speed, cost. It was for the future in their view important to keep fares high.

Juan Trippe always maintained that the world's future was a race between air travel and the atom bomb. His order of priorities was cost, speed, comfort. He was already pressing for a single fare of $275 and $495 return.

Once again, British and American ideas on the North Atlantic were different. Because they had no suitable aircraft, the British wanted regulation of flights by quota and strict fare and frequency control. While the days of the Gentlemen's Agreement were over, it was clear that, particularly with so many other national airlines on the course as well, there was every possibility of bitterness and misunderstanding. While competition was excellent, cut-throat trading would be to nobody's benefit. The North Atlantic was not a closed shop. A viable and respected form of international control was imperative.

\*　　　\*　　　\*

This need for international regulations had been raised at the 1910 meeting, when the question of the sovereignty of the air above each country had been raised. Further need for internationalism had been apparent in 1919, when the French started the first regular weekly service from Paris to Brussels and the British began to operate the London–Paris route.

Lawyers from several countries began to assemble a body of Air Law broadly based on ground precedent. Six countries started the International Air Traffic Association that same year, and its rules were kept few for flexibility.

The two big problems were navigation and weather. Quick reporting of weather conditions for pilots was soon introduced, but it was not until 1930 that a Technical Committee was established, which amongst other things recommended standardisation in aerodrome lighting, the direction of propeller rotation and distress procedure. Not until 1932 was it agreed that throttles should move forward to advance and backwards to decrease power. Later still it was agreed that the needles on the instruments should move 'in a clockwise direction to correspond with the turning movement of the screw'. Yet while international agreement was slow, the Committee showed itself remarkably far-sighted in urging, as early as 1935, that suitable wireless stations should be set up all over the world and that 'international airports should be provided with radio-electric devices with short-length wavelength reserved for blind landing'. And in 1937 there was instituted an Air Traffic Association code and an international teletype reservation system.

Then came the Gentlemen's Agreement row. It turned out to have far-reaching consequences for good, in that it brought realisation of the enormous administrative problems ahead. It precipitated civil flying out of the nursery and into the realisation that though it belonged to the same family as shipping and railways, it had a life and dimension exclusively its own. Most important of all, it could not be other than international.

In 1939, the Air Traffic Association was going to extend world-wide with Juan Trippe as President-Elect. Then the war intervened.

It was not until 1944 that aviation authorities met in Chicago. The nations were emerging from the war with far different attitudes to aviation. They had (at least for a time) learned the grim lesson of its misuse.

As a result of that conference, two of the most important bodies in civil flying emerged, the International Air Transport Association (IATA), successor to the earlier International Air Traffic Association, and the International Civil Aviation Organisation (ICAO).

The interested countries bickered over the economic regulation of traffic over the water jump and other routes. How many services? How many passengers? Who was to carry the mail? Who was to operate and what were to be the fares?

In 1946, a bilateral Anglo-American traffic meeting was held in Bermuda. By now, American Overseas Airways as well as Pan American were operating five services a week to the United Kingdom. The Civil Aeronautics Board had allowed both American airlines half the Atlantic frequencies each. They were also allowing Trans-World Airlines (TWA) in. BOAC tried to play the American companies off one against the other. But, despite the atmosphere in which it had begun, the conference proved a success.

Though there was no agreement on frequencies, an understanding was reached on the bases leased by Britain to America—and it was agreed that IATA should recommend the rates in regular Traffic Conferences, though each government reserved the right to approve the rates and fares before they became effective.

It is this use of universal free agreement that has been the hallmark of IATA's success. Accusations that it is a cartel have been levelled at the Association—but cartels allocate markets, control production and fix rates, and IATA does none of these things. Markets are allocated by inter-government agreements, and production is regulated by the capacity provisions of the same agreements. It is governments which have recognised that scheduled international air transport cannot be conducted without some form of price regulation, and who have decided to delegate this unenviable burden to IATA. Inevitably, with price control comes basic product uniformity. So free drinks may only be served in the First Class, and there are other limitations.

But areas of competition remain. Each airline can still entice the floating traveller by its décor, the number of its toilets and the length of its stewardesses' skirts. There were rows at one time on what constituted a sandwich, but there were also disputes on more fundamental things such as collision-avoidance over the Atlantic. Aircraft separation for safety evolved from the mass bombing raids. For the first ten years after the war, eastbound trips were flown at odd altitudes, westbound at evens, which was considered sufficient to avoid collisions.

In 1940, there had been only twenty-six North Atlantic movements. A year later Trans-Atlantic Area Control was set up in the drawing room of Redbrae House, Prestwick, and military and civil traffic movements increased enormously till in 1944 they numbered 16,218. From the end of the war till the mid-60s, oceanic control and radio communication was maintained by Prestwick and Shannon. By that time, crossings were over 70,000 a year, and it was agreed to centre oceanic control at Prestwick and the radio communication centre at Shannon.

But traffic went on increasing, so that there were 100,000 big jet crossings a year as well as a large number of propeller aircraft trips. Most eastbound traffic wanted to leave New York in the early evening. Most westbound traffic wanted to leave Europe in the early afternoon. There was a further complication in that the jets wanted to fly at their most economic altitude (around 33,000 ft).

A vast conglomeration of aircraft resulted, not only round the terminals, but also along the Great Circle crossing which they all preferred because it was shortest. In summer it was three times more congested than in winter, due to the influx of American tourists. There were no route restraints. Aircraft left from a variety of departure points, all with different upper wind forecasts and all with their own ideas for selecting the optimum route. So intertwined were the flight paths that it became a fairly common expression in Air Traffic Control circles to refer to the Atlantic as 'a bucket of worms'. There was no obligation to stay on the planned route, and ATC's job became increasingly difficult when one or more aircraft 'followed its nose'. The risk of collisions increased daily, particularly as most aircraft flew at Mach .82 (82 per cent of the speed of sound).

A system had been introduced, aiming at affording a degree of organisation by the definition of a daily track structure for the mainstream Atlantic traffic. Tracks were evolved one above the other, 120 miles apart, Gander Oceanic Control being in charge of all traffic to 30° West, Shanwick Oceanic Control from 30° West in the particular area of the Atlantic.

But this meant that aircraft might have to fly 250-odd miles north or south of their desired track in order to get on their allotted tramway. That meant delays on schedules and more fuel being used. The airlines, through IATA and ICAO, sought a 90-mile separation, saying that their navigation was accurate enough never to need 120 miles to allow for possible errors.

The International Federation of Airline Pilots Association objected. They demanded 120 miles, and would not fly 90. Various radar tests on Atlantic navigation errors were carried out and eventually, after much argument, agreement was at last reached on a new idea—staggered separation—that pleased almost everybody. Instead of controllers having to reassess aircraft movements and being in a state of continual conflict between detection and resolution, now they feed aircraft out along trans-Atlantic tramways where they stay, all automated by means of an Apollo computer.

As you fly in your Jumbo, you will have aircraft at the same altitude but 120 miles away north and south, aircraft above and below you separated by 2000 feet, and aircraft 60 miles away north and south at 1000 feet above or below you.

So now fuel and time have been saved. And the risk of a collision is millions to one against. There never has been a collision on the Atlantic —and with the marvellous accuracy of the Inertial Navigation System, the probability of large errors of navigation (and therefore of your aircraft being out of position and constituting a collision risk) is extremely low. Safety is the number one priority on the water jump. Logic, commonsense and cooperation triumphed again.

Out of the conquest of wind and weather, the exclusions and the squabbles, has been born a new internationalism. Virtually any nationally accredited airline may join IATA on equal terms regardless of size, with an equal vote. Any binding agreement within a Traffic Conference can be vetoed by one member airline. And even when decisions have been taken by IATA, the governments concerned need not implement them. There are 1500 resolutions in the IATA Traffic Conference agreements alone, and with such flexibility it is difficult to see how anything manages to be achieved. Yet less than five per cent of the 1500 Traffic Conference resolutions have ever even been partly disapproved by any government.

Though ICAO has been the centre for developing international legal conventions, IATA has exercised much initiative in conventions on every aspect of liability, offences, security and safe carriage. In the field of the environment, it advises on noise and aircraft emissions. A world-wide service provides up-to-date aviation information, issuing studies on traffic and fare trends, forecasting the future, providing possible solutions to problems, making suggestions to improve profitability.

The Traffic Conferences make resolutions on tickets, waybills, baggage handling, customs, cargo, the whole machinery of moving people and goods internationally. With ICAO on all aspects of safety, with the International Telecommunications Union, with the World Meteorological Organisation and the International Organisation for Standardisation, IATA works to simplify and speed up airline operations across all international barriers.

Amongst IATA's achievements is the Clearing House, brainchild of KLM. This free service allows world airlines to settle centrally monthly accounts, often running to millions of dollars, for interline revenue transactions. A passenger may travel by several different airlines to his destination. The Clearing House, set up in London, sees each airline is paid for its own part, which saves a huge amount of complex accounting, often in many different currencies.

Round the fuselage of your Jumbo jet is an invisible cloak that has kept pace and faith with the technical developments of aviation. Because of this you fly safely over numerous national frontiers quickly, freely, unharried, and it has all been done by common consent and common sense in the furtherance of common interests. English is the common language.

Look at the sky! Watch the towering build up of clouds! Catch a glimpse every now and then of the dark foam-flecked sea below!

This is the terrible North Atlantic, the cruel sea—the safest, most highly technical, most efficient, best governed, most democratic, most international, least inflationary piece of the world's surface.

## *Fourteen:* Selling the Water Jump

For some time past now, there has been activity in the aisles. The cabin crew have been going up and down. The elevators to the galleys in the lower deck have been in operation. If you are in the First Class, you will have been served with pre-dinner drinks or champagne. You may have gone up the winding stairs to the lounge (on Pan American it is a dining-room) and studied a colourful eight course menu. In the Tourist Class, trolley carts have appeared, tables are pulled down for passengers from the seat in front, and your meal is served on a tray.

Initially after the war, there was only one class, and all airlines were trying to outdo the Atlantic liners and each other to make their service the best. Of the three selling factors—comfort, cost and speed—bearing in mind the luxury of the ships, initially the airline accent was on comfort. Passengers would be attracted to fly by the provision of the most succulent meals, served by the most competent stewards and the prettiest stewardesses.

The British were first to introduce a cabin attendant, and were also the first, in 1927, to introduce a luxury service with drinks and a five-course luncheon on the Imperial Airways Silver Wing service between London and Paris. The stewards had been through the hotel business, and quickly built up on the Paris run and the Empire boats an enviable reputation for courtesy and efficiency.

On Pan American's flying boats, too, the service was immaculate. Frozen food was carried, thawed out, and cooked in the air. In addition, experiments were carried out to find out how altitude affected cooking, which uncovered the facts that there was no effect on drip-coffee, but that water takes longer to boil and half a minute extra must be allowed on a three-minute egg.

Airlines were cossetting the passengers—turkey and cranberry sauce would be served on Thanksgiving Day and a full Christmas dinner, with all the trimmings, on 25th December.

Comfort was further enhanced by the Imperial Airways lightweight

[206]

chair, prototype of the one on board present-day airliners, in which a passenger could sit upright for meals, loll to read, recline to sleep.

Air France began to employ stewardesses in 1931. In America, Boeing Air Transport and United began to introduce them. They were regarded as airborne nurses to cope with air-sickness, ailments and accidents. Then World War II dried up the supply of nurses, and the airline accepted instead a high-school diploma, attractive appearance, pleasing personality and not over 5 ft 8 in in height.

Pan American at first employed none. In 1941, they admitted that 'passengers who have travelled extensively via domestic airlines frequently ask why Pan American Airways has stewards rather than stewardesses. The answer of course, is that the Clippers make long flights over great distances through isolated territory, and the job has always been considered a little too strenuous for a young woman.'

BOAC had similar sentiments. During the war, stewardesses had been operating on Sunderlands between Poole, Shannon and Lisbon. As soon as the war in Europe was over, the Corporation had begun exploring the possibility of employing more girls as stewardesses—but without enthusiasm. However, the Chairman had been approached by people with daughters who were keen to fly. He visited the USA and found that Pan American had selected eight girls and put them through training school at the end of 1943. Pan American's change of attitude was explained by the statement that, 'the assignment of each girl to flight duty will, in effect, relieve a man for war duty, since they will supplement the present staff of male stewards.' Pan American's ideal stewardess was 'blue-eyed with brown hair, poised and self-possessed, slender, 5 feet 3 inches tall, weighs 115 pounds, is 23 years old, actively engaged in some participant sport, an expert swimmer, a high-school graduate, with business training—and attractive.' Those first eight did so well, winning their wings and the right to carry merchant seamen's papers (another hereditary relic), that further courses and regular recruitment were arranged. Their uniform was light blue with a white blouse. It is now a stronger blue, with a pull-on cap. British Airways 747 uniform remains dark blue, but otherwise appears subject to as frequent change as Chairmen.

BOAC New York Sales Department emphasised that from a selling angle stewardesses must be employed on the North Atlantic. BOAC could get 'just as good-looking girls in England and the difference in their ways and speech may be an asset.' Back in London, the airline executives commented 'should be British—preferably lightweight', and 'they must be willing to undertake the duties of their task which should be described to them as similar to those of a domestic servant.'

On his return from America, BOAC's Chairman gave instructions that stewardesses were to be recruited for the North Atlantic. The reluctant

**The BOAC Catering School in 1947. The instructor demonstrates to trainees the correct method of balancing a tray.** (British Airways)

**BOAC Stewards and Stewardesses are inspected for clean hands and fingernails before going on duty.** (British Airways)

Catering Department approved the uniform which would 'consist of a replica of the steward's uniforms—in other words, the same white Eton jacket with facings and, in lieu of blue trousers, a blue skirt.'

The appointments would be, for the time being, confined to the North Atlantic and the age limits were 23–30 years. The pay offered was hardly an inducement. Even three years after the war, Stewards Second Class only received £189 a year, plus £78 cost of living, and no tips were allowed. Stewardesses were not to wear jewellery, other than wedding, engagement or signet rings. The girls would be required to undertake a ten-week course of training at the Catering Training School in the various aspects of the work, 'particularly as to the duties required of them as waitresses and elementary first aid.'

The training school was strictly disciplinarian. The exact height above the collar that stewardesses might wear their hair was demonstrated to them. One training school centre was held in an old convent school. After roll-call, hands and nails were held out and inspected for dirt or nicotine stains. Collars were checked for dandruff, stocking seams for a mathematical straightness. Trainee stewardesses waited at table, learned the theory of flight and the hierarchy of the Company. Facilities were not good and classes were sometimes held in the open with the trainee catering crew waiting on their instructors, who sat incongruously at perfectly set tables positioned on the grass.

Eventually on 4th November 1946, four stewardesses were posted to the North Atlantic run. BOAC issued press releases stressing they were stewardesses, not air hostesses, wanting particularly to avoid 'glamour and frivolity'.

So stewardesses became crew members on the Constellations on which I was then flying as First Officer. Whatever the initial forebodings might have been, they were a great success.

There remained the vexed matter of where the girl should sit. And more vexed still whether she should be allowed in the galley or the crew

**Stewards at the Catering School watch Stewardesses practising the art of picking things up off the floor while carrying a loaded tray.    (British Airways)**

compartment. It was discovered that 'the Standing Instructions for most of the American airlines are that entry into the cockpit is very emphatically laid down not to exceed 30 seconds.' The resultant British order stated that 'the stewardesses' duties do not require them to enter the Galley or the Crew Compartment and they are to remain in the Passenger Compartment throughout the flight.'

In July 1947 the instruction had been modified—the stewardess was now allowed in the galley to prepare baby foods. However, a month later, the British Airline Pilots' Association had expressed dissatisfaction with the rule regarding entry into the crew compartment, and the Catering Department was asked for any sound reason why the embargo should be maintained.

So, step by step, the North Atlantic stewardess won the freedom of the ship. Just as the women pilots had shown the men that they could do

**A BOAC** Stewardess with a typical meal served to passengers travelling in a Constellation.                                                                **(British Airways)**

JETPLANE · AVIÓN A CHORRO
8 MILLAS POR MINUTO (8 MILES A MINUTE)
A 8 MILLAS DE ALTURA (8 MILES HIGH)
"SIN VIBRACIÓN (NO VIBRATION)

**The BOAC Catering School prepares for the worldwide impact of the Comet airliner in 1952.** **(British Airways)**

the water jump in the early days, so the stewardess showed her mettle. For the trip was a gruelling one—they were continually on the move and the stewardess was always walking up and down the aisle, bringing trays, drinks, coping with children, hour after hour. Then delays were frequent. In 1947, fifty per cent of BOAC's Constellations arrived in New York 24 hours late (now the figure is 1 per cent or less for the big jets).

BOAC began to think they had overdone the frivolity bit, and now began to be concerned about fatigue and sickness. The girls on American Overseas Airlines all slipped (that is, changed crews, the aircraft going on) at Gander. It was pointed out that the BOAC westbound schedule, 'specifies for departure London Airport at 10 o'clock at night, and although the trip Rineanna/Gander is made during the night, whereby the stewardess may, or may not be able to sit down, the meal schedule instructs that a full lunch is served Gander/New York. This meal, therefore, is served when the Catering Staff have already experienced some 16 hours, at least, from time of departure London Airport. A further full-scale meal is served to members of the crew between New York and Montreal—some 21 hours after leaving London Airport. The arrival at Montreal is scheduled for 11 pm GMT, the total run occupying 25 hours in all . . .'

On the Tourist service, there was only a steward and a stewardess for 68 passengers and six operating crew on a Constellation. In the First Class the work was just as strenuous.

But more and more passengers were buying tickets for the air Atlantic crossing. In 1949, 273,000 did the water jump, about a quarter of the total traffic. And while the number of sea passengers increased sedately, the number who went by air did a big jump every year.

\*       \*       \*

While Pan Am's profits and those of other airlines were increasing, BOAC's world-wide losses were £8 million at the end of 1947. What was needed was a more positive approach at the top to selling, and Sir Miles Thomas was appointed Deputy Chairman of BOAC, preparatory to becoming full Chairman and Chief Executive.

Sir Miles had been asked to get things moving, to bring action and profitability into British involvement in the water jump. But like Griselda, he was asked to make gold from straw. The essential ingredient, a viable British North Atlantic aircraft, was missing. What was present, according to Sir Miles, was a big gap between dreams and implementation, accounts in a mess, an abundance of Whitehall interference and a belief that money did not matter.

There was now in charge someone who had that quality with which Woods Humphery had been branded—commercialism—and one who had vast engineering and selling experience in the motor industry.

He slashed spending, reduced staff, cut the Corporation's aircraft types from nine to five, improved maintenance. According to those who worked under him—particularly on the engineering side—there were no hesitations with Sir Miles. He never interfered, but was there when he was needed, and knew enough about engineering to talk their language.

Within the Corporation, he had found a shy-violet approach to advertising and public relations. It was British to be tight-lipped and modest. The Civil Service avoided standing up for itself or its associates. The press had had a heyday, pointing to the Air Terminal clock being slow as epitomising British civil aviation.

A marketing operation was mounted. Sir Miles had first to sell the idea of selling to the salesmen of BOAC, then to project the Corporation, to sell British courtesy, sell British competence even if he couldn't yet sell British aeroplanes.

BOAC on the water jump began to do splendidly, in 1948 completing 503 crossings, carrying 12,981 passengers, 150,786 kilos of cargo and 180,794 kilos of mail. The Corporation had the highest average actual payload of all carriers and carried more passengers per aircraft than any of the other eight operators—KLM, Air France, Pan Am, AOA, TWA, SAS, Swissair and Sabena, all operating American aircraft, mostly Constellations and DC4s.

The other airlines on the water jump began new techniques to attract passengers. Pan American introduced the new Boeing Stratocruiser to

Trans Canada Airlines operated North Star Airliners across the Atlantic—modified and pressurised DC4's with Rolls-Royce Merlin engines.　　　　　(Air Canada)

The Stratocruiser *Cathay*, engines running, glittering from nose to tail, about to taxi out to take off on BOAC's first Stratocruiser service, 6 December 1949.　　　(British Airways)

the Atlantic on 2nd June 1949. This aircraft was a natural for passenger appeal, with its twisted turret staircase leading down to a cosy downstairs bar, and it also had a number of bunks.

BOAC had also eventually obtained Treasury approval and bought ten Stratocruisers at a cost of $1.5 million each, and now went to work with great zeal on preparations for their introduction.

At that time, comfort was still favoured as the main selling factor. There was still a feeling amongst the British, inherited from the Grand Tour, that travel was the prerogative of the rich. They were very conscious that people were apprehensive of flying, particularly over a vast ocean, and needed cossetting. The superb luxury of the liners' grand saloons made eighteen hours cooped up in a tin box undignified, unBritish, and certainly not worth the same money. The air passenger must be made to feel a king.

It was proposed for the inaugural Stratocruiser flight that a famous personality should be carried, preferably Winston Churchill. The Port of New York Authority promised the attendance of its Chairman. At that time the Authority was in the process of transferring its operations from La Guardia to Idlewild (now Kennedy) and it was decided that a plaque should be carried to Idlewild, a present from Heathrow as a 'hands across the sea' gesture.

But Winston Churchill was not free on the day of the inaugural flight, so Sir John D'Albiac, Commandant of London Airport and Lady D'Albiac agreed to be the VIPs aboard. There was one other highly secret final sales touch—a bulldog was to be carried as a personification of the British fighting spirit. The secrecy surrounding this passenger was partly for surprise effect, partly because it might die en route. Despite the special oxygen tent which had been made for it, canine experts feared the dog might have breathing difficulties in flight.

The dog was to be called CAVU, a meteorological term meaning Ceiling and Visibility Unlimited, symbolising British high hopes on the water jump. According to the official handout, scheduled for safe Idlewild arrival, CAVU 'will not only have travelled in the height of luxury aboard a Stratocruiser, but, in addition, will be dressed in the height of dog fashion in a smart coat embossed with a Speedbird and collared with a plaque, giving vital statistics of its mission in life.'

After suitably lavish farewells, the first Stratocruiser service departed from London on 6th December 1949. The aircraft had originally been bought by the Scandinavian Airlines system (SAS), which had decided that Stratocruisers were too costly to operate. Polished a glittering silver, this was its big night. Besides Sir John and Lady D'Albiac, journalists and other passengers and CAVU, Charles Smith, Chief Statistician of BOAC was on board. He had written the Stratocruiser Cruise Control Charts, but he had an added responsibility—that of looking after CAVU. The firm who made the oxygen tent had leaked the story to the press, so that the dog was already famous. It was, therefore, vitally important that he arrived at Idlewild in good shape.

The North Atlantic winter and the strong west winds awaited them. Because of the strength of the headwinds there was no possibility of flying to New York direct, despite the relatively light load and full tanks. The captain decided that even Gander was too far, and set course for Keflavik in Iceland.

Of that first Stratocruiser service, Charles Smith wrote, 'at intervals, between checking out my Cruise Control manual, I patrolled the passenger cabin to find CAVU, on one occasion, being sick as a dog. On arrival at Keflavik, we were told that a Constellation, en route for Gander, was returning with a sick engine, and please, could we take on their load. The Captain decided that this would be in the firm's best interests, on the argument that if we arrived at New York with a 100 per cent load factor, this would indeed impress the waiting multitude.

'In the event we spent about 6 hours at Keflavik because the first attempt to load the baggage into the Stratocruiser's holds proved abortive and consequently the whole lot had to be re-packed from scratch, in torchlight so as to preserve the aircraft's batteries for start-up. The Captain then discovered he couldn't make New York non-stop so we set off for Gander. During that sector, we ran into a jet stream of 180 knots on the nose.'

'Arriving at Gander later than the flight plan, we landed in light slush but with no obvious problems. A 45-minute transit was declared, so we all went "ashore" for a leg-stretch. Five minutes before we were due to re-board, the engineers appeared on the scene to say that the light slush had caused damage to our landing flaps and, therefore, there would be a delay. Shortly afterwards, I discovered my canine friend prostrate in the Flight Operations office showing all the signs of immediate heart failure. Finding a suitable piece of rope, I then took him for "walkies" which was fine for him but hell for me because I kept falling down on the ice. Even so, I soon realised that this Arctic climate was not his "cup of tea" either (this after I'd had to cut him free from a tethering icicle which formed every time he cocked his leg).

'Four hours later we were told that the flaps had been repaired. You can imagine our reactions, however, as while the passengers were in the process of boarding, freezing rain started to fall. This left no option but to call a night stop so orders were given to get the passengers' light bags out of the holds. This led to the discovery that the water pipes had burst and some 55 gallons had cascaded down into the holds. I have a vivid memory to this day of Lady D'Albiac emptying out a good eight pints from her night-stop bag. We, therefore, set up a series of washing

**The flight deck of a Stratocruiser coming in for a night landing.**
(British Airways)

lines in one of the hangars which added a note of pre-Christmas festivity to the scene. Apparently the pipes froze up while we were delayed at Keflavik and thawed while the aircraft was on the ground at Gander.'

Back in the Public Relations offices of London and New York, apprehension, concern and frantic rearrangements of ceremonies and parties was going on. There were fears that the British journalists on board and the American journalists hanging around Idlewild would have a field day. The Chief Information Officer signalled the New York PRO, 'I trust you will be able to persuade Miss Patricia O'Brien, who is writing the story for the *Daily Mirror*, to deal gently with us.'

The Stratocruiser finally arrived in New York twenty-seven hours late, the Constellation for which it had done its Good Samaritan act at Keflavik having arrived ten hours earlier.

The bruised and battered New York PRO signalled back to his Chief, 'You will, I think, agree with me if I suggest the less anybody says about this, the better. It was unquestioningly one of the most revolting lash-ups in the history, and my personal opinion is that BOAC seldom has a lash-up, but when it does, it is a proper one.'

A lash-up? Not at all! The journalists had in fact been gentle. The important thing was that they had got there, and all in one piece. BOAC had learned more about operating Stratocruisers in those two days than they would have done in two months.

CAVU arrived fighting fit, and according to the PRO 'was a howling success with the Port of New York Authority and everybody else'. He posed with aplomb. Photographs in the newspapers showed him wearing a helmet riding in a Port of New York Authority Fire Car, and sitting on BOAC's counter at Idlewild. The PRO had signed off, 'Yours for no more inaugurals.' But in the event, it had all been a success.

Now BOAC proceeded to organise a regular luxury service on their Stratocruisers. In June 1949 Pan American had put on their first *President* service. Seventeen berths were provided plus 39 sleeperettes, seven-course dinners with champagne, orchids and perfume for the ladies and cigars for the men. The cabin staff comprised four stewards and a stewardess. Air France had put on its ooh-la-la *Parisienne* service. TWA was operating luxurious *Ambassador* flights. BOAC's Advertising Manager in New York was having difficulty working out a good plan of attack to counter the selling points of these services. Some action equivalent to the provision of orchids for the ladies and red carpet on the tarmac for despatch and arrival would, he thought, become standard drill, and he wrote to London for further suggestions for BOAC's super-luxury service. The Sales Manager felt that the only considerable advantage the American luxury services offered was the provision of an extra steward. Nevertheless, BOAC went ahead with its own plans.

First of all, the name: what was more impressive than a President and an Ambassador? Charles Smith quoted to the Information Department two sentences from an article on British butterflies: 'The Monarch is unique in that it comes to us across the Atlantic from North America, which is its real home. It is longer than any of our native species, rich chestnut-brown in colour, with black veins and a few small white spots.'

The name *Monarch* was decided on. Further suggestions were that a short distance of rubber matting with white rails be provided before

**Left :** CAVU on arrival at Idlewild (now Kennedy), with BOAC Receptionist Sheila Bevan, Air Marshal Sir John D'Alblac, Lady D'Albiac, and Mr Erik Nelson (Deputy General Manager, Western Division.
*Above :* CAVU acknowledges his welcome at New York from the BOAC ticket counter.
(British Airways)

the steps for mounting the aircraft (accepted). Another was that the symbol should be a golden crown (accepted). Another was that there should be a detachable archway on which was blazoned *Welcome to London* or *Welcome to New York*, as appropriate (accepted).

A suggestion that the downstairs bar should be called the Savoy Lounge was discounted. The General Manager preferred 'something rather British. The George and Dragon occurs to me, rather too many words for good advertising, I agree, but perhaps better than the King's Head or the Queen's Arms.'

In the end, it was agreed that for a small surcharge on the Monarch (but smaller than that charged on the Pan Am President) the passengers would get free cocktails followed by a dinner of caviare, turtle soup, cold Inverness salmon, spring chicken with Wiltshire bacon and peas, Hampshire strawberries with fresh double cream, frivolities, cheese and fresh fruit. There was to be free champagne and any other liquor. Free Monarch ties were to be provided for the men, Monarch luggage labels for the crew. The only thing missing in comparison to the President was the orchid.

The inaugural Monarch service was scheduled for departure at 18.30 on 1 March 1951. The one fly in the ointment was that due to the Strato-cruisers' limited range a refuelling stop at Gander was necessary on the westbound flight, and BOAC's pre-service advertising had been a trifle too enthusiastic. The Advertising Manager wrote to the Chairman, confirming that instructions had been issued to delete 'Non-Stop service London/New York from such press advertising wherever possible. Non-stop will be changed to Direct.'

Of that successful first Monarch service, one enthusiastic journalist wrote that after the gourmet dinner bedtime came, 'and it really was bedtime for a number of the passengers. True, they paid extra for their beds, but they had the comfort of mattresses, pillows, blankets and crisp white linen sheets. The bunks pulled down from the side of the aircraft, where in daytime they're hidden.'

The lowering of the bunks and the making up of the beds was arduous for the cabin crew—indeed their work on the luxury service was non-stop. The Monarch departed London at 20.00 GMT where they had already been on duty nearly three hours. Then there was the serving of the elaborate meals, with one steward on duty all the time in the downstairs bar. The service arrived in New York at 15.45 GMT (10.45 am local).

Other selling factors were thought up by airlines. In the early days, a dollar bill suitably signed was given to those who had done the crossing, and was called a 'short snorter'. BOAC modified this idea and gave each passenger an illuminated scroll, signed by the Captain, declaring them members of the Winged Order of Pond Hoppers.

'Phoebus Apollo, the Sun God, Monarch of the Sky', it read, 'have under my special care those who perform the Biggest Hop of All—namely across the Herring-Pond, as the Atlantic Ocean has been vulgarly termed by mortals; and hereby declare that Hoppers of the Herring-Pond shall henceforth be set apart from all men—and that embraces women too.'

But scrolls and presents and super-luxury gradually gave way as big selling points for the majority of passengers—though first class at a premium continued to be maintained.

Attention now began to be diverted from comfort to *cost*.

\*　　\*　　\*

There was a ready-made low-fare westbound market for ships: the emigrants. Between 1815 and 1854 over four million left for North America from British ports alone. The fare was cheap, but the emigrants were treated like slaves. They had to bring their own food and cooking facilities. During Atlantic storms, they were battened down in the holds. Disasters were common. In 1848, the *Ocean Monarch* caught fire and all four hundred on board were burned to death. In 1854, the *City of Glasgow* departed Liverpool with 480 souls and was never heard of again. Cholera raged. Many of the early passengers either died or were drowned en route. Driven to do something, the American authorities fined captains ten dollars for each corpse delivered to the New World.

Now after the Second World War, emigrants were comparatively few, but they travelled safely and comfortably—the vast majority of them still by ship. For the water jump, businessmen and the rich were considered the sort of people to attract. The rest had not yet cottoned on to air travel. Salaries were small in comparison to those paid in America, and far more people wanted to visit Europe than the USA. In addition, the Stratocruiser and the Constellation 049 were the only Atlantic aircraft BOAC had, and neither were really suitable for conversion to the high-density seating of tourist travel.

In comparison, Juan Trippe had long propounded the philosophy of cutting costs, maintaining, as do the charter operators today, that neither speed nor comfort could compare with the hard fact of a rock-bottom priced trans-Atlantic ticket. 'The tourist plane and the bomber,' Trippe said, 'have for years been racing each other to a photofinish. In my opinion, however, the tourist plane, if allowed to move forward unshackled by political boundaries and economic restrictions, will win this race between education and catastrophe. Mass travel by air may prove to be more significant to world destiny than the atom bomb.'

Pan American began pressing for Tourist fares in 1948. But the stumbling block was the newly formed IATA regulation which required that fares be unanimously agreed and approved by all members' governments. Agreement was not reached. Another argument started, this time under the banner of cheap North Atlantic fares.

Because they did not have the right aircraft, once again the British were forced into the role of reactionaries opposing progress. They had now put their money on speed. The pure jet Comet and the turbo-jet Britannia when they came into service would warrant a surcharge even over the first-class fare, which would hardly go with cramped conditions.

But at that same time, the Americans were pressing to *reduce* fares. They wanted a tourist service—and once again they had the right aircraft for the job. In September, 1950, Juan Trippe had ordered 18 DC6Bs. If the laurels for conquering the North Atlantic winter go to the Liberator, if the laurels for the first scheduled year-round pressurised service as we know it today go to the Constellation, then the laurels for the tourist water jump belong to Douglas's band of brothers, bigger brothers and biggest brothers.

That family is a clear example of American aviation heredity. The DC4 had a wingspan of 118 feet, length of 94 feet, and all-up weight of 73,000 lb and a speed of 192 mph. The DC6 had the same wingspan, but was longer and faster. The 6B again simply had its fuselage stretched to 109 feet, and now the all-up weight was 127,000, and with 3350 horse-power engines giving more than twice the thrust, the speed was up to 340 mph. The last of the piston-engined line, the DC7C's span was increased to 128 feet and its length to 113 feet, so that now its passenger load was over a hundred.

Seats in the 6B were arranged five abreast, so that now 82 passengers could be accommodated instead of 52. It was proposed to introduce simple meals on a tray with coffee and the minimum of cabin attendants, but such spartan packaging was relieved by mid-blue seat covers and carpets, white headrests, cream walls and pink curtains.

The other North Atlantic airlines began to do their sums. As always, BOAC considered every alternative in their hand. The new Rolls-Royce-engined DC4s called Argonauts were a possibility. Another war-time derivative, the Hermes IV, this time from the Halifax bomber, was another possibility, but production had fallen behind schedule. The Boeing Stratocruiser's tourist potential, with 84 seats, was examined, but then what would operate the first-class service? The only possibility was to cram 68 seats into BOAC's six 43-seater 049 Constellations, and the cost of conversion would be £50,000 each aircraft, over twice the previous estimate.

Meetings on tourist fares were convened at Bermuda and in New York in 1951, at which the invaluable Charles Smith was BOAC's delegate. Not surprisingly, his brief was to say no to everything. Not surprisingly either, Pan American gave as little information as possible, and made sure that they did not agree to anything that would tie their hands in the future. They reckoned on no appreciable loss from first-class travel. TWA calculated the diversion would be as high as 80 per cent. BOAC sales side guessed 40 per cent, but thought it might be possible to carry first-class and tourist in the same aircraft. BOAC also tried to restrict the DC4 type, though they knew it would be impossible.

Pan Am were pressing for a year-round first-class reduction from $395 to $375 one-way New York–London with a 10 per cent discount for return, against a tourist fare of $225 with the same discount for the round trip, to undercut the ships. They tabled a paper at Bermuda to make their point, which was a most significant document. In it, they pointed out that the present first-class air fare was 10.87 cents per mile compared to 10 cents first-class sea fare. But the tourist sea fare was only 4–5 cents a mile and they feared a flood to the ships. They quoted the *Queen Mary* return fares: on season $750 first, $470 cabin and $340 tourist: off season $730, $450 and $330, and warned that it was significant that for every three air passengers, seven still went by sea. Pan Am reckoned airlines could easily afford the low fare, in that the cost had been calculated as $144.02 flying operations, $38.26 for maintenance and $18.67 for depreciation, adding up to $200.95 per North Atlantic aircraft hour.

Such costs were compared with the Brabazon's £400 an hour estimate, and the figures sent a shiver down BOAC's spine. The one ray of light was that the CAB had rejected the Bermuda resolution on tourist operation, and this was interpreted as meaning that the Board would insist on a seating density that would compel a certain amount of discomfort to discourage first-class travellers from using the service. BOAC policy for future meetings was to limit the maximum space for each tourist passenger to 8.2 square feet (including lavatories and galleys) against the 12 square feet of a Stratocruiser. The service planned was to be as spartan as possible 'with no alcoholic drinks, lunch boxes only and a maximum of one cabin attendant', no newspapers, no nightstop bags and free luggage limited to 20 kilos. In this approach, they had the backing of the Treasury which did not want to see the Cunarders forced out of business and everyone flocking to the DC6Bs.

No agreement was reached on any of the main points. BOAC alone opposed complete freedom on the number of services to be run per week and the meeting came to a standstill on the tourist fare to be charged. TWA proposed $285, Pan Am $250. An almost infinite variety of fare combinations were suggested by the BOAC delegate, but he found Pan Am 'entirely proof against my arguments, to the effect that it might be wiser to start with the higher fare and reduce it later if it was found possible'.

From New York in November, 1951, the BOAC Chairman reported that the Atlantic tourist rate, 'seems to be on in a big way'. Simple arithmetic showed that 43 Constellation seats at $395 each produced only 53 dollars more than 68 at $249. BOAC bowed to the inevitable, but briefed its delegate for the IATA meeting at Nice on 27 November not to go below $250, and to 'guard against the facilities provided being so good as to destroy the whole conception of tourist services, and thus make a very heavy dilution of the first-class traffic quite inevitable.'

Operators without the right aircraft opposed tourist fares at Nice, but the concept of the cheap water jump had been established. The British government agreed that it was quite impossible to prevent the idea of cheap fares from spreading. The only real point of issue was the fare.

Having accepted the tourist concept, BOAC wanted to make sure they were the first to operate. The Sales Director wished 'to ensure that BOAC operates the first North Atlantic Tourist service out of London, suggested 1 May 1952, on the following schedule:

| | | | |
|---|---|---|---|
| Depart | L.A.P. | 00.01 | GMT |
| Arrive | Prestwick | 01.45 | |
| Depart | Prestwick | 02.45 | |
| Arrive | Keflavik | 04.45 | |
| Depart | Keflavik | 05.45 | |
| Arrive | Gander | 10.15 | |
| Depart | Gander | 11.15 | |
| Arrive | New York | 16.00 | (11.00 local) |

But things did not work out that way. The Constellation 049s had to be flown out to California, to wait their turn in the queue at Lockheed for conversion to tourist carriers. Meanwhile BOAC ran into friction with its North Atlantic crews. The management had seen this as the opportunity to dispense with North Atlantic pay for pilots operating tourist services.

North Atlantic pay (£300 for captains, £250 for first officers) was introduced when the North Atlantic was being pioneered and considered dangerous. It was regarded as anomalous by BOAC pilots on other routes, particularly as the North Atlantic was shaping up to being the best organised and safest in the world. Nevertheless it was administratively unwise to dispense with it at this time when tourist captains (of which I was one) were being asked to carry loads with correspondingly less fuel in discomfort round the houses. After protest and argument, the matter was settled amicably with the tourist pilots retaining North Atlantic pay.

On 24 May, three weeks after the hopeful date set for the beginning of the tourist service, I flew as a passenger to California by an American airline to pick up a converted BOAC 049. On the morning we took off from Burbank to go back to New York, a yellow smog covered the airfield, and I was somewhat concerned about the hills surrounding it. Easy Mike had a notoriously long take-off, but on this occasion she leapt into the air and I climbed merrily up onto airways over Arizona.

On my way west as a passenger, the continent had been covered in cloud. Now for the first time I watched America go by under my wing from coast to coast. I went back into the passenger compartment and was for the moment overwhelmed by the spectacle of all those neat blue rows of empty seats. There seemed to be many more than twenty-five above the forty-three of the first-class service. I sat down in one of them and was surprised at the leg room.

Flying east, night falls fast and over the Ohio plains it was already dusk. A hundred miles away we saw the big bonfire of glittering New York and half an hour later the tiny necklace of perimeter and runway lights on the dark peninsular of Idlewild. Ten minutes later we were in the circuit, and I followed a Pan Am DC6B tourist service from London down to land.

Pan Am had beaten BOAC to it. They had inaugurated the first tourist service on 1 May 1952 in *Clipper Liberty Bell*. One-way fare had been agreed as $270 ($486 round trip) and the operation was called 'The Rainbow', still the name for Pan Am cheap flights.

BOAC went on operating the 049s. In actuality, we managed to avoid going to Keflavik every westbound trip by careful routing via the winds on the top of low-pressure areas. The passengers seemed to be quite comfortable, but there were queues outside the toilets. Two differences, however, were marked. On the first-class service, it was usual for the Captain to go back and talk to the passengers, but now there were too many. And up front, due to the pressures on the one steward and the absence of a stewardess, the number of cups of tea and coffee that came up to the cockpit fell sharply.

But receipts rose. Very rarely was there an empty seat, and usually there was a long waiting list to get on. I saw the *Queen Mary* in mid-Atlantic that winter, looking minute from 23,000 feet. We were as usual crammed to the gills, and I wondered how much spare space she had on board.

In fact, the tourist fares made a much bigger hole in the Atlantic liners' hulls than the super-luxury service. But the ships were still afloat and paying for themselves between New York and Europe. Three years after the introduction of tourist services, ships were still beating aircraft in numbers of passengers carried across the Atlantic—though the airline percentage of the total traffic had risen to 46 per cent.

Like comfort, cost had not proved lethal. Now of that trinity of water jump selling points, there remained only—speed.

*     *     *

Watching the swift expansion of mail and passenger traffic over the water jump after the Second World War, the thoughts of airline operators next turned to the possibilities of air cargo. Bennett had shown the way in his 1938 Mercury flight. But comparing the huge capacity of trans-Atlantic shipping with the tiny and operationally expensive holds of aircraft, cargo possibilities still looked restricted. Such freight as was carried was of the kind for which speed or special care was essential—gold, jewels, flowers, oysters, grouse, fashions, newsreels, cream and animals.

BOAC, with its background of operating the old Empire routes, had carried in their antique Yorks from India to the UK a variety of animals—monkeys, tigers, horses, elephants and every sort of snake. They had gained valuable experience in the handling of this traffic half-way between 'human and cargo'.

Cargo can be called the catalyst of civil aviation. For cargo in the form of mail was the generating force for most airlines. Imperial Airways was created primarily as a mail carrier, particularly of diplomatic mail to the Empire, and the first cargo container was the dustbin bolted to the floor of a flying boat that served as a diplomatic mail locker. In the days of the Buttercup Route across the water jump I have carried diplomatic mail and gold bars in a tin cupboard that rarely shut, let alone locked, though happily none ever went missing. The Empire flying boat ran principally for the mail, with a dozen passengers squeezed in when possible.

American civil aviation had begun with the army mail run between New York and Washington in 1918. Pan American had expanded world-wide financed by mail contracts, and by 1951 the concept of large-scale freight over the water jump was well advanced in America.

The Berlin airlift of 1948/49, in which BOAC and Pan Am participated, showed that if enough money was spent, the most bulky cargoes could go by air. The onward carriage of monkeys across the water jump was a further factor encouraging BOAC to turn its thoughts towards increasing North Atlantic air freight. Thousands of monkeys were flown by Yorks into London from Delhi and Calcutta. They were on their way to America where a tremendous effort was being made to fight polio. Monkeys were also being used for other medical experiments and psychological tests, and the transport of them built up steadily in the early 1950s, accelerating even more with the Salk vaccine breakthrough and its availability to the general public.

On 21 June 1951 the Commercial Director of BOAC wrote to the Traffic Manager that in recent talks with the Sales Director 'we touched on developing monkey traffic over the North Atlantic by means of a weekly freighter, estimated to earn $250,000 westbound.' Much discussion followed this suggestion. The traffic was profitable. But monkey transportation had its own peculiar problems, and could the aircraft be spared?

The possibilities were examined. A Boeing Stratocruiser was rejected as the hold would only carry 250 monkeys, and of a full load of 500, half would have to be accommodated in the passenger cabin.

BOAC had learned by bitter experience on the Yorks that even after repeated fumigation and steam hosing, it was not possible completely to deodorise the cabin after the monkeys. That meant that if they sent a plane-load of monkeys to New York, on the return eastbound flight they could carry no passengers. Huge losses were estimated for the round trip.

On the other hand, by not offering onward carriage of monkeys to New York, BOAC was losing out to competition such as KLM, who did.

By mid-July 1951 there was a fear that BOAC might lose the Eastern monkey traffic altogether, unless a through service to New York was forthcoming. York aircraft, flying via the Azores or Keflavik, were considered, then the Argonauts. But there were no Argonauts immediately available, and even if there were an annual operating loss of £90,000 was gloomily forecast.

Meanwhile, an independent company, Airwork, had applied to the Minister of Civil Aviation for permission to operate a freighter service over the water jump.

Without a suitable aircraft, and now under political pressure, an undertaking was given by BOAC not to operate freighters over the Atlantic for a year. The Corporation got the monkeys across in the belly holds of passenger aircraft, but it was obvious that the Corporation must have its own cargo aircraft.

In the end, three events decided the cargo issue.

In the year 1952 Pan American began an all-cargo trans-Atlantic DC6A freight service in competition with Seaboard and Western, who were already operating DC4 freighters. At about the same time, BOAC operated a Constellation to New York and return as a freighter, and it was a great financial success. Thirdly, KLM began stepping up their cargo frequencies.

Three months later, a team from BOAC, amongst them Mr Koster, present Cargo Manager (Europe), arrived in New York to see just how the American air-freight business was done. They were deeply impressed with what they saw. They found one all-cargo line, Slick, which charged the Navy only 11 cents per ton mile, due to a 100 per cent load factor and a nine-hour-a-day aircraft utilisation. The American operators had undertaken a vast market research study. They were of the unanimous

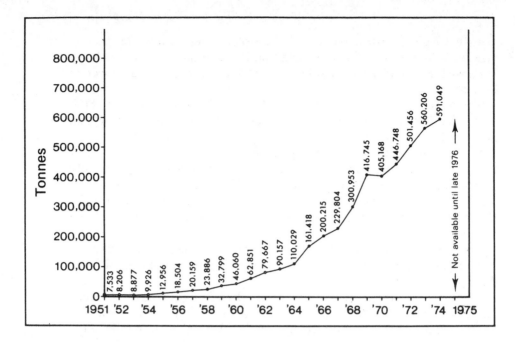

The growth of cargo handled by IATA carriers on the North Atlantic route.
*(figures obtained from IATA and CAA)*

opinion that air freight was a specialised operation, best organised separately from the passenger side.

On the team's return to the UK they recommended exactly that, a separate air-freight division and wrote, 'the North Atlantic is the most important part of our international route operating pattern . . . our competitors are already taking business away from us and priority should, therefore, be given to the North Atlantic.'

One official wrote 'this is one route where there is no justification for a freighter. Several of our competitors have tried and subsequently cancelled the service.' There was much to support his view. The 53,329-ton *United States* had been launched and was to smash the *Queen Mary*'s fourteen-year-old record and win the Blue Riband on her maiden crossing in 3 days 10 hours and 40 minutes. The ships in 1952 were still doing well.

Nevertheless, an Atlantic freighter service was agreed. The turbo-prop Britannia was the obvious choice of aircraft, but it would be years before a freighter version could be developed. BOAC sought quotations from American and British charter companies to operate a freight service for them. Slick were too busy to bother. Flying Tigers quoted $1.48 per ton mile for the New York to London round trip. The British airlines' rates were even higher.

The modern way with cargo: containers being loaded into a 747.          (British Airways)

So once again, the British had to be cautious. The generally held view, reflected in technical books and newspapers, was that the aeroplane might possibly keep pace with trans-Atlantic liners on passengers, but would never have a hope of competing on cargo. The British shipping companies were now beginning to be concerned about diminishing passengers, but they rarely gave a thought to the capture of freight. The opinion even within the airlines was that air-freight space exceeded demand. Besides they had no spare aircraft for freight.

But as progress in aircraft design accelerated, more older aircraft insufficiently speedy to attract the traveller were modified for freight, and the cargo fleets rapidly expanded. BOAC and Pan Am ran DC7Cs, and with the arrival of the jets many propeller-driven aircraft were turned over to cargo.

For cargo was now big business. Early in 1966 BOAC had ordered two 707 all-cargo aircraft, and a further one was ordered a year later.

Other airlines were doing the same thing. The accompanying graph will show just how the freight built up, how it compared with the experts' forecasts, and how despite the handicaps, the air cargo business cleared the water jump with a clean pair of heels.

And the monkeys? They still continue to fly the water jump, not only more swiftly, but more comfortably. Strict IATA regulations for animals are laid down, which say what leg, or beak, or tail room they must have, what they shall be fed and when, each species has its cage requirements and attendants specified, its behaviour pattern anticipated from aardvarks through dolphins, maggots, magpies and hippopotami to woolly monkeys and zebras. There are excellent animal hostels both sides of the water jump. They have moved from midway between human and freight to a little nearer human.

Forms and facilities have been speeded up, and round-the-clock customs introduced wherever possible. IATA introduced its own standardised Air Waybill which covers every item of movement and charges, for standardisation is essential for fast trans-Atlantic freight movement. Though IATA has nothing to do with deciding what airlines fly what routes or with how much capacity, at its world-wide conferences recommendations are made on uniform cargo rates on a voluntary and self-regulating basis.

At the same time, more cargo is attracted not only by the most efficient automatic handling and computerisation, but by a special discount system.

By the mid-1950s, the idea of bringing all packages that a consigner was sending into one package caught on, leading actually in the late 1950s to the first container programme. IATA had done much research on bulk containers, and now further discounts were offered for goods in standardised containers which were specifically designed for aircraft cargo compartments. Those containers became more sophisticated, and are now of two basic types—one of tri-wall cardboard boxes for comparatively small loads, and the other a really strong container carrying huge amounts which is fastened to the aircraft structure.

Up and up went the air cargo, and it is estimated that 20,000 million ton kilometres will be flown in 1975, doubling by 1980. Of that, a large proportion will be across the water jump. And now there are 747 freighters.

But nothing is certain, nothing is quite as expected. No one *knew* how much air cargo over the North Atlantic would increase or how to deal with it. When it was clearly a roaring success, instead of tents and huts, huge warehouses were built and every sort of mechanical handling and storage device was introduced. Millions were spent by the big companies, until it was realised that too much mechanical handling was altogether too slow. Small parcels were going round a Heath Robinson network of assembly lines and racks—and then getting lost. If a machine broke down, it cost thousands of pounds. Men were the only known devices that were capable of operating, in shifts, twenty four hours a day, throughout the year. Much of the expensive mechanical handling and storage equipment was pulled out.

Demand also changes. Growth is not constant. As with passenger seats, now there is for the time being cargo over-capacity. Yet, with those steep upward graphs, who would have anticipated it? And how long will the over-capacity last? Commodities change—new fibres and fashions are introduced, new types of goods specially suited for air travel come into demand.

Almost everyone thinks they can see forward. Particularly in the air cargo business, they have to think so, because they have to plan and buy and build. On what fragile bases they have to act, the history of air cargo across the Atlantic is witness, from monkeys to vast ships' screws weighing thousands of kilos, from leaking tents to three quarter filled warehouses. Yet the future may hold startling developments—huge cargo flying boats or airships, and a German proposal is that passengers should be fitted into a giant container, so that the passenger lounge at the airport in which they sit is simply slid whole into the aircraft and slid out again at the destination airport.

Only one thing is certain: it will be different tomorrow.

## *Fifteen:* **The Race to be Fastest**

Speed—the Brabazon Committee had given the British a blueprint. Whittle had given them a clear lead in jet engines. One jet type was used to turn a propeller, as in the Proteus engine. The pure jet type dispensed with propellers, and was being developed for the Ghost. These engines were to power the aircraft recommended by the Brabazon Committee— the Proteus for the Princess flying boat, the Britannia and perhaps the Brabazon, the Ghost for the Comet.

But in 1949, all these aircraft were still in the process of production. For the interim period, there was government pressure on BOAC to introduce the Tudors onto the North Atlantic, despite the Corporation's view that they were unsuitable. As a precaution against the Tudor's inability to do the water jump, BOAC had ordered more Boeing Stratocruisers. But beyond the immediate present, the British future for speed looked bright.

Pan American had ordered six Consolidated Vultees, capable of carrying 209 passengers non-stop over the water jump in the height of luxury, as their answer to the Brabazon. But this idea never materialised: Trippe had ordered neither turbo-props nor pure jets, gambling on the turbo-propeller as being an unnecessary intermediary and the Comet being too small to operate the North Atlantic. At the end of the 40s and the early 50s, he relied on Stratocruisers. TWA, Air France and KLM flew various versions of Constellation, while SAS and TCA operated mostly DC4s. Meanwhile, with all airlines operating American aircraft of much the same power, the only commercially viable way to increase speed was to try to cut transit times.

BOAC Sales grumbled because their New York to London Constellation schedule was 12.15 hours with 2.30 hours on the ground, compared with Pan Am's 11.45 with 45 minutes on the ground and AOA's 11.05 with 1.45 hours on the ground. The operational side declared that to achieve such speed, AOA must have adopted constant power cruising with sacrifice of payload. All transit times were reported and analysed.

In 1950, Pan American obtained control of American Overseas, and therefore now had only TWA as an American competitor.

Meanwhile the development of the British Comet was proceeding fast. With great foresight, a repetition of what had been done with the Empire boats, BOAC had ordered fourteen of these jet airliners from De Havilland right off the drawing board, at a cost of £236,000 each. In spite of loud and repeated predictions that passengers did not want to fly so fast and that jet civil aircraft drank fuel and would never be a commercial success, the project was pushed forward with energy, enthusiasm and immense skill. A beautiful aircraft, totally streamlined, the engines deeply embedded in the wings, the Comet gave the impression of a huge silver gull. It could carry forty passengers in comfort at speeds of over 500 miles an hour.

The jets promised far easier maintenance than the cumbersome piston-engines, far greater utilisation in aircraft hours per day, far less vibration and noise in the passenger cabin, a far smoother ride above the weather at over 30,000 feet—and a far faster ride.

And Britain was well ahead of every other country.

\*     \*     \*

But now the production of the Brabazon and the Britannia started falling behind schedule. Only the Comet was well up to time. The prototype first flew in 1951, and in a series of impeccable test flights exceeded its guaranteed performance. It looked as though the pure jet would be in airline service before the turbo-prop. Trippe now placed orders for Comets, and his forecast regarding the intermediary nature of the turbo-prop for long-range civil aircraft looked like being fulfilled.

Now there was further trouble with the Tudors. The Proteus engine was producing difficulties. The cost of the Britannia was rocketing. All other trans-Atlantic operators had dispensed with their flying boats, and only BOAC continued to operate them. It was becoming apparent that BOAC would therefore have the crippling costs of maintaining marine bases exclusively for their own aircraft. Perhaps because of their marine tradition, the British had hung lovingly and uneconomically on to flying boats. Now the future of the British giant Princess was bleak.

In the race to be fastest, the Americans were not simply standing still. American aircraft designers had seen the flight of the Comet at the Farnborough Air Show, and had been deeply impressed. It was obvious that they would now concentrate on the development of new jet types rather than further expanding their piston-engined aircraft. The Deputy Chairman of BOAC, Whitney Straight, pointed out that 'from the civil viewpoint, the most economical method of developing a radically new aircraft is through military channels. The USA were in a position to

**The Tudor, intended for the North Atlantic, flew the Mid-Atlantic for British South American Airways, before being withdrawn after two disappeared in the area of the Azores and Bermuda.** (British Airways)

embark on the civil application of jets with a greater background of certainty and related development than was available to us in the case of the Comet.'

The President of Boeing had said that he would build a prototype jet transport in eighteen months. Whitney Straight thought that the Comet could hold its own against American aircraft of its size, but was sure that the Americans would be going in for something substantially bigger. It was known that Boeings had completed a civil study of the XB52 bomber, a pure jet capable of flying the Atlantic non-stop in either direction with 100 passengers at 500 miles an hour. Whitney Straight prophesied that such jets would be 'the sort of aircraft that our Brabazon and SR45 (Princess) will have to compete against,' and warned that 'the fact that we have an apparent advantage in the field of jet transports provides no reason for complacency, in view of the possibility of rapid and effective competition from American aircraft—especially on the Atlantic route.'

Unwelcome words—but as usual all too true. De Havillands had taken a brave gamble developing the Comet cold without any help from military prototypes. But the aircraft had been designed for the medium-range Empire routes. Could it be stretched for the water jump?

To exacerbate the problems, there was yet another dollar crisis, BOAC's Atlantic Division had been moved *en bloc* to Filton at the end of 1948 to save hard currency. Here the Brabazon was being built in an airship-size hangar specially constructed for it that towered above the Gloucestershire countryside. Coming to the aerodrome one morning from my new home on the edge of the Downs, I saw a huge black silhouette blotting out the sun. The Brabazon was airborne, and I watched the twinkling eight contra-rotating propellers as it flew ponderously overhead. Someone beside me said, 'That proves conclusively one thing. A big aeroplane flies slowly.' History was to show otherwise. In fact, the Brabazon was a Jumbo before its time, a good-looking aeroplane, but it needed powerful pure jet engines which were not then available. The British had put their money on turbo-props for their long-range aircraft. Wisely as it turned out, the Americans did not.

Further operating cost analysis were done on all British aircraft. The Britannia had fallen further behind. There had been an alarming incident during a demonstration flight when a Britannia was ditched in the Bristol Channel. The Brabazon was proving a white elephant. The cost of the three Princess flying boats had risen from £2,800,000 to £4,500,000.

The nub of the problem had always been the need to produce the *right* aircraft for the Atlantic. Instead, the British had spent most of their time disposing of the *wrong* ones. Basically, they had got their timing wrong—they were usually ahead of the field, producing good aircraft at the wrong time, or too late.

The Deputy Chairman of BOAC wrote, 'the Corporation have not the freedom of action in respect of aircraft that is enjoyed by the airlines of

**The Bristol Brabazon, first of the Jumbos, designed for a luxury Atlantic service which it never flew, outside the hanger that was specially built for it at Bristol.** **(BAC)**

The Princess flying boat, designed for the Atlantic, which was cocooned before finally being scrapped.
(Flight)

The Comet I is given an enthusiastic send-off by BOAC staff at Heathrow before departing on the inaugural flight of the first ever scheduled jet service on 2 May 1952. The same aircraft crashed near Elba on 10 January 1954. After the Navy recovered pieces from the sea, a massive and successful testing programme was undertaken which benefited the world.
(British Airways)

all other countries ... whether we like it or not, we are in fact, subsidising the British aircraft industry.' Sir Miles Thomas could do no more than streamline the fleet and try to dispose of aircraft ordered years before he became Chairman.

The Minister was asked to hammer home to the Cabinet, 'the financial and other implications of the "Fly British" policy during the interim phase, in view of the serious losses which are inevitable under it.' Unwillingly, the Cabinet agreed to dispose of 26 Tudors. The Brabazon was scrapped in 1952, which in many ways was a pity. The huge aircraft was described in later years as the 'last of the thick-wings-and-staterooms approach to trans-Atlantic flying'. All work on the giant Princess flying boats ceased. They were cocooned like vast white snowmen, and stood mummified at Calshot for years before following the Brabazon to the breakers' yard.

All the cards in the British hand had crumbled with the exception of the Comet. But there were now rumours that its Ghost engines were under-powered. Certainly the Comet I was not up to the North Atlantic operation.

There were two possibilities. A stretched Comet with bigger engines, such as Conways. Or it was back again on the snakes and ladders board to that 1930s stop-gap device to give an aircraft the range to do the water jump—flight refuelling the Comet I.

*          *          *

The first Atlantic flight refuelling trials had taken place on the Empire boats in 1939. In the spring of 1948, I had taken part in a further series, this time designed to extend the range of aircraft like the Tudor, and possibly the Comet and Britannia, in the hope of doing the water jump non-stop.

In Liberator Yoke Dog we would leave Montreal to rendezvous with a silver Lancastrian of Flight Refuelling Ltd a hundred miles or so off Gander or Shannon. Contact was made by radio homing, and then we talked to each other over the R/T. The rear of the Liberator had been modified and a line was extended with a weight on the end. The Lancastrian would fly across and above us, pick the line up on a grapnel and attach it to a hose.

Then the Lancastrian pilot would formate on us, twenty feet or so above our heads, while in the Liberator tail the lead was winched in, this time with the hose attached. The end of the hose would be connected to pipes leading to our petrol tanks, and we would tell the Lancastrian to start refuelling.

Joined together by the hose, the Lancastrian above the Liberator, the two aircraft would continue in formation for ten minutes. By this time, six hundred gallons would have been transferred by gravity feed into the

A night photograph of Liberator YD being refuelled from a Flight Refuelling Ltd Lancastrian flying above it. The connecting hose can be seen on the left. The rapidity of the exposure was such that the airscrews are seen stopped in their tracks. (Flight Refuelling Ltd.)

Liberator's tanks. The signal to break away would then be given. A slight jerk could be felt as the hose was pulled out of the socket in the Liberator and wound back into the tanker aircraft. Then the Lancastrian pilot would wave to us, waggle his wings, and go back to his base, while we continued our way across the Atlantic.

Altogether I did eight flight-refuelled trans-Atlantic crossings, and I found them easy and efficient. We never had any trouble, though the smell of petrol at the back was strong for a while. The Liberator was faster than the Lancastrian, and I had to throttle back, while during refuelling the aircraft became a trifle tail heavy. The Flight Refuelling pilots were extraordinarily skilful at picking up the drogue and in formating, and I never had either a premature breakaway or a failure. In fact, as an interim measure before the arrival of aircraft with sufficient range, I was convinced that flight refuelling could prove successful.

Others thought differently. There were incidents when no contact was made between the Liberator and the tanker. On one occasion, the Lancastrian pilot complained that the Liberator appeared to have put on maximum power and taken avoiding action. I was going to do the first night refuelling over the Atlantic, but the crew put in a demand to the Corporation for danger money, so it was altered to another day refuelling.

The final report on the trials was lukewarm. Out of 43 scheduled refuellings, there had been three failures to refuel. Thirty irregularities had been reported, mainly failures to refuel at the optimum position.

BOAC considered that there were many technical and operational factors still to be overcome. Flight refuelling must stand on economics. To be of value, it must lead to significantly higher load factors, a more attractive service and cheaper overall costs. The cost of maintaining tankers at Gander and Shannon was considered prohibitive.

However, the Ministry of Civil Aviation had other things to worry about, particularly the fact that the Comet and the Britannia had been primarily built for the Empire routes while it was at last clear to the government, particularly as the Empire was rapidly disappearing, that the North Atlantic was by far the most important. So the Ministry had to find a means of turning both aircraft into Atlantic fliers and flight refuelling was at that time the only answer. The Minister was also fearful of the effect of a possible shut-down of Flight Refuelling Ltd, in which event there was 'certain to be controversy'. A subsidy of £55,000 was offered to BOAC for work performed in connection with new flight refuelling trials on the North Atlantic.

Considerable progress had been made in connection with new probe and drogue equipment. Here the receiver aircraft nosed its way in to a socket at the end of a hose streamed by the tanker. Flight Refuelling Ltd wished to demonstrate this to BOAC. But the airline, as they had always been, were much keener to get an aircraft which could operate non-stop on its own devices. Sir Miles Thomas expressed his view that passengers would not by choice fly in an aircraft, however fast, that was 'going to be subject to new and strange manoeuvres in the air'.

The makers of the Comet, De Havilland, supported Flight Refuelling and in 1950 produced a paper showing that a scheduled non-stop Comet flight could easily be maintained. Against average winds, estimated time westwards was 9.5 hours against the fastest current schedule of 18.2. Eastbound time was 7.5 against 12.6 hours. Payload would be 11,609 lb, with 1860 gallons being transferred over Shannon and 1426 over Gander.

'Flight refuelling,' wrote De Havilland, 'will always pay a dividend because it permits the use of, or the design of, what may be called normal aeroplanes for Atlantic service rather than great fuel carriers. This consideration overrides any question of the economics of more frequent landings versus flight refuelling.' Calling for active encouragement from all parties, the conclusion was 'the prize—an unassailable competitive position on the world's most important long-range air route—is worth the effort involved.'

In May 1951 a flying trial using the new equipment was laid on. The Comet pilot had difficulty in flying the probe into the cone streamed on the end of the pipe from the tanker. The operation took forty-seven minutes, and the connection quickly broke. The BOAC pilots who were watching were not impressed. Further refinements were necessary.

In any case, by this time another star had suddenly swum into BOAC's ken.

In 1951 the Ministry of Supply had asked Vickers to consider a design for an RAF transport aircraft, based on the Valiant bomber. BOAC were also interested in such a jet for the service across the Atlantic, and had joined in the discussions. As a result, in October 1952 Vickers were authorised to build a prototype called the V–1000—a much larger Comet-type civil aircraft with an Atlantic range.

So that was apparently the end of flight refuelling on the water jump. In the event, flight refuelling has been a great military success, taken up by the Americans a long time before the British RAF, and big jet bombers are kept constantly on strategic patrol by this means.

Would it have worked on civil aircraft, enabling Britain to be years ahead with a fast non-stop service over the water jump? Pan American had always considered that passengers would not tolerate it. But in the end would they have got used to the idea, preferring it to the inevitable stops at that time at Gander or Keflavik? While the actual technicalities for the fuel transfer operation could have been achieved in time, at the back of many people's minds was the danger of possible collision. Given a trouble-free service, it might have been a great success as an interim measure at that time—but the cookie did not crumble that far, so nobody knows. Now again flight refuelling is being considered—this time for the supersonic Concorde.

\*     \*     \*

Then disaster struck the ace card in the British hand. In May 1953 a Comet disintegrated, apparently in a storm over India. Eight months later, another exploded off Elba, and the aircraft were all grounded. Nothing could be found wrong, but no sooner had they gone back into service than, on 8th April 1954, another disintegrated near Naples into the Mediterranean.

What had happened?

Before there could be any answer, the aircraft pieces had to be recovered from the seabed. The Navy equipped two salvage vessels with under-water television, special grabs and deep-sea divers. They located the Elba aircraft, and piece by piece, with immense skill, brought two-thirds of it up to the surface.

These were brought to the Royal Aircraft Establishment at Farnborough where in the manner of a crossword puzzle, they were fitted to a wooden skeleton of the Comet fuselage to try to locate possible weaknesses. Simultaneously, another Comet fuselage was immersed in a huge tank of water, leaving its wings protruding. The cabin was tested by repeated pressurising and depressurising, while huge hammers methodically pounded the wings.

The Vickers 1000—the big four engined jet that might have given the British a lead over the Americans, but which remained only a model. (BAC)

These methods simulated the stresses in actual flights. And after the equivalent of three thousand real flights, suddenly a cabin window-frame cracked.

The cause had been found—metal fatigue. BOAC had the tragedies of the Comet accidents. Now all the Comet Is were removed from civil operation: at one stroke, the Corporation lost one-fifth of their aircraft capacity. Not only did they now not have the right aeroplane for the Atlantic, they had nowhere near enough aircraft to operate their world-wide network. In a sellers' market, BOAC representatives had to travel the world, trying to pick up aircraft.

In such a dire situation, it would have been expected that the British would regard their ambition to run the first fast jet service across the Atlantic as now hopeless. But with BOAC support, De Havilland intended to turn their attention away from Comets II and III to the construction of the stretched Comet IV which had a trans-Atlantic capability. By doing this, they could still beat the American Boeing 707, now being designed, by two years.

However, the government would not agree. They insisted that the Company first design the Comet II for the RAF, thus absorbing De Havilland's energies at a crucial time.

What the government had agreed to was the V–1000, and in 1954 a production order for six had been placed with Vickers. A year later, there was concern about rising costs and the non-delivery of British aircraft (notably the Britannia), and the government cancelled the V–1000, on which £3 million had been spent.

The V-1000 might have beaten the 707 on the Atlantic. The Parliamentary Secretary was to look back at the cancellation of the V–1000 as a 'terrible tragedy'. Certainly it meant that the British were 100 to 1 outsiders for the first fast jet service across the water jump.

They were also virtually out of the race to run the first non-stop service from London to New York. The Britannia had fallen further behind. There was still trouble with the Proteus engine. Ice repeatedly developed at the back of the air intake. There were flame-outs on all four engines simultaneously on several Britannias, and there was considerable backfiring when flying through clouds at altitude. Heating the air-intakes cured the trouble—eventually.

The other contenders for the non-stop race were the L–1049 Super-Constellation of TWA and Air France, on the further extension of the DC6, the DC7C. The 'Seven Seas' was certainly the favourite. Its Wright 3400 hp engines, though initially giving trouble, could be said to represent the ultimate in aircraft piston engines, just as the DC7C, with its long fuselage and comfortable cabin accommodating up to 91 tourist passengers and cruising at 353 miles an hour, was the ultimate in piston-engined aircraft.

This was the golden era on the water jump. Traffic and profits were expanding annually. Huge increases in tourist demand had followed the cheap fares, and up went the load factors to 67 per cent and higher. Thirty per cent more passengers crossed the Atlantic in 1952 compared to 1951, and regularly each year up went the number of passengers and down went the cost per ton mile. Sir Miles Thomas had pulled BOAC out of the red with their first net surplus in 1951/52 of £274,999, and had been increasing their annual operating surplus till the tragedy of the Comet. Even so, by careful management, BOAC had begun to recover from that setback.

The big problem was still aircraft—particularly for the North Atlantic. De Havilland and BOAC were now working on the Comet IV, on which great hopes were placed. Sir Miles wanted it to be powered with the big new Avon engine, giving more power and range, but the Minister would not agree at that time.

On the other side of the Atlantic, with record profits succeeding record profits annually, in October 1955 Juan Trippe confidently signed huge orders for large American jets, carrying twice as many passengers almost twice as fast. These were for 20 Boeing 707s and 25 Douglas DC8s at a cost of $269 million. This order was quickly followed up by other airlines.

Still without an Atlantic aircraft, BOAC had to seek government permission to buy foreign. Eventually in 1956, the Minister agreed to the airline buying fifteen 707s for £44 million, mostly in scarce dollars— but they were to be powered by the British Conway engines that were

**Passengers disembarking from a DC7C—the ultimate in piston-engined aircraft.**
**(British Airways)**

to have powered the scrapped V–1000. The Minister said that permission had been given 'in order that the Corporation may hold that competitive position on the North Atlantic route from 1959 to 1960. At that time, no suitable aircraft can be made for that purpose—the purchase is an exceptional measure to bridge the gap.' The government warned BOAC that it was the last American aircraft they could buy.

That same year, in June 1956, Pan Am won the race to put on the first non-stop service between London and New York with the DC7C, no longer stopping at Goose or Gander. It was right that a piston-engined aircraft should win the non-stop race. Piston-engined aircraft had built up the water jump from the early exploratory beginnings to the huge commercial success that it was in the 1950s. They had brought safe, comfortable, regular, cheap and finally fast North Atlantic travel to millions. It is to the piston-engined aircraft that the accolade for the opening up of the North Atlantic sky must go—rightly personified by the most sophisticated example of the type, the Douglas DC7C.

The non-stop service was the final blow to the liners. In 1958 the number of passengers that travelled by air over the water jump first exceeded the number that travelled by sea. In every succeeding year the ships lost more passengers to the tourist-filled aircraft. The non-stop DC7C had sealed the fate of ships like the *Queen Mary* and the

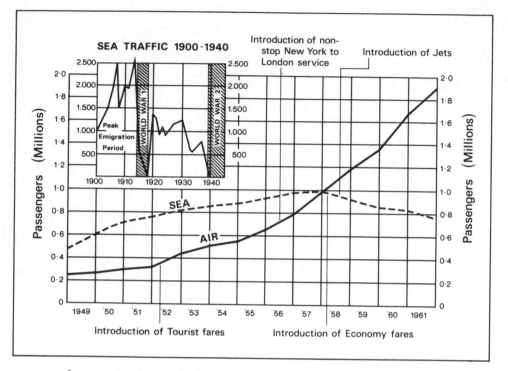

**Comparative figures for North Atlantic passenger traffic by sea and by air.**

*Queen Elizabeth.* What had been regarded as impossible only twenty-five years before was now an actuality.

Not till 19 December 1957 did the British succeed in putting a British aircraft in service on the water jump. The turbo-prop Britannias, first envisioned by the Brabazon Committee in the darkest days of the war, at last came into service. These were fine aircraft, comfortable and silent. Regrettably they were years too late, and they were obsolescent by the time they started. The much faster pure jets had caught them up. For a few months, they did succeed in capturing passengers from Pan Am and TWA, but in two years they were the only propeller-driven aircraft in BOAC. Instead of providing the fast super-luxury service for which they were originally designed, they were allowed by IATA to charge special low fares, below jet economy class, for being propeller-driven. The DC7Cs, their hatchet job completed on the ships, were gradually changed into cargo carriers.

For the jet age on the water jump was about to be born.

As for the race to be fastest—in spite of all their difficulties, the British won it. After a huge programme of costly research which benefited all the world's airlines, the weakness on the Comet had been rectified, and the Comet IV had emerged. Its cost was £1.25 million, five times that of the earlier model, but it was to prove itself a fine aircraft.

On 4 October 1958 BOAC began the world's first scheduled jet service over the water jump from London to New York via Gander with Comet IVs, flying at 500 miles an hour.

The turbo-prop Bristol Britannia, a good aircraft with a magnificent safety record which arrived on the Atlantic at the end of 1957—too late—and was quickly made obsolete by the pure jets.                                                                 (British Airways)

## *Sixteen:* The Age of the Big Jets

A tiny scratching sound on your porthole now . . . what is it? Looking out, you see a scattering of crystals, like a spilt spoonful of sugar, on the top curve of the glass. Peering ahead, you can just make out the tufted tops of cloud. Gently, the wings of the big jet rock. You begin to wonder. Odd tags and phrases about the North Atlantic weather come into your mind. What will happen? What are you in for?

Even above the vast span of the water jump, men feared the North Atlantic weather—and it was natural that the British should fear the North Atlantic most. Their fickle and uncertain weather was ruled by the Atlantic. Over the years they had lost many ships in that ocean.

The majority of people had proclaimed the North Atlantic weather to be all-powerful and went on prophesying disaster to aviators who took it on. Even as late as 1940, when the Ferry Service started the water jump, the British had expected only around half of the aircraft to get across.

The first big menace to aircraft was the wind. Some early aviators even sacrificed their sandwiches for just those extra few ounces of petrol.

Then it was the violence of the storms, the up-currents that could smash an aircraft to bits. Huge cumulo-nimbus anvils had the destructive energy of a nuclear explosion. Flying through them in the piston-engined days, the aircraft used to buck and bounce. The wings fluttered. The engines coughed. The whole sky would go as black as ink, as both pilots wrestled with the controls. Going through a severe front (the word comes from the battle 'front' of the trenches of the First World War) between Atlantic air masses, resembled an almost endless ride on a bronco till suddenly and with relief you saw the line of light, hundreds of miles long, slanting across the horizon ahead.

High cloud, impossible to surmount, blotting out the sun and the stars, had been the scourge of early Atlantic navigators.

Fog was another hazard—particularly at Gander, where the Labrador current round the Newfoundland coast is like an ice-cold magic wand to any warm air that comes drifting in from the Gulf Stream. Many times, as I descended over the coast in perfect visibility, I could see Gander fifty miles away and would already be cleared for a visual straight-in approach to land. Then suddenly a wraith of white would curl like smoke around the rocks and firs and over the lakes. And the next moment— nothing: Gander had vanished. Instead, a thick soft uniform bandage now appeared to cover the whole world. And I would be on the R/T, getting a clearance to an alternate, like Stephenville, or even Sydney, three hundred miles south-west.

Goose was four hundred miles away, and could close, too—though not as suddenly as Gander. The practice usually followed, when Gander forecast temperature was teetering on the brink of the dewpoint, was this: to flight plan to a point between the two aerodromes—a longer way round but leaving your options open till an hour or so before arrival. Because of the considerable distances between them, the big danger was of becoming committed to a landing at one aerodrome in bad visibility and thereby given a deadline before which you had to get in.

Hailstones diminished visibility. The noise was intense. A thousand armourers appeared to be intent on beating their swords into plough-shares on the fuselage, the hailstones sometimes denting the skin of the aircraft. There was always rain—the North Atlantic rain is endless. But it was usually of that thin mizzling variety, that small rain brought in by the blowing of the western wind, that is the mainstay of the British weather. Though sometimes water used to turn the windscreens myopic, for a landing the wipers could cope with everything except heavy rainstorms—when the visibility was nil.

Nil visibility included snow, which to the North Atlantic pilot was almost synonymous with fog. Up in the air, it could do no harm. The whole effect was rather Christmassy, as though an endless stream of accurately hurled snowballs was hitting you on the nose. But trying to land was a different matter, particularly at night when the landing lights simply turned the air ahead into a solid wall of glittering diamonds. Snow, like fog, blinded you, day or night, but had the advantage of usually being well forecast and therefore could be tactically avoided.

Nil visibility certainly killed. But the number one killer on the North Atlantic was ice. Sometimes, half-way across the water jump, as the Liberator pushed its blunt nose sturdily westwards through innocent-looking cloud, suddenly the needle on the airspeed indicator would start going back 160 . . . 155 . . . 150 . . . 145 . . . Looking out over the wings, I would see nothing, and then all at once a thin white line piping the leading edge.

Ice.

'Prop anticers on! Rated power!'

The throttles would go almost to the stop as the aircraft climbed. It was essential to move quickly out of the temperature at which the ice was forming. Going down would be warmer—it *might* melt the ice. But if it did not, your fate was sealed. You climbed higher into colder air where the air at lower temperatures was drier and could not hold the moisture.

It was often a nerve-racking experience. The ice would accumulate, slowing the climb. The engines would fade and you would have to go into hot air, keeping ice from the carburettors but reducing the power. The needle on the airspeed indicator would fall back towards stalling. Inching up higher and higher, the Liberator would struggle, till all the crew were on oxygen and the Liberator was wallowing in the tops of the cloud at 25,000 feet.

I had always flown low down on anti-submarine work, and I knew next to nothing of wing ice, propeller ice or carburettor ice. In the same way, only ten years before, the Imperial Airways pilots had flown on the hot weather eastern runs and knew little about icing. Even as late as 1938, though great strides had been made in other areas, ice still remained a little-known quantity. After the highly successful flight by Howard Hughes, in the latest Lockheed to Paris, as they took off into heavy storms on their way round the world, it was only ice they feared.

Fortunately for me, by now the veteran BOAC Captains had become highly experienced in icing conditions, from operating the Return Ferry Service throughout the year. Some of these same pilots had been involved in the row before the Cadman Committee, when they accused the management of being indifferent to providing suitable icing equipment.

The management was not so much indifferent as ignorant. On 14th September 1937, in one of their trans-Atlantic telephone conversations, Trippe had told Woods Humphery that he was fixing up de-icing rubber shoes on the wing leading edges of his boats, and said he would tell his engineers to give all the assistance to Imperial Airways that they needed. He added it was 'absolutely necessary to have some sort of equipment to cope with the conditions, if we intended to operate all through the winter'.

BOAC's Bennett had done research into Kilfrost. This was a yellow paste that was used on the railways to try to prevent points freezing up. It used to be smeared onto the leading edges of the wings. It did in fact have some effect against airframe icing, but unlike Pan Am with their Alaska operations, the circumstances of Empire Routing had precluded real experience in cold conditions. The Empire Boat Atlantic proving flights had been carried out in the summer and mainly in the warm air at 1000 feet.

The Empire *Cavalier* had operated a solitary service against the Pan American flying boats on the New York–Bermuda run for eighteen months. Its comfort and regularity had been much admired—but there were problems in the winter with ice. The engines particularly would fade. The Captain had reported this yet again at New York in his voyage report when he had come up from Bermuda in January 1939. On the trip back, two engines began fading again. It was clear that the carburettors were icing up.

Watching the engine power fade is a frightening experience when you can do nothing about it. The carburettor anti-icing equipment was clearly inadequate. Sometimes by juggling the throttles, you could back-fire and shatter the ice that was forming on the intakes.

Not on this occasion. The captain tried everything. Unable to maintain height, he sent out a distress signal, then prepared to land on a big swell. He had the two outer engines only, and set the boat down as well as he could. But the hull had been damaged. Water came pouring in.

Soon it was evident they were sinking. The flying boat was abandoned in good order, and the crew and passengers linked hands in a circle. The captain kept up morale. The daylight faded. In the darkness, two of the passengers and one of the stewards, who had exhausted himself swimming round giving help, died. Ships were seen twice, and loudly hailed, to no effect. On the third occasion, the voices of the survivors were heard and they were rescued by the *Esso Baytown*.

Many of those who disappeared in the early flights and on the Ferry Service almost certainly came down due to ice—mostly carburettor ice, but ice in other forms too. On an aircraft, ice could form in the pitot head—as it did with Alcock, cutting off all airspeed indication. Ice could form on the propellers, rapidly diminishing their efficiency. The ice slung off the propellers against the fuselage made a noise like gunfire on all aircraft and could actually hole a flying boat below the water-line. Ice frequently formed on the fuselage, and also on the leading edge of the wing. Particularly on the thin-section Davis wing of the Liberator, the slightest amount even of rime (or opaque) ice was enough seriously to affect its aerodynamic qualities and the aircraft would begin losing the ability to fly. One Liberator took off from Montreal on an Atlantic flight, and, unable to get higher than a few feet above the ground under such conditions, began milling around between trees and church steeples. Fortunately, in spite of fog, the captain found a runway and skilfully put the aircraft down.

But the most dramatic form of ice came from freezing rain. Air temperature generally falls at a reasonably standard rate with height. But sometimes a bank of warm air overlays colder air, a situation called an inversion, and if precipitation is induced, rain from such a layer can turn an aircraft on which it falls into a solid block of ice in a matter of minutes. Then the sheer weight of ice is enough to force the plane down.

One by one, such forms of ice began to be conquered. Very early on, the pitot tubes for the airspeed indicator were provided with electric heaters. Alcohol was piped onto the propellers to stop ice forming. The leading edges of the wing were fitted with inflating and deflating rubber boots. In a 314, Churchill saw 'a large rubber tube which expanded and contracted at intervals'. He was told it was to prevent icing. 'We saw, from time to time the ice splintering off as it expanded.' But you had to be careful, lest ice formed beyond the travel of the boots and then could build up unmolested. Then hot air along the leading edge was used. Hot air from the exhausts could be diverted into the carburettors at temperatures between +1 and −10° centigrade. Again care had to be taken not to turn on the heat at lower temperatures, since research had shown that this simply brought the carburettor back up into the critical temperature range. For freezing rain, nothing could be done except to stay on the ground, but with more reporting points now, accurate forecasts of inversion situations could almost invariably be given.

All this information was hammered home to me and the other ex-RAF pilots by the Training Section and the veteran Captains: 'Next to your artificial horizon, your temperature gauge is your most valuable instrument.' I used to watch it like a hawk. The theory that ice could not form at temperatures below −10°C was already being disproved by the discovery of super-cooled water drops that could cause ice at almost any temperature. 'As soon as you see ice, climb!' I climbed as high as I could get. I did what others had found out and told me, and I never had any trouble.

Then came the jets, and it was reckoned that engine ice would be a thing of the past. This hope proved premature, particularly on the turbo-prop. The Proteus engine of the Britannia had endless icing troubles, and was one of the main reasons why the aircraft was held up for so long. All four engines used to fail simultaneously in flame-outs that were very frightening. Two engines were lost over the Atlantic because of the round compressor case being twisted into an oval, because of ice.

The pure jets surely would be far too hot and had no carburettors to worry about. But now a different problem arose. Because they flew so high, in cold weather the kerosene began to turn into wax. This was such a problem that Boeings originally were going to use petrol on their 707s. But BOAC, De Havillands and Shell had had this trouble and originated a new kerosene fuel with a freezing point of −50°C. This solved Boeing's problem—yet another example of the cooperation between airliners and aircraft manufacturers.

The top of the Atlantic cloud used to be reckoned at 15,000 ft. In 1946, it had gone up to 25,000. Now cloud is known at 30,000 and above

—but at 38,000 ft, which is a common height used by Atlantic jets today, at last almost invariably you are above the weather. Certainly (very rarely) you can get rocked by Clear Air Turbulence. But gone are the bumps, the cloud turbulence, the rain, the snow, the hail, the ice. Gone are the carburettors and all engine ice. Gone are the propellers and the alcohol. Gone are the inflating rubber boots on the leading edge, since the friction of a fast-moving jet generates enough heat to keep ice away. The bite of strong westerly winds has largely been neutralised by speeds of over 500 miles an hour. Fog is still there, but what with every sort of landing aid, like the Instrument Landing System, Ground Controlled Approach and the robot autoland at the Atlantic terminals and accurate forecasting, it has lost most of its terrors.

The meteorological service remains as efficient as it always has been. The weather briefings we got on both sides of the Atlantic were excellent —and after the war there was the benefit of a great many reports. As more and more aircraft flew across, more and more hourly weather reports came in. ICAO had taken on the idea of the weather ships and built up to a fleet of nine dotted over the Atlantic, taking radiosonic soundings, sending up balloons and repeatedly transmitting reports on all aspects of weather conditions.

It was lonely and must often have been boring for the 120-man crew on these ships, particularly Weather Ship Charlie stationed half-way across the water jump at longitude 35° West. Each ship had a radio beacon which could be picked up a couple of hundred miles away, and since Charlie was on the Great Circle route, most aircraft flew over her, talked to her on the R/T and got the winds at their altitude. One night, the veteran BOAC Captain, O. P. Jones, was approaching the weather ship and picked up his microphone to make contact. However, a sailor was having a conversation with the stewardess on the American aircraft ahead, and all he could hear through the headphones was . . . 'I'm twenty-two, five feet four inches, thirty-five, twenty-two, thirty-five, blonde hair, blue eyes. My flat is in 16 Brooklyn Park, telephone 5652 . . .' 'Jesus honey, we're practically neighbours. Can you cook!' . . . 'Everybody says my apple pie . . .' 'Honey, I'll be right over. That is in three weeks and two days and five hours time.' Eventually there was a break in the conversation and Captain Jones spoke: 'This is Speedbird Easy Love . . . I'm fifty-one years old, five feet nine inches tall, forty-two, thirty-two, thirty-five, blue eyes, a torpedo beard . . . I'm interested in breeding bull terriers and I live in Sussex, England. My cooking is well known. Do you want my telephone number?' There was an astonished silence before the one word . . . 'No-o-o.' 'Then can I,' said Captain Jones, 'have the wind at 19,000 feet?'

The weather ships did sterling service over thirty years—in meteorology, navigation and also in air-sea rescue. But again, scientific progress has begun to make their value less and inflation has made their cost more. Three were withdrawn in 1972. Others may soon follow. Pilots used to call up the weather ship automatically, but now that ICAO have instituted a charge for their services, orders have gone out from cost-conscious airlines for them not to do so, except in emergency. The pilots can manage perfectly well without them. The weather ships too are moving into history.

And though meteorologists are essential for a wide number of activities, their use on the water jump is lessening. The wind forecasts still come in to flight planning. But the jets are now above the weather. They look down on rain and hail, snow, lightning and turbulence. Speed has made even the terminal forecast less important—and less difficult to do. The captain these days is mainly interested in the actual weather at his destination before he even takes off. In seven hours—and the time is shrinking all the time—he will be over the water jump and *there*.

That rash of little crystals on your porthole is spreading. But your jet aircraft stays where it is. The noise of the engines never changes. Nobody is concerned. Nobody takes any notice. If you brought the attention of your young stewardess to these symptoms of disease, she would not know what you were driving at. In today's aircraft, ice is something she puts in drinks.

*        *        *

There is the ice now—floating in the whisky in your hand. As you take your eyes away from the porthole and look around in the cabin, the huge size of the Jumbo again strikes you—and yet how quietly and effortlessly it flies.

In this seating arrangement, there are 376 Economy class passengers comfortably seated in three compartments, separated by ninety-inch wide galleys located at the crossroads between aisles. Down in the lower deck, there are two more galleys where the food carts are prepared and brought up by elevator. Also on the lower deck are the huge cargo compartments with over 6000 cubic feet capacity. Forward sit the 26 first-class passengers right up to the nose, two seats side by side at 38 inch spacing, in comparison to the economy 34 inch, with very wide aisles and a separate galley. Altogether, there are sixteen flushing toilets spaced throughout the cabin. On these walls is a mottled blue and cream motif, picked up in the carpet and the seats—but each company chooses its own decor. Over on the starboard side is a little striped tent in which the stewardesses relax and have their meals.

It is the number of windows that is surprising—more window than fuselage so that you can see under the wing the big annular ring of the turbo-fan by-pass on the Pratt and Whitney engine, now cruising at 10,000 lb thrust against 46,000 on take-off. Such a by-pass design means

The family likeness—the Douglas jet brothers, the DC 10, DC 8 (middle) and DC 9.
(Douglas)

20 per cent less fuel consumption and far less noise. Shrouding the engines like a huge parasol, the wings that sweep back like a boomerang are one huge fuel tank carrying a load of kerosene equivalent to three and a half Constellations at all-up weight. The spoilers and flaps are tucked away and snug now, flush with the wing skin.

Controls and systems are duplicated, triplicated or quadrupled—four ailerons, four elevators, two rudders, and none of the controls now are manually operated. Roll, pitch and yaw movements are all power-driven by four separate hydraulic systems. Everything is built for safety, comfort and quietness—the temperature and heating controlled by hot air from the air compressors, the pressurisation held at 5000 feet above sea level. The seats recline easily and the windows have blinds. Forward from the passenger cabin, a spiral staircase exactly like the Stratocruiser's leads up to the top deck where there is a lounge bar with a curved bay seat at the far end and red armchairs by the window.

This aircraft arrangement holds 402 passengers, but it can be converted to hold over 550. Soon the stretched versions of big jets will arrive with 750, eventually 1000 passengers. Or the seats can be easily dismantled and the whole aircraft, or part of it, can be turned into a cargo carrier, capable of transporting 170,000 lb of freight across the Atlantic in fully automated holds. For the whole essence of survival in the competitiveness across the water jump is flexibility—rearrangement of the aircraft interior to carry out any combination of demand for first-class or economy seating, together with every shape and size of freight.

How was it that this aircraft, enormous, and yet so fast and adaptable and easy to fly, came into being? And what was its effect on the water jump?

*     *     *

The British victory with the Comet IV, first commercial jet across the Atlantic, had been short-lived. Twenty-two days later, on 26th October 1958, the Pan American 707, *Clipper America*, completed the water jump from New York to Paris, carrying 111 passengers, though it still made a refuelling stop at Gander. For eleven years, the 707 and DC8 and later the British VC10 were to rule the Atlantic.

Juan Trippe's double gamble on not ordering turbo-prop Britannias or the small Comet was clearly paying off. As always before, his intuitive sense of timing had been superb, as indeed had been the whole way the Americans had tackled the introduction of jet civil transports.

They had learned from the German He178, the first jet to fly a few days before the Second World War, and essentially from the British

**The Boeing 707 could do the work of three big piston-engined aircraft and, with the DC 8, revolutionised Atlantic air travel.** (Boeing)

Whittle jet engines. They had also gained valuable experience from the Comet. But they had also learned two lessons themselves: first, that aircraft come in families and should be built as natural progressions: second, that military aircraft are not basically different from civil aircraft and, wherever possible, should father them. The DC4 emerged from the C54, the Constellation from the C69 military transport. The B29 and the C97 transport fathered the Stratocruiser. Boeings had built the B47 Stratojet with its swept-back wing, its four podded engines, the first bomber designed to carry post-war thermonuclear weapons. They also built the B52 Stratofortress in 1952, which was not only a bomber but a tanker (the Americans had seized on the refuelling idea originated by Sir Alan Cobham for their strategic Air Force) and a military transport. It was directly from along this hereditary line that there had emerged what Boeings called Dash Eighty, the eightieth configuration of the C97, which the world soon knew as the 707.

The jets brought their own problems. Flying the 707 was not easy. Coming in to land demanded the reverse of what pilots had learned from their *ab initio* training—height was now controlled by the control column and speed by the throttles. The very speed at which the aircraft flew demanded quicker reactions on the part of the crew, more things to be done in drills and less time to do them. Then the jets brought noise and nuisance to the environment. The early engines produced a deafening high whistle and poured black smoke from their exhausts. Protests from people living around airports multiplied, and a huge research programme was undertaken to clean up the aircraft. Cluster-type tail pipes were devised as sound suppressors, and new by-pass ideas for exhaust gases explored. Year by year, even as the engines grew bigger and more powerful, the smoke was gradually eliminated and much of the noise suppressed.

Maintenance now became much easier. There were far fewer moving parts in jets in comparison to piston engines. Utilisation went up from around seven hours a day on piston-engined aircraft to twelve on jets. Cruising at 575 mph, the 707 could carry nearly 200 passengers, and was soon, in a stretched version with new turbofan engines, operating direct London–New York. It was boom time on the North Atlantic. Pan American's profits went up from $17 million in 1959 to $79 million in 1963.

The selling factor of good service still remains. On a Jumbo, there are usually sixteen cabin staff to serve First Class and Economy passengers from trolleys in the aisles. Because the jets move so fast they are all pressed for time, even though these days there is no washing up on board; bars are exchanged at every station.

But the cabin crew conditions have changed for the better. Hours on duty are limited to a maximum of fourteen. Training is given in proper mock-ups for each aircraft type (including the Concorde), so that the catering crew learn to operate the exact equipment on the ground that they will be using in the air, and in the same cabin and galley environment. They are trained by those who have been in the aircraft catering service all their lives. Now instead of being expected to leave after a few years, stewardesses can become pursers with possibilities of further promotion.

A further selling factor has been the introduction of in-flight entertainment. British South American Airways had films on their Yorks in 1948, hiring the equipment at nine guineas a week, plus the cost of the film. BOAC saw no future for films on Constellations—the passengers would all be asleep. However, in 1949 the Catering Manager did indicate that as they were being used by some American and South African aircraft, perhaps BOAC should follow suit. But they did so slowly. However, now there are four screens on board a Jumbo, and on some airlines two separate full-length films are shown.

But there was now more competition. Lufthansa had come back into the game in 1955. Captain Meyr, the Captain of the Do–X, became Chief Pilot. Most of the Luftwaffe aces who had been in various occupations for a dozen years outside aviation were contacted. So Lufthansa

**Head-on view of the British answer to the American big jets—the VC 10, climbing above Atlantic clouds.** **(British Airways)**

started with the cream of the Luftwaffe. Captain Pretsch, an old TWA Captain, an American with German forebears, and other TWA and British pilots trained the Germans. Lufthansa bought Constellation 1049s and carried out their first commercial Atlantic crossing on 8 June 1955. Once again, the Germans were to show their fantastic capacity to organise and press ahead. Again from practically nothing, they built up a huge and efficient airline network. Why what is now called the German economic miracle should be such a surprise is strange. It could be predicted from the history of the water jump. Twice on the Snakes and Ladders board they were sent back to the beginning after each of the World Wars, restricted on building aeroplanes and engines —and twice up they came amongst the leaders again, in eighteen years from 1958 increasing sixteenfold the numbers of Atlantic passengers carried.

Air Canada, Air France, KLM, TWA were all doing well. BOAC, hampered by the exceptional burden and expense of introducing new types of British aircraft and by their extraordinary government financing arrangements, still managed to increase its North Atlantic business. But the whole financial organisation of the Corporation was still basically unworkable for a commercial airline. On top of it all, there was another British aircraft—the VC10—of which BOAC under some pressure had ordered 45 of various marks. Again as late in the day as this, it is strange that the original VC10 was designed basically as an Empire aircraft best suited for comparatively short stages and for operating into short hot airfields. The aircraft thus had a comparatively low wing loading and behaved like a real lady, unlike the more difficult 707. But the standard VC10 was too small for the Atlantic, being over-powered and under-bodied. So the Super VC10 was designed with a lengthened fuselage, copying the 707 in certain respects.

In the end, the VC10 turned out to be a good aircraft, safe, comfortable and quiet with the most spacious flight deck of modern aircraft and easy to fly. But as was the usual and in certain respects inevitable British practice, it was a custom-built 'one-off' production, with no military antecedents and no family history. From the operators' point of view, the VC10 was no improvement on the 707, significantly more expensive to buy, yet going into service six years later—and in spite of disposing of some to the RAF, BOAC were still burdened with too many.

However, for passengers this new jet-age was a revelation. High above the weather at over 30,000 feet, the flights were smooth, quiet, vibrationless and comfortable. Airsickness became almost a thing of the past. The flights were regular and on time, and returns to the ramp for mechanical reasons were rare.

**Night reflections at London Airport—the VC10.** (British Airways)

Safety, comfort, regularity, speed—all the requirements of the passenger were now being met by the jets. But the big thing was that all these services, comfort and speed were being provided at no extra cost—in fact, the price of a ticket over the water jump was going *down*. Instead of Tourist was introduced an even cheaper fare called Economy Class.

Far more services were being offered, Pan Am alone increasing from 170 in 1958 to 258 in 1965. More and more passengers, particularly tourists on package tours, came over the water jump. It was the death knell of the big ships: one by one, they disappeared off the Atlantic. The *Queen Mary* became a tourist attraction at Palm Beach. The *Queen Elizabeth* was sold to be made into a university and caught fire in Hong Kong. The *America* rusts beside the quay, no one knowing what to do with her. Only the *Queen Elizabeth II* still plies between New York and Southampton, and then only between May and November.

Not only was the big jetliner itself a streamlined symbol of speed and comfort and efficiency—everything servicing or appertaining to it had to match the aircraft or the whole operation became spoiled. After an Atlantic trip, the skin film from the salt air and the residue from the exhausts was quickly washed with special cleaning fluids so that the appearance gleamed. The interiors, decorated to the users' own ideas, were colourful and kept spotlessly clean by vacuuming and disinfecting. The servicing of a jet on the ground, instead of being manual and somewhat haphazard, now became a highly organised, largely mechanical process in which specially built refuellers, bulk cargo loaders, food and water trucks, maintenance vans, lavatory trucks and containerised lockers, together with cleaners, would deal with a big jet en route in twenty minutes or a turn-round in half an hour. Everything possible was done for the passenger far more quickly and efficiently than on any other form of transport.

And for the airline operator, both the DC8 and 707 were godsends because deliberately they were made so adaptable. A tremendous amount of market research had gone into them, and as a result all sorts of adaptations could be arranged easily and cheaply. Passenger seating arrangements were almost unlimited, because of the wide cabin interior with galleys and lavatories installed at each end. In the fully stretched DC8, 240 seats were installed. In the 707–320C a high density of 215 passengers with 29-inch seat pitch could be arranged, or any mixture of economy class and first class, with an eight-place lounge if required.

**The Jumbo takes off.** (Boeing)

Inside the Jumbo. (Boeing)

Instead of the six flying crew of the piston-engined aircraft, these large money-spinners were operated by only four—Captain, First Officer, Navigator and Engineer. Voice and not morse was now used on the radio right across the Atlantic.

Airlines could cut their fleets, since a big jet carried three times as many passengers as a piston-engined aircraft. And the passengers liked them so much that load factors began as high as 90 per cent. Every year, more people wanted to do the water jump—two million in 1963 increasing to five million in 1966. Up and up went the cargo carried by an average of 15 per cent a year.

There appeared to be no end to this ever expanding traffic on the North Atlantic. Pan American built a huge new overhaul base to cope with the jets, and introduced a world-wide computer system to cope with bookings and reservations. TWA had led the way with a vast modernistic passenger terminal at Kennedy to make embarking and disembarking easy, with aircraft actually coming into bays like ships into harbour. Pan American had followed up closely behind with their own passenger terminal known as the 'Worldport', later to be followed by BOAC.

Everything that the North Atlantic sky touched seemed to turn to gold. It was against this apparently endless golden background, with Pan Am profits leaping from $26.2 million in 1961 to a record $132 million five years later, that, on 13 April 1966, Juan Trippe signed a contract for 25 Boeing 747 Jumbo jets at a total cost of $525 million

As with the 707 contract, that order helped Boeing enormously, and was an act of faith and confidence that was to bring the world's airlines queueing for this private-enterprise aircraft.

\*    \*    \*

The Americans had pointed the way—and inevitably the other operators followed. It has always been a maxim on the water jump that all players must have similar equipment, or be forced out of the game. The one with the edge in speed, comfort, novelty or cost will win the jackpot.

For years now, the North Atlantic had been the Queen's Route, the most prestigious in the world. It had become a matter of national shame *not* to operate it. All the European countries and Japan had been competing with each other and the Americans for a long time, but now the developing countries, too, felt that they should not be excluded. Jumbos and their equivalent wide-bodied three-engined jets, the DC10 and the TriStar, were ordered by countries all over the world. Air Canada, Air France, Air India, Alitalia, Lufthansa, Iberia, El Al, KLM, Japan Airlines, Sabena, Quantas, TWA, Aer Lingus, Olympic, SAS and others all ordered 747s for the water jump.

In BOAC, the early years of the big jets had not been such happy ones. By 1963 there was an accumulated deficit of £77 million. Another government-induced British aviation heart-searching exercise was inevitable. In 1963, the Minister appointed an accountant, Mr Corbett, to look into the matter, and though the details of what he found were kept secret, a White Paper entitled *The Financial Problems of British Overseas Airways Corporation* was highly critical of management. In circumstances reminiscent of Woods Humphery, the Chairman and the Managing Director resigned.

The new Chairman, Sir Giles Guthrie, was both a pilot and a banker. Before he agreed to take the job on, he wisely insisted on a change in the system. As a result, at last BOAC was put on the same footing as Pan American and other airlines—it was a *commercial* airline that chose its own staff, routes and aircraft and the accumulated deficit was written off. In historic words that should have been spelt out forty years before, since in essence they embodied the Hambling Committee recommendations, the Minister agreed, 'the choice of aircraft is a matter for the Corporation's judgment ... there is a fundamental responsibility for the Corporation to act in accordance with their commercial judgment. If the national interest should appear, whether to the Corporation or to the Government, to require some departure from the strict commercial interests of the Corporation, this should be done only with the express agreement or at the express request of the Minister.'

Sir Giles now pruned his routes, decided on his fleet—cancelling thirteen VC10s that had been ordered—and settled on the necessary number of staff.

At last, the Fly British and the All-Red Route policies were (officially anyway) dead, but they had needed a lot of killing. The Empire might have hastened Britain's pre-eminence, but it also hastened her decline.

Against this background of reorganisation on commercial lines and careful control, and in order to supplement its fleet of 707s and VC10s, in 1966 BOAC also put in a modest order for six Jumbo jets.

This was a time that British caution and the British economic predicament paid off. BOAC increased their Jumbo fleet by degrees, easily absorbing training and the phasing out of older equipment, and were thus in a better position to cope with the two big bumps that lay seven years ahead—the fuel crisis and the economic recession.

\*        \*        \*

Meanwhile Boeing, Douglas and Lockheed were actually building their three huge wide-bodied jets—respectively the 747, the DC10 and the TriStar.

It had all started, as usual in America, with a military aircraft contract—this time for the C5A transport.

All three companies entered, but the contract went to Lockheed. Undeterred, both the other companies went out on their own, both starting with an intensive market research exercise. All over the world, their representatives travelled, asking the airlines searching questions on their plans and what they required for future operation, at the same time trying out on them various designs. Both companies had decided on a really big aircraft—Douglas were going to build a thousand-seater, but halved the size after their investigations. Both companies were worried by the big question as to whether airlines could afford around $20 million each for these leviathans—more than the price of the *Queen Mary* and twice as much as the total market value of all American civil aircraft in 1938.

As it turned out, the Lockheed C5A bore little resemblance to the TriStar, but much of the military transport's technology—particularly in regard to engines and navigation systems—was used in all three big jets.

Between Boeing, Pan Am and Pratt and Whitney, the engine manufacturers, there was the closest cooperation. Various early designs were made, including one with a mid-wing and two decks, before deciding on a low-wing, wide-bodied aircraft with a cathedral-size interior, having along two aisles ten seats abreast for 450 economy passengers. All-up weight was to be 710,000 lb, and the power plants were to be huge J79D high by-pass engines that eliminated smoke and muffled noise, twice the

The TriStar—Lockheed's three-engined wide-bodied Jumbo. (Lockheed)

size of previous jet engines, and with a huge fan in front to increase thrust power.

It was the 'impossible' aircraft for the 'impossible' route.

And now, the Americans showed their immense organisational and construction abilities. An entirely new manufacturing complex was set up; the buildings, the hangars, the costs were all huge. In addition, a component structure complex was built at Auburn.

The total production bill for the 747 was over a billion dollars. Because of the high cost and because of the enormous construction requirements that were achieved, it is clear that no other country in the world could have built it. The building of very large civil aircraft has become an almost exclusively American domain, and is likely to remain so in the future. And yet for all its size, the Jumbo acts like a lady— quiet, steady, easy to fly, able to take off and land from comparatively short runways, coming in on approach at low speeds.

Juan Trippe had signed the first contract with Boeing on 13th April 1966. On 30th September 1968, to the strains of *Pomp and Circumstance*, the hangar doors were opened and out came the Jumbo to be christened with champagne by twenty-six stewardesses from all the airlines that had ordered the aircraft. On 9th February 1969 the 747 first flew, and on 12th December of that same year, the first Jumbo was delivered to Pan American.

As the British are apt wistfully to remark, 'When you order an American aircraft, all you have to worry about on the day of delivery is whether it will be handed over before or after lunch.'

In fact, the Americans have made the age of the big jets peculiarly their own. Over the water jump, the USA is largely supreme. International regulations certainly control it, and the airlines of many nations operate it. But it is American aircraft that almost exclusively fly it. American instruments guide and guard them. American operating procedures have been inherited and are used.

It could be said that the sky is the American empire. But all the time, their rule is being challenged.

A European consortium is building the A300 Airbus, a big jet capable of being further stretched which will certainly be a challenger on the North Atlantic. Then there is the British/French supersonic Concorde.

Will the American sky empire go, too—like all other empires before it? Or are we still in the childhood of flying, and will the numbers of passengers and tons of cargo crossing the Atlantic again accelerate in a steep upward curve?

**Air Canada Jumbo at altitude.**                                    **(Air Canada)**

# *Seventeen:* Landfall

Round about now, the early pioneers would be getting a little worried. Five minutes or so from estimated time of arrival for crossing the coast, and only sea below and cloud ahead.

With the exception of Service navigators, few of them had much idea of navigation. As late as the mid-thirties, Imperial Airways had few First Class Navigators, and air navigation was still taught at their school at Croydon along mainly marine lines. Even the experts like Byrd got lost. As for the pioneers, it was a matter of little importance to Hoiriis and Hillig that they arrived at Krefeld in Germany when they were aiming at Copenhagen in Denmark. When Major Cooke of the R34 was commended for his accurate navigation, he remarked modestly, 'America is 6000 miles long and it would have been surprising if we had not hit it.' Gatty, who navigated Post, thought he was coming up to Ireland when he was actually over Lancashire. Amy and Jim Mollison never really mastered navigation and were pilots by instinct. On his first crossing, Mollison had no idea where he was when he landed. The Russians Kokkinaki and Gordienko were hundreds of miles from where they thought they were when they made their wheels-up landing at Miscou Island.

Of course, the pioneers had almost no aids to help them and little accurate wind forecasting. Even if they had known much about astro-navigation, it would not have helped them a great deal because of the solid cloud layers and the Atlantic storms. Radio aids were few and often unreliable. They relied very much on their flight plan, made up on the ground, on ships, on their airman's sixth sense and their own individual homemade ideas on how to 'home'.

As always, Lindbergh was the opposite. He had his tracks laid down, his distances marked, his maps neatly folded. But even he reckoned that he could be hundreds of miles off track towards the end of the crossing.

Eriksson and the early Norwegian navigators across the Atlantic had used shields to measure the altitude of the sun. They also carried pigeons (so did the R34), and when in doubt, one was released. The direction the bird took was towards land, and the ship altered course accordingly. When Bleriot crossed the Channel, his intention was to follow a fast French destroyer *Escopette* making full smoke. Unfortunately, he overtook the ship and landed on the other side of the Channel not knowing where he was. He took the right direction to Dover, but crashed on landing. In fact, the ground looks very different from the air, and aerial map reading takes some learning. In the early days, towns had their names spelt out on beaches or on roofs of railway stations and over land following railway lines was normal practice. The apocryphal story is that early Imperial Airways pilots in their open cockpits would let down over Croydon when they could smell the gas works.

The big problem on the North Atlantic was a beam wind which could blow a slow-moving aircraft miles off course in no time. Such drift in wartime was measured by the rear gunner, on a bag of aluminium dust or dye, by day, and a flame float by night, thrown from the aircraft. He would keep his guns on the float and read off the drift on the quadrant marked on the turret. The most ingenious method of navigating was certainly Chamberlin's, who carried the *New York Times* giving the shipping list on his day of departure. Totally lost, he spotted a big ship and recognised the four red and black funnels of the *Mauretania*. He ascertained that she was outward bound to New York, calculated her position from the sailing date given, and set course along her length eastwards for England.

Captain D. C. T. Bennett reorganised Imperial Airways navigation so the crews could cope with the Atlantic at about the same time as Pan American were building up their school for the Pacific run. Most British pilots, as I did, learned their navigation from his and Francis Chichester's books, and the RAF publication 1234, where each chapter is headed by a quotation from *Alice in Wonderland*. Bennett's succession of flights with inexperienced navigators across the water jump on the Return Ferry Service were a complete success, largely because he planned them so well and managed to instil into the crews, during a couple of training flights in Montreal before departure, more astro-navigation than they had learned throughout their whole training. Afterwards, Bennett was to organise and lead the Pathfinders of Bomber Command.

There had been a big advance in almanacs and precomputation tables when I learned astro. More than once was I comforted by the ancient engraving on the cover of the air almanac of a navigator using a primitive sextant above the words *Man is not lost*. And when I came on the Buttercup Route in 1946, such had been the multiplication of radio aids and the increase of experience that navigating over the water jump presented few problems. The radio compass had long been in use.

Instead of the complications of a loop bearing, a needle round a dial in front of the pilot indicated automatically, when the right frequency had been selected, exactly the direction in which a radio beacon lay. Over the VHF, the pilots would be talking to stations a hundred miles away, a great advance on the old TR9 radio with which communication was often impossible. Courses were still plotted on a Mercator chart, and the basis of the navigation was still dead reckoning. But if we were above cloud the navigator would use a bubble sextant through the astrodome to shoot the stars. Or he would use Loran to obtain a fix—a hyperbolic navigation system that is based on measuring the time taken for pulses from two known transmitters to reach the aircraft. Since radio waves travel at 186,000 miles a second, it is possible to obtain a position line from the time interval between the arrival of the two signals. Apart from the middle of the Atlantic, where there was somewhat of a blind spot, positions up to 1000 miles away could be obtained, accurate to around ten miles. In addition, there were D/F beacons on weather ships, radio ranges on all principal airfields, and if necessary a QDM (course to steer) could be obtained from the ground.

Gradually, the mechanics of navigation advanced even further. As additional aids to safety, further refinements of radio altimeters were developed: terrain warning was given by flashing lights and bells. Phase comparison systems, called Decca and Dectra, were introduced. Then an entirely new idea, Doppler, was introduced which gave the pilot not only his drift but his groundspeed and the distance in nautical miles that he had travelled. Moreover new Atlantic routes were being flown, notably the one via Greenland to the American west coast, pioneered by the Scandinavian Airlines System. This route, which was first flown in a DC6B on 15th/16th November 1954, took ten hours off the Copenhagen –Los Angeles run, as compared to the trip via New York—but navigation was more difficult due to the difficulty of flying close to the magnetic pole.

Up front in the 747 on the left of the Captain is now a radar with 30, 100 and 300 mile ranges. The beam can also be directed ahead, left or right. Radar shows storms ahead which can then be circumnavigated. Coastlines, lakes and rivers are clearly indicated up to around 100 miles ahead. Other aircraft show up fifteen to twenty miles away as little bright pimples. In addition, there is the Distance Measuring Equipment working on VHF Omni-directional Ranges, and this again gives an accurate fix that need not be plotted. There are three quite separate ones on the flight deck of a 747, showing the miles that have been flown.

With the introduction of so many jets on the Atlantic (500 and more a day) travelling so fast, it was essential to ensure that pilots knew where they were all the time with even greater accuracy in order to maintain their allotted airlanes. And so an entirely new system of navigation came to be introduced—first on the 707s and then in a more advanced form on the Jumbo. The Inertial Navigation System has been hailed as 'the greatest advance in aviation since the artificial horizon'.

It is, in fact, on the same system as that invaluable instrument, the gyro. Three gyros maintain a platform fixed in space, but it is balanced to move freely, north or south, east or west. Also fitted are two detectors which monitor every movement and feed it to a computer. Into this computer is fed all relevant navigation information, such as course and airspeed and time. At the start of the flight, the Engineer of a 747, by means of push-buttons, sets up the latitude and longitude of his position which registers on an instrument. This setting is checked independently by both other members of the crew—since it is of course absolutely vital that the starting position is registered correctly. As the flight progresses, the INS registers like a taxi meter the new latitude and longitude in neon-light type numerals, and the windspeed and direction can be found at any moment by turning the appropriate switch. The automatic pilot is connected to the INS, and the flying of the course and the logging of the trip are both entirely mechanical. And there is not just one of these machines—there are *three* of them. One steers the aircraft and is on watch. It 'reports' if it becomes unserviceable. The second monitors the first. The third machine is the 'hot spare'—all ready to be brought into use if either of the other sets fails. And now, an even simpler navigation system has been introduced, the Collins AINS 70, where all the routes that may be required, amended up to date, are contained in a cassette which is simply slipped into place as though into a tape recorder, and the aircraft flown according to its stored information.

So now the lengthy and painstaking navigation log such as Whitten Brown kept has gone. Instead a condensed flight log is kept, with much of the information already printed on it. Gone too is the Mercator chart with its arrow-headed position lines and its little cocked hats of fixes.

There goes the coastline of Newfoundland! Up front, the crew will be visually pin-pointing Gander ahead through the cloud breaks and comparing the position with the reading on the INS.

After 2500 miles, how far out? Maybe a couple of miles, maybe less. And the pilots have been talking on the radio, reporting their positions and getting the latest weather right across the Atlantic.

The ADF needle is tuned to Channel Head. Far below can dimly be seen the runways and buildings of Gander—so crucial in the history of the water jump, now no longer necessary. Gander Centre clears you to proceed to Kennebunk.

The First Officer selects the new course of 276°. Automatically, the Jumbo swings to the left down the airway towards New York.

\*       \*       \*

Now night has fallen—slowly as it always does flying westwards. Down below, it is raining, but every now and then through ragged breaks in the cloud you glimpse flat coastline, the bright neons on roads and a sparkling of lighted houses.

The visibility on the ground may look bad, but in these days of radar and automation, bad weather has lost much of its dangers.

Side by side with advances in training have come advances in auto-landing. Twenty years ago, a military aircraft flew over the water jump automatically controlled all the way. Since then, new techniques have been perfected whereby auto-landing can be carried out with complete safety in very bad visibility. At present, most airlines, including Pan Am and British Airways, operate to Category II—200 foot ceiling and 440 yards visibility. Such bad conditions are rare, but even so when more modern equipment is used and there is greater experience, the airlines will be able to operate if need be in near zero-zero conditions.

Safety, reliability, regularity, comfort, cheapness—all those required standards that seemed so impossible forty years ago have been achieved. In the past few years, however, it has been not mechanical trouble that has been feared, but hi-jacking. Political extremists have sought to rule the sky with bombs and pistol point. A world-wide security net with careful X-Ray and search procedures with international cooperation is slowly bringing this new danger under control.

**Seat occupancy rates for scheduled IATA carriers on the North Atlantic.**
*(figures obtained from IATA and CAA)*

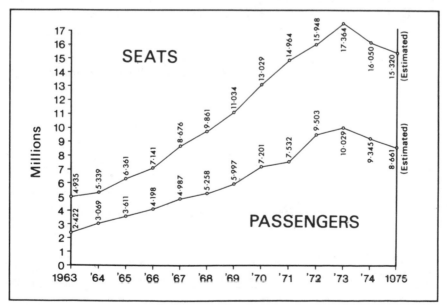

There have been other new problems, often produced by the very technical advances that have brought progress, but many of these have been solved. Much has been done on the reduction of noise and pollution of the big jets, and the big problems now are administrative and economic. World commodity prices have risen sevenfold since 1962. Aviation fuel is nine times the price it was in 1970. Inflation is rampant bringing with it higher wages and higher landing fees. And this period has been just the time that large numbers of wide-bodied jets have been coming onto the Atlantic, together with more Charter operators (particularly American, previously on military charter to South East Asia). Non-scheduled, non-IATA traffic has grown from 510,000 passengers in 1967 to 2,437,000 in 1973 and is still rising sharply.

The situation is difficult. Even though passenger and cargo growth on the North Atlantic is still increasing, too many seats are now chasing too few passengers. As a result, many airlines have plunged into the red. One of the few exceptions is the Overseas Division of British Airways (there has been another government reorganisation and BOAC and BEA have been amalgamated into one airline) which made a profit in 1974/75 of £20 million.

A price war has inevitably resulted, and a wide assortment of different fares in addition to First and Economy were brought in, such as affiliation groups, youth organisations, bulk and future bookings, none of which bring anything but loss to the airlines.

Charter companies, like Laker in Britain, offer a low return fare to New York. They are also pressing for a walk-on Skytrain service, where you buy your ticket on board—though this has at present been refused by the government. Whether such charter companies should be encouraged or controlled is an open question that governments must solve. Protectionist measures have not succeeded on the water jump in

**North Atlantic passenger fares, London–New York, 1939–1975.**

*(statistics by courtesy of British Airways)*

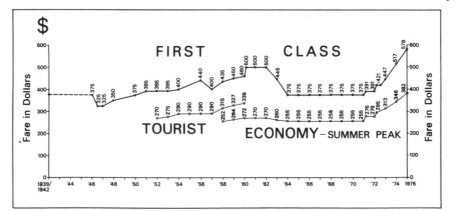

the past: it is unlikely they will succeed in the future. The eventual evolution of compromise arrangements is perhaps more the solution.

But the passenger is given the best bargain in the world. In twenty years, the trip has been cut from 22 hours to 7. There is much more comfort and entertainment, less noise and vibration. Yet the remarkably steady rate of scheduled trans-Atlantic fares over the years can be seen from the chart. This phenomenon of low fares is unprecedented in an inflation-ridden world. And there are even lower fares offered by scheduled operators for charter, special groups and future bookings.

Fares have been kept down so spectacularly primarily by speed and efficiency and by introducing safe, large, comfortable, economical, easily maintained aircraft like the 747, TriStar and DC10.

Airlines had streamlined their fleets. The Overseas Division of British Airways now have nineteen 747s, fifteen 707s, nineteen VC10s and three Concordes with more on order. The entire Pan Am fleet have only three types at present—707s, 727s and 747s.

The British, who held most of the chips in 1919, but lost many of them in the twenties and thirties, at last appear to have got their financial and managerial priorities right. A more technical and less politically orientated approach has been introduced by the Civil Aviation Authority, which is outside the Civil Service. The Flight Operations Department of the British Airways Overseas Division is managed by pilots with long experience of the Atlantic, who can plan the right equipment for the routes. The financial system, a compromise between nationalisation and free enterprise, has been changed. And the Overseas Division are making regular profits. They carry over a million passengers annually across the Atlantic, becoming in 1974 number three after Pan Am and TWA and number four in freighting, and leading in 1975.

Pan Am lost out to TWA as number one, but is now coming into profit again as so often in the past. On the water jump, all airlines owe Juan Trippe and Pan American an enormous debt, for they have in so many ways led the way forward and acted as pacemakers. Yet TWA has also contributed much, as have the British, the French, the Germans, the Dutch, the Italians, the Swiss, the Belgians, the Scandinavian countries, the Canadians and many others right from the early beginnings. They had competed with each other, quarrelled, tried to out-do each other, but at the same time contributed a vast pool of technical knowledge free—finally arranging their affairs and administration on a world-wide, not a narrow national plane.

In the past, impossible problems have come up, one by one have been solved, and from the solutions issue more impossible problems which in their turn are solved too. For aviation is well ahead of other human organisations in realising and accepting that the choice is between international cooperation or extinction.

Behind you now is the Atlantic, flecked with white, that has been there for millions of years, and in crossing it within the last five hours, you have compressed almost a lifetime.

But all that is already in the past. What will the future bring?

Further advances, certainly—particularly in speed. In 1935 the Chairman of Imperial Airways toured Africa at a speed of 100 mph. In 1951 civil aviation entered the era of the jets at 600 mph. Now is beginning the supersonic age at speeds of 1350 mph.

The United States alone spent $1000 million on the research and development of a supersonic airliner, before, in 1971, putting it into cold storage. It was the large-wing, 1800 mph, titanium Boeing 2707.

The British and the French called their aircraft Concorde—a name that could hardly be less appropriate for the aircraft that has produced more controversy than any other. Having had bad luck in losing the race with the Comet, the British pursued it in an effort to be first in the next stage of the race. The estimates for its building were wildly low, and as costs mounted, so did the political intrigue. There was every sort of problem. An alliance with the French was made after an unsuccessful attempt to woo the Americans into a joint enterprise. Even the name caused trouble; the British for years insisted on spelling it Concord. It has taken twenty-six years to develop, and the ever-increasing costs have now reached £1154 million. Built for strength, weighing rather more than half a 747, basically it resembles a dart. This is particularly evident on the flight deck which is long and thin, and in the passenger cabin with its narrow aisle.

Its appearance is now well known—the prehistoric-bird-like take-off, with its tiny head and down-pointing beak with outstretched wings, has figured in the news the world over. The 'beak' is the visor nose lowered to give the pilot better visibility. Flying twice as high and two and a quarter times as fast as a Jumbo, on a clear day it provides for the passenger through inky blue light a perfect picture of the rounded flank of the earth. The portholes are small and (when flying supersonically) warm to touch. The comfort is the same as that of first-class Jumbo. It is perhaps a little quieter in the cabin. Navigation aids and blind-landing aids are much the same, and it is operated by the same number of crew—three. Carrying up to 128 passengers at 1350 mph, it can land at New York one and a half hours earlier, local time, than it took off from London, easily beating the sun. The Concorde's appeal would appear to be mainly to businessmen whose time is big money, rather than to the tourist on a package holiday.

As technical difficulties mounted, so also there developed a huge international anti-Concorde lobby. Environmentalists, economists and politicians ranted against it. In 1964 the British government, as so often previously on aviation projects, appeared to want to pull out.

There have certainly been problems with the Concorde. Its cost is enormous—at present around £30 million each, reflecting the high research and development expenses of this totally new type of airliner—again 'one-off' and custom-built with no military ancestors. At a time when most world airlines are heavily in the red (due to over-capitalisation on big jets, the number of unsold seats on the North Atlantic, the high cost of fuel and charter competition) they say they cannot afford this huge new advance so soon. In 1973 Pan Am and TWA cancelled their options on the aircraft, and all the other airlines, except Air France and BOAC, Iran and China followed suit.

The Concorde was regarded as too expensive to operate. There is in fact evidence that businessmen would be prepared to pay the surcharge over the first-class service for the supersonic crossing. The manufacturers have claimed that break-even can be obtained at around 50 per cent capacity, and put the total operating costs per hour at slightly less than the 747, and in that one hour Concorde can do twice as much work. But such figures depend very much on the cost of fuel and the effect of inflation.

Head-on view of the Concorde—showing its perfect streamlining, the thin wing section and the air intakes of the four Olympus jet engines.

A marshaller guides the Concorde onto the ramp at Heathrow.

Then there is noise. Due to shock waves produced by all supersonic aircraft, the Concorde produces a sonic boom heard on the ground like distant thunder as it flies over. Because of this, some countries prohibit supersonic flying over their territories, in spite of the fact that military aircraft do it regularly. In addition, the Olympus engine is a straight jet and cannot be modified into the much quieter high by-pass ratio engine of the Jumbos. The British and French have spent millions on noise reduction. They claim that the Concorde's noise is now within the present regulations, and further improvements are being considered.

The environmentalists have also cited pollution against Concorde. Coils of black smoke could be seen streaming from the engines on televised take-offs of the prototype. Even though this pollution was minimal—apart from electric vehicles, aircraft are the cleanest forms of mechanical transport, much more so than the totally accepted motor car—concern was naturally felt by those living round airports. But in the production engines, this smoke (which is basically unburned fuel) has been all but eliminated by the incorporation of a new annular chamber with a vastly increased combustion efficiency. Then concern has been expressed that oxides of nitrogen, emitted into the strato-sphere by supersonic exhausts, might cause a chain reaction with the ozone, thus depriving the earth of protection against excessive ultra-violet radiation, though a major survey shows no real evidence of this effect.

Some authorities were worried about radiation. We are exposed to some radiation from many sources, such as luminous dials, television, X-Rays and those have been accepted as normal. In addition, there is cosmic radiation which is composed of stripped atomic nuclei particles that normally do not penetrate the shield of the earth's atmosphere. However, about twice a year—often connected with the appearance of sunspots—the sun ejects streams of particles in a solar flare, some of which may have sufficient energy to reach the thin top of the atmosphere through which both subsonic and (higher still and therefore more vulnerable) supersonic aircraft fly. All jets are, in fact, regularly tested for radiation activity, but in addition on the Concorde, there is a radiation meter which continually measures radiation and gives an early warning system to the crew. If the needle points to rising radiation,

On 21 January 1976, British Airways Concorde took off from London Airport for the first commercial supersonic flight, with 100 passengers on board. At exactly the same time, the Air France Concorde took off from Paris. (British Airways)

all the captain has to do is to descend under the thickness of the atmosphere shield.

In spite of these problems, under the usual intense competition, work progressed. The French made the first supersonic flight, to the chagrin of the British. There followed a programme of tests that lasted three years and were the most stringent conducted on any aircraft yet. At the end of 1975 the Concorde was ready to start civil operations. The big problem was, where to? No country wanted supersonic flights over its territory. The North Atlantic would clearly be the obvious route, but the Americans refused to allow a service—some say because they had no supersonic aircraft to match it, some say because of noise and pollution.

And so with the same sort of ballyhoo that heralded the Monarch service, but only on a much larger scale, on 21st January 1976 two Concordes opened the supersonic era—Air France to Rio de Janeiro, the British Airways to Bahrein. The stewardesses had seventeen different combinations of clothes, including for the first time trousers, in which to serve gourmet meals. Special Concorde Royal Doulton fine bone china was made. At London an exclusive Concorde terminal was constructed, where all the formalities are speeded up so that almost immediately passengers can board the aircraft waiting just outside.

Huge crowds, reminiscent of Lindbergh, watched the take-offs from London and Paris. Millions more watched both at the same time on television. For just like Imperial Airways and Pan American on the Atlantic flying boat proving flights nearly thirty-nine years before, neither the French nor the British would allow the other to start first.

And through the benefit of radio advancement, both aircraft took off at 11.40 and fifty seconds precisely. On the ground, noise abatement supporters recorded 134 perceived noise decibels on their instruments as against the 110 limit.

And now what happens? So far there has been no success selling Concordes to other nations, and without more places to fly to, the British and the French are not sure what to do with the ones they have. Routes over Russia and Africa are possibilities, and a UK–Australia service has been agreed. There is still, at the time of writing, deadlock on flying into Kennedy, but this may be resolved.

As regards competition with the subsonic jets, Concorde is handicapped by its consumption of a gallon a second, and has to come down to refuel on long routes like UK–Australia. A tortoise and hare situation then develops whereby very long-range subsonics catch up the time that the supersonic has been on the ground. So now the British are again actively pursuing the possibility of flight refuelling in the air—such as they did over the North Atlantic on the Empire boats and the Liberators thirty and forty years ago and which the air forces of the world still rely on.

But then any new era in civil aviation has always looked bleak. In 1934 Woods Humphery was lamenting the many difficulties, 'and of these none is greater than those presented by international politics.' That these difficulties will be overcome by technical advance and changing circumstances is certain.

The Concorde is basically in the same category as the Comet I—a leader, a research vehicle that nevertheless has commercial possibilities. The sort of Atlantic supersonic that is more commercially viable would need to carry 300 passengers, have the capacity for being 'stretched', and fly at above 2500 mph. Such aircraft are actively being considered by the Americans. Further 'impossible' problems then arise, particularly as above Mach 3.5 conventional jet engines are ineffective. A 'cleaner' fuel might be used, such as hydrogen, or the aircraft might be powered with a nuclear reactor. The sonic boom may be largely eliminated by new airframe design, and engine noise and pollution further reduced.

For clearly supersonics are now the logical next step. Their arrival is a matter of timing.

The history of aviation shows life is a series of 'impossible' problems that are then solved. Their solution on the supersonics will produce spin-offs in solving problems (as with the Space Programme) not directly connected but similarly part of the advancement of civilisation.

For supersonics bring speed—and speed always sells because it is archetypal in man. Saving time means saving a tiny piece of life, and in a sophisticated society aimed at maximum achievement in the short span of human existence, that is essential. Out of that passenger-attracting trinity—comfort, cost and speed, speed is the only absolute which cannot be changed—you cannot fly supersonic in a subsonic.

Concorde has done the water jump flying it twice (east and west) faster than a Jumbo flew it once, and in 1974 set up a record of 3 hours and 9 minutes for a flight from Paris to Boston.

When there will be a regular London–New York service is, at present, still a question mark. The American government have agreed, the Port of New York Authority has refused. Flights to Washington for a limited period by Air France and British Airways began on 24th May 1976, taking just under four hours—half the normal subsonic time. There was great interest and a huge waiting list of American passengers to fly Concorde has resulted.

As regards the long-term future, there will be the usual number of people saying *no*. The cookie will be tossed, as always, by political pressures, military needs, international prestige, environmental problems, world strategy, economic crises, lack of reciprocal agreements and inadequate knowledge.

But when commercially viable supersonics regularly cross the Atlantic, as has always happened before, the other big airlines will have to match that equipment or quit the game.

The French and British are half-way there, but the big problem is how the development of a really commercial supersonic can be funded. Future Concorde production has been slowed down until firm orders have been obtained from other airlines. If they are not going to continue to the logical end, then the project should never have been started. For the only thing to do is to go on or again give all the expensive research away to someone else who will. Already Boeing are working on a design for a much larger and faster supersonic for the 1990s.

For as has been shown in the history of the water jump, man leaps into the unknown. If he doesn't jump, the archetype on which man's advancement depends is that eventually another man will.

# *Eighteen:* Cleared to Descend

Six miles below they have been expecting you. Everything is organised. No long spiel of complicated instructions comes up these days from the ground as you report at Kennebunk. Your aircraft is given a Star—a Standard Terminal Arrival Route.

Laconically Control confirms that you are to 'continue as filed to a Saybrook 2 Arrival'.

You are cleared to descend to Flight level 31. The nose of the 747 dips. The tops of the cloud are coming closer.

With the clearance comes the weather forecast for Kennedy—continuous rain, cloud base 200 feet, visibility 1/4 mile, wind north-east twenty, gusting thirty. Four years ago, the pilots would have exchanged grimaces. Now there is no reaction. Only the autopilot, locked to the airway heading, continues to fly the Jumbo on a south-westerly course above the sandy beaches of New England.

It is remarkably quiet on the flight deck, which is smaller than that of a Stratocruiser and much neater. The instrument panel has been streamlined and so have all the circuit breakers on the roof, which used to give the impression of myriad little shells sticking to the arch of a cave. The Jumbo cockpit is dominated by the automatic flight-control systems on the console, which are connected to the Flight Director and the Initial Navigation System—this last no bigger than an electric type-writer. The autopilot has taken you across the Atlantic. Now it is flying down the beam to the Bohemia Holding Point.

Down on the ground, the Jumbo has been picked up as a little spot on numerous radar screens. It has entered the highly computerised auto-matic control system of Kennedy Approach. Its position and speed are continually checked, being carefully separated from other aircraft. In essence, the whole descent and landing operation in bad weather is like a liner being brought into harbour by the pilot, though the pilot in this case stays on the ground, watches the obstructions, the other traffic and the danger areas electronically, warns and advises the aircraft Captain.

Half an hour later, you are still in cloud. You are vaguely conscious that the aircraft keeps altering course and height, though you are not sure whether you are going port or starboard, up or down. The Captain's voice comes over the public address system. 'There's rather a lot of traffic into Kennedy. So we've joined the stack.'

You are circling at allotted altitudes, gradually being brought by thousand-foot stages to the bottom of the stack at 10,000 feet, from where you will be siphoned off for a landing.

*     *     *

Looking out into the opaque grey mist, in spite of the lack of concern of the cabin crew already clearing up for the end of the flight, again you may begin to wonder.

A typical modern Approach Control—this one is at London.          (CAA)

The Boeing Stratocruiser Flight Simulator—the first electronic flight simulator built by Redifon for BOAC in 1950. (Redifon Ltd)

How *is* the pilot going to land? How can he be trained to bring safely down to earth through all this smog and cloud something flying so fast and weighing so much?

In the early days, the pioneers had flown by sucking-and-seeing. They had taught themselves. Then a more experienced pilot indicated to a pupil the controls and instruments and what did what. The accident rate was phenomenal. It was not understood that man was very handicapped without a horizon, and many were killed spinning in out of thick cloud.

Pilots were given blind-flying instruction on the ground in Link trainers, which were simulated cockpits with hoods over them. Dual instruction on flying technique was given in the air. Military flying schools had been established as early as 1912 when the British Central Flying School opened. Civil flying schools developed later. But pilots were difficult to teach. Even as late as 1930, a demonstration in an Avro with a folding hood shutting off the horizon was necessary to show RAF pilots that they could fly in blind conditions for a maximum of eight minutes before losing equilibrium and spinning in. It was then that gyro horizons began to be standard equipment—the first over the Atlantic being used by Post and Gatty in their 1931 round-the-world flight. The pilot's cockpit drill was by a mnemonic—F for flaps, M for Mixture, G for Gyro. Each pilot was a law unto himself, and flew the way he wanted. Then aircraft became too complicated—and a big advance was made by the introduction of Pilot's Notes and Check Lists for take-off and landing and emergencies.

Operating procedures were still passed on largely by word of mouth, until again these became too complicated and Operational Manuals began to be produced.

By the end of World War II, Atlantic training procedures were based on American and Canadian methods. There was a heavy emphasis on basic instrument flying, using the same few instruments as the pioneers, along the beam of the Radio Range.

But this training was for captains: co-pilots were still regarded as office boys who put down the flaps and raised the undercarriage and obediently carried out the captain's orders. Since most co-pilots had been military captains, this led to friction. The compulsory introduction of type rating qualifications for co-pilots in 1947 was grudgingly interpreted on BOAC's Atlantic Division as half a dozen touch-and-goes (landings followed by immediate take-offs).

Each Atlantic Baron had his own way of flying. The individualism that sparked everything off on the water jump initially could now become a difficulty, and the co-pilot's lot was not always a happy one. In a novel, I described my own Atlantic co-pilot experiences: 'There was always another man sitting in the left-hand seat. Nearly always a different man, with different ideas, and with different ways of doing things. They all worried about something different. This one loathed crosswinds on runways: this one wouldn't go near a thunderstorm: this one had a phobia about short runways: this one hated taking off at maximum all-up-weight: this one didn't like going to Iceland: this one wouldn't go into a cumulo-nimbus cloud: this one banged them down: this one greased them in: this one shouted when he was anxious: this one whispered. Talk about the Ten Little Nigger Boys! Saracen sat there smiling in the right-hand seat, saying "Yes, sir!" and "No, sir!" and nursing his own little worry, too: how to become a Little Nigger Boy himself.'

The first improvement in training standardisation came when Pan Am introduced a Stratocruiser simulator, later followed by BOAC. Instrument ratings and checks on emergency procedures were carried out every six months for all pilots. Because every sort of emergency could be simulated electronically, at first the checkers were emergency-happy. No sooner had the checkee settled in his seat than he got an engine fire, followed by hydraulic failure taxiing. Three-quarters of the way down the 'runway', he got an engine failure, followed by another engine going as he lifted off. Staggering up to cruising altitude, he got an explosive decompression or a fuselage fire, and had to come down to 10,000 feet. Only gradually was the simulator used properly to allow a full assessment of basic handling skill and crew coordination during normal operation, with a selective testing and training in emergency procedures.

As Captain Jack Nicholl, BOAC's former General Manager Flight Training put it, 'So the simulator was the first nail in the coffin of the old

Atlantic Baron—no longer quite so much the proud independent but every six months exposed to the rigours of an absolutely standardised simulator check, with a co-pilot alongside him able to observe how well he did, not just another captain and colleague!'

Atlantic co-pilots by the mid-50s began to be given a comprehensive training on the type of aircraft they were operating. Now, as well as captains, co-pilots were taught the same standardised handling procedures. Along the route, they were given more take-offs and landings. Instead of a Baron and an office boy, a team of two pilots sat in the nose of Atlantic aircraft.

The shade of the Atlantic Baron lingered on in that he still got special pay and privileges. But with the introduction of the 7Cs and Britannias, BOAC pilots from other Divisions were posted to the Atlantic. No longer could it be regarded as a 'special' route requiring 'special' crews, since these aircraft could almost always operate non-stop to New York, thus avoiding the bad winter weather of Gander and the Maritimes.

The 707 did the hatchet job on the Atlantic Baron. Pay differentials were for bigger and faster aircraft, not for routes. Soon big jets were operating throughout the world, and route and pilot specialisation for the Atlantic had disappeared.

**The 747 Redifon Flight Simulator is mounted on a six degrees of freedom motion system (pitch, roll, heave, yaw, sway and surge) and is equipped with a realistic colour visual system.** **(Redifon Ltd)**

More and more the emphasis was now on standardisation. There had been operating procedure differences with the 707 when BOAC first introduced the VC10, but Jack Nicholl bulldozed the differences down so that the operation was almost identical with the American aircraft. The idea of Standard Operating Procedures was established throughout the BOAC network. Now that BOAC and BEA have amalgamated into British Airways, standardisation will need to go one step further.

For standardisation has now become not only inter-company but international. With the arrival of the 747, TriStar and DC10, far better communication between aircraft manufacturers, airlines and administrations has been achieved.

Key airline personnel are now trained on new aircraft by the manufacturers. On the 707, Boeing had come under some criticism for dictating to airlines how best to operate, while knowing little about the airline business at first hand. They learned their lesson, and with the 747 they held seminars and conferences on the training side for all their customers with a complete two-way exchange system of teaching and learning.

As a result, the training on all the wide-bodied jets became much more standardised throughout the world. There was an international exchange of problems, syllabi and procedures, coordinated through the manufacturers so that the same high standard of operation was achieved internationally. This standardisation is maintained by regular meetings of the IATA Committee on flight crew training.

It is also now accepted that the operation of the aircraft is a team effort. There is a concept of *crew* operation, each man operating to exactly the same standard and each monitoring the others. In the 747, this means that just as there are three quite separate Inertial Navigation Systems monitoring each other, and three auto-pilots doing the same thing on the auto-land, there are three men checking all vital actions in the cockpit. Each of the items on the Take Off and Landing Check Lists are checked by at least two, and most by all three crew. When the reading of the INS is changed, the new pinpoint position is fed in under three pairs of eyes. The whole concept of operation is geared to monitoring and guarding against human slips. The Engineer Officer is given courses in certain hitherto all-pilot preserves, such as airways flying, and acts in many ways like a third safety pilot.

This further concept of standardisation has been made possible by the introduction of even more sophisticated simulators. The big 747 simulator, moving on all three axes, is moored to a quay protected by rails, and looks at first glance like the tethered head of a huge white whale. Where before initial training and checks had to be done on the aircraft itself at an astronomical cost per hour, now almost all of it can be done on the ground. With the advent of digital simulators, an

The instrument panel of the Vimy.    (Science Museum)

The instrument panel of the 747.    (British Airways)

astonishing realism is achieved so that every indication is given that the pilots are flying actual aircraft. Computers control the view from the windscreen to simulate exact actual conditions in making a night approach and landing onto a lighted runway. The visibility, cloud base and weather can be altered at the instructor's wish.

Every little movement of the controls, every change of speed or altitude correctly changes the picture ahead, so that pilots can be taught to take off and fly and land without ever having been in the aeroplane. This new technique is such an improvement on the earlier film and television visuals that a 747 new pilot will be given around forty hours on the simulator and only three or four hours on the aircraft itself, basically only to give him confidence, as against thirty-six hours on the simulator and fourteen hours on the aircraft in 707 training. The saving is of course enormous; a simulator hour costs only a fraction of that of a big jet. Every conceivable emergency can still be fed into the simulator and the drills practised to such perfection that the licensing authorities have accepted such teaching and checking as completely on a par with the real thing. Even so, pilots are still required after training to be checked on the simulator every three months, and have a thorough medical twice a year.

In ground school, too, training ideas have changed. When I took my B Licence thirty years ago, I had to learn a lot of useless information on tides and lights on flying boats and methods of navigation from an aircraft carrier. Now there is a need-to-know approach to training. TWA claim to be the forerunners here, providing training courses with every sort of audio-visual aid geared to what the psychologists call Specific Behavioural Objectives. If it is not necessary to actual operation, then it is dispensed with. Instead of cluttering up aircrew's minds with a lot of abstruse facts, the whole training system is streamlined for safety and simplicity and is operationally orientated. The training is designed so the aircrew can perform correctly and quickly all the actions required of them. Anything that it is not necessary to know is not taught. So on many airlines that operate inertial navigation systems, navigation courses have been stopped, as a First Class Navigator's ticket is no longer required. And the actual operation of the aircraft has been simplified. On the 747, there are only 22 items on the Before Take Off and only 10 on the After Take Off Checks.

Gone is the pioneer, gone is the individual, gone is the Atlantic Baron—all their work complete. Up front in your 747, now a three-man crew operates the aircraft on international standardised procedures.

The flying trapeze has been replaced by the safest long-range air route in the world.

## *Nineteen:* The Happy Landing

'. . . you are now Number One. Cleared for an approach to Runway Zero Four.'

The Jumbo is leaving the bottom of the stack. As it descends from 10,000 feet, maybe now is the time when you think of all those skyscrapers on Manhattan. After an Atlantic crossing in 1942 to see Roosevelt in the White House, Winston Churchill also had such high hazards in mind. As the Boeing flying boat descended to the Potomac river, he remarked that they were the same height as the Washington Monument, and how unfortunate it would be if they were to hit this, 'of all other objects in the world'.

The weather now is only just above Category II—200 feet cloud base and a quarter of a mile visibility. But these days, it is the radar from Control that guides your aircraft through the mist towards the Kennedy Instrument Landing System beam.

The First Officer sets the course selector of the autoland to 043 (the exact heading of the runway) and tunes the Automatic Direction Finder to the Outer Marker Beacon. The Engineer calls out the Approach Check. The undercarriage is lowered. Speed is reduced to 220 knots with 5 degrees flap.

Gradually, the aircraft is brought lower and placed on the extended centreline of the runway. The Captain moves the autopilot mode selector from Heading to Land. B and C autopilots are engaged, so now *three* autopilots are monitoring each other. The chances of a mistake being made are millions to one against.

Now the indicator shows the localiser beam central, and the autoland 'captures' it.

The First Officer calls, 'Nav green!'

Slowly, the glide slope descends on the indicator and is captured in the centre. The autopilots and the autothrottles are now locked on the descent.

[285]

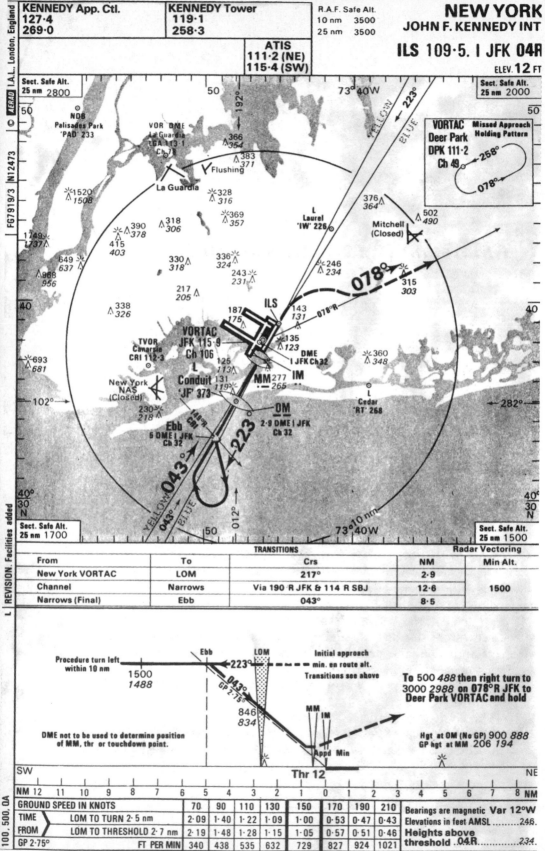

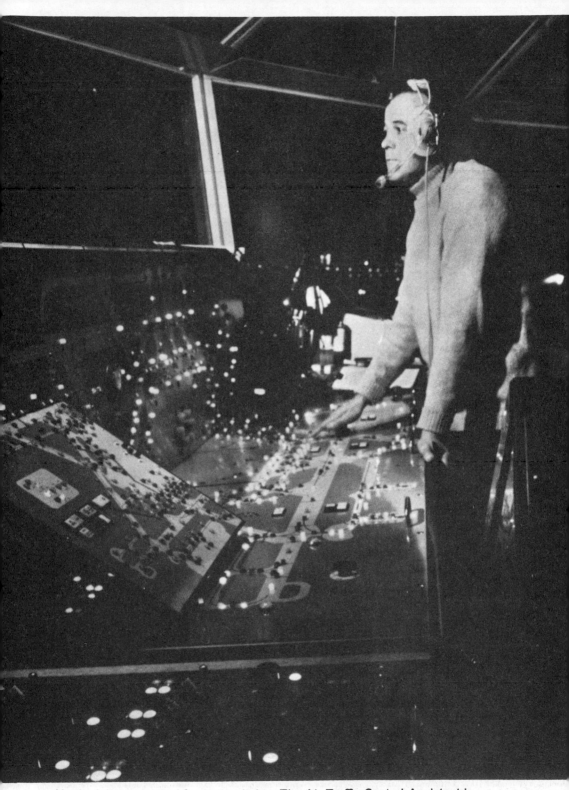

*Above:* A lighting panel for airport lights. The Air Traffic Control Assistant is controlling the lights on taxiways and runways by listening to the Ground Movement Controller's instructions to aircraft moving on the ground. (CAA)

*Opposite:* Let-down procedure at Kennedy.

The Captain's left hand is poised over the autopilot/autothrottle disconnect button on the left-hand spectacle of the control column. His right hand rests lightly on the four throttles.

The First Officer calls '1000 feet! No Flags! Landing Flap set!' The needle on the ADF turns right round. 'Over the Outer Marker!'

Controlled by the autoland, steadily the 747 descends at five hundred feet a minute. Nothing can be seen outside, except black rain streaming down the windscreen. The throttles make tiny movements backwards and forwards, keeping the speed at 140 knots. The aileron control moves to starboard as it picks up the port wing caught in a gust.

The altimeter reading is 600 feet . . . 500 . . . 400. There is still no sign of the ground outside. An amber light flashing on the instrument panel indicates the Inner Marker.

300 . . . 250 . . . the altimeter needle is still unwinding. At 200 feet there is a faint glimmer of a lead-in light.

'100 decision!' calls the First Officer.

Now wisps of dark mist stream over the wing as though the leading edge is cutting the cloud to ribbons. A line of muzzy green lights marks the runway threshold.

'Decision height, sir!'

The runway and approach accurately simulated by Novoview, the latest type of visual system. This is the pilot's view during a night approach. (Redifon Ltd)

'Continuing.'

The degree of braking required has been selected on the automatic speed brakes. At fifty feet, a green light glows.

'Flare green!'

The nose is lifting for the flare-out. Like great yellow blobs of wet flak, the runway lights can now be seen coming up on either side. Up and up comes the Jumbo to a 4° angle of attack to achieve maximum drag.

The throttles close with a decisive click. The sixteen main wheels touch. The two nose wheels connect. You are down.

The Captain presses the button and disengages the autoland. He puts reverse thrust on the engines. Rapidly, the Jumbo decelerates to a jog-trot, and angles off the runway onto the rain-soaked taxi-track.

As the aircraft moves sedately between an aisle of blue lights, through the window, you see not tents or a makeshift hut but a palatial docking area with individual docks towards which your 747 moves.

Up front, the Captain is guided by two vertical lines on the wall of the Terminal ahead—one now red, one green. He steers till both are green, getting the nosewheel right on the white line on the ground. Down below, a marshaller makes a cross with the beams of two torches. The engines stop.

You unfasten your belt—the belt that was introduced after Lieutenant Towers' fall in 1919. You get up from the modern equivalent of the old Imperial Airways light-weight seat. You collect your hand luggage. You move to the front, past the descendant of the Strato-cruiser staircase up to the lounge, then towards the door where stand the purser and stewardess.

'Thank you for flying with us,' they say. 'Hope you enjoyed your trip.'

Out into a long convoluted elephant's trunk of a movable corridor, carpeted in red. Before you turn the corner, take a look back and see in the huge nose of the Jumbo the ghost of the Empire flying boat. Heredity runs right the way through aviation.

Now you are approaching Immigration, where your passport is checked, then on into the Customs' Hall. Already your luggage has come down a moving belt, is rotating like a horse in a merry-go-round, called in fact a 'carousel'.

You find a Customs Officer. You have nothing to declare. The doors open.

This is New York.

It seems ages ago since you were in London—more than half a century. Yet it is not yet seven o'clock local here and you left London at four in the afternoon. But as you walk outside to get a taxi, the shadows of so much of what has happened before will be following you

—Commander Read in his Nancy, Alcock and Brown spinning in mid-Atlantic, Scott serenely flying the airship R34 over, Eckener sending his son out on the Zeppelin to mend the tail with blankets, the ships that guided the aircraft and the seamen who rescued the airmen, the Army Douglas seaplanes, Lindbergh leading off the others in the greatest international flying circus of all time, Von Gronau's three flights in the little Wal flying boats and Jim Mollison's three crossings, the epic of the Do–X, the flight of the R100, Captain Wilcockson and Captain Gray starting the commercial proving flights together, the success of Graf Zeppelin and the mystery of the *Hindenburg*, the establishment of the international organisations, the Germans flying their catapulted seaplanes a few feet above the water from the Azores, Bennett flying the first non-stop mail service in the top part of the Composite, the magnificent return flight of the Condor, the luxury of the 314 flying boats, the Return Ferry Service Liberators conquering the North Atlantic winter, the Connies and the Strats and the Seven Seas, the tourist services that Juan Trippe so passionately believed in, the jets and the Jumbos, and all the aircrews and the groundcrews and the aircraft manufacturers and the salesmen and the promoters and the meteorologists and the instrument makers and the administrators and all the others who achieved the impossible.

Now you have joined them. You have completed the water jump.

Yet your crossing has been so safe, so carefully watched, so comfortable, so fast, so cheap, so beautifully organised, so friendly, so completely without problems. Perhaps there is something in the claim that the water jump is the finest international technical and administrative achievement of all time, and yet . . . it has all been so simple.

Whatever did they mean when they said it was impossible? And what are they saying is impossible today?

# Selected Bibliography

*Our Trans-Atlantic Flight* Alcock and Brown (Kimber, 1969)

*Airships* Patrick Abbott (Adams and Dart, 1973)

*Hitch Your Wagon* Bernt Balchen (Bell, 1950)

*Great Mysteries of the Air* Ralph Barker (Chatto, 1966)

*Pathfinder* D. C. T. Bennett (Muller, 1958)

*The Second World War* Winston Churchill (Cassell, 1950)

*Through Atlantic Clouds* Collinson and McDermott (Hutchinson, 1934)

*History of the World's Airlines* R. E. G. Davies (OUP, 1964)

*Airlines of the United States since 1914* R. E. G. Davies (Putnam, 1972)

*The Blunted Sword* David Divine (Hutchinson, 1964)

*The Broken Wing* David Divine (Hutchinson, 1966)

*Atlantic Air Conquest* F. K. and E. Ellis (Kimber, 1963)

*Airline Detective* Donald Fish (Collins, 1962)

*A History of the Air Ministry* C. G. Grey (Allen and Unwin, 1940)

*Our Atlantic Attempt* Hawker and Grieve (Methuen, 1919)

*Merchant Airmen* HMSO

*Britain's Imperial Air Routes 1918–1939* Robin Higham (Foulis, 1961)

*Air Travel* Kenneth Hudson (Adams and Dart, 1972)

*History of Navigation* A. J. Hughes (Allen and Unwin, 1946)

*747* Douglas Ingells (Aero Publishers, 1970)

*My Flying Life* C. Kingsford-Smith (Aviation Book Club, 1937)

*Listen! The Wind* Anne Morrow Lindbergh (Chatto, 1938)

*We—Pilot and Plane* Charles Lindbergh (Putnam, 1937)

'An Aircraft Collision Model' Robert Machol (*Management Science*, June 1975)

[292]  *Selected Bibliography*

'Atlantic Wings 1919–1939' Kenneth McDonough (*Model Aeronautical Press*, 1966)

*Playboy of the Air* Jim Mollison (Joseph, 1937)

*The Hindenburg* Michael Mooney (Hart-Davis, 1972)

*Pictorial History of BOAC and Imperial Airways* Kenneth Munson (Allan, 1957)

*Air Dates* C. G. S. Payne (Heinemann, 1957)

*Around the World in Eight Days* Post and Gatty (Hamilton)

*The Seven Skies* John Pudney (Putnam, 1959)

*Into the Wind* J. C. W. Reith (Hodder, 1949)

*The Reith Diaries* Ed. Charles Stuart (Collins, 1975)

*Vickers* J. D. Scott (Weidenfeld and Nicolson, 1962)

*Slide Rule* Nevil Shute (Heinemann)

*Amy Johnson* Constance Babington-Smith (Cassell, 1967)

*Pictorial History of Pan American World Airways* P. St. J. Turner (Allan, 1973)

*The Flight of Alcock and Brown* Graham Wallace (Putnam, 1955)


Also Jane's *All the World's Aircraft*, Putnam's Aeronautical Series, *Aerospace*, the Journal of the Aeronautical Society, particularly the text of lectures by Captain J. C. Kelly-Rogers on commercial Atlantic operations (January 1976) and John Grierson on Lindbergh (October 1975), the Centenary Journal of the Royal Aeronautical Society, *Flight International*, Shell *Aviation News*, various publications of the Smithsonian Institution, US Navy, the Boeing, Lockheed and McDonnell Douglas Corporations, British Airways, Pan American World Airways, the Sperry Gyroscope Division, IATA, ICAO, Bristol Aeroplane Company, BAC, and numerous contemporary papers, letters and documents from various archives, record offices and private collections.

# Aircraft and Engines

# Index